CHARLES DICKENS' LONDON

Mark Davis & Zara Liddle

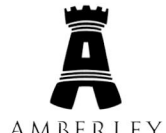

Dedicated to the memory of Catherine Dickens (19 May 1815–22 November 1879)

'Because he loved me once...'

First published 2022

Amberley Publishing
The Hill, Stroud, Gloucestershire, GL5 4EP
www.amberley-books.com

Copyright © Mark Davis & Zara Liddle, 2022

The right of Mark Davis & Zara Liddle to be identified as the Authors of this work has been asserted in accordance with the Copyrights, Designs and Patents Act 1988.

ISBN 978 1 3981 0989 6 (print)
ISBN 978 1 3981 0990 2 (ebook)

All rights reserved. No part of this book may be reprinted or reproduced or utilised in any form or by any electronic, mechanical or other means, now known or hereafter invented, including photocopying and recording, or in any information storage or retrieval system, without the permission in writing from the Publishers.

British Library Cataloguing in Publication Data.
A catalogue record for this book is available from the British Library.

Typesetting by SJmagic DESIGN SERVICES, India.
Printed in Great Britain.

INTRODUCTION

Born Charles John Huffam Dickens, Charles Dickens as we know him less formally was without doubt a true literary genius and to many, he was and still is regarded as the greatest of all Victorian novelists. As his works enjoyed huge popularity during his own living lifetime he is as ever-hugely popular in 2022. Christmas in my household, as in countless other homes, would not be Christmas without watching a version of *A Christmas Carol*, my favourite in particular being the 1951 black and white version starring Alistair Sim as *Ebenezer Scrooge*. It was standard Christmas Eve viewing as a child for me, and remains so to this day.

Given that *A Christmas Carol* is firmly set in London, as were many of his novels, we decided to quite literally walk in Dickens' footsteps, seeking out the city Dickens both loved and wrote about. Dickens' ability to weave magic with words is legendary, but his ability to find inspiration from both the people he knew intimately and others he met more briefly, and the places he visited or had knowledge of, is where his true genius lies.

Dickens didn't just write about people and places; he visited the prisons, workhouses and slums that housed those unfortunates of Victorian society. He had no problem with

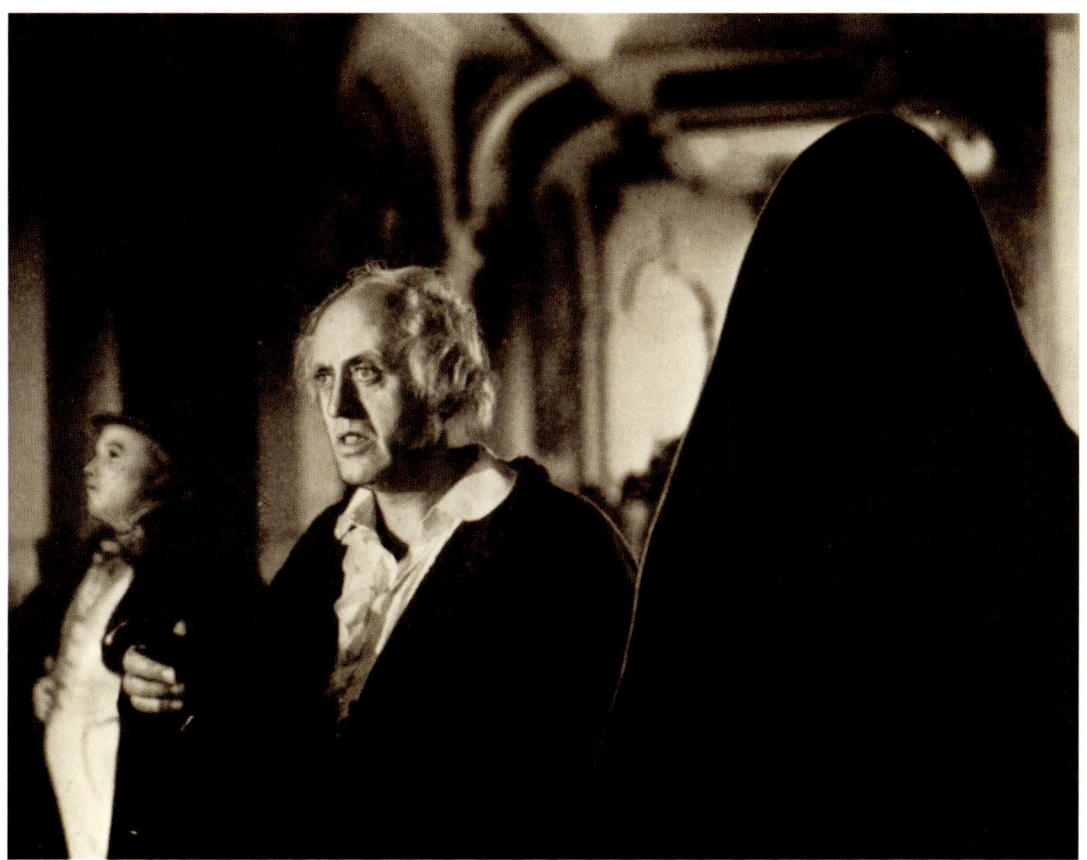

walking 10 or 20 miles around London taking in the sights, the unique smells and the living, breathing life of what was then, during Victorian times, the largest and most spectacular city in the world and the most powerful global trading centre on the planet.

Often at night he would wander like a ghost through the gas-lit streets observing and interacting with all walks of life. In terms of London geographically, he knew it all; the city was his inspirational wonderland. Incredibly many of the buildings and places he knew remain to this day. If Dickens was to rise from his tomb at Westminster Abbey, he would quite easily be able to circumnavigate the new, modern London and make his way to Whitechapel, Camden, Fitzrovia, Southwark or even stop off for fine dining in 'Rules' restaurant in Covent Garden.

Born in February 1812, during his lifetime Dickens would welcome three new monarchs to the throne. He would live in an era of remarkable changes in the metropolis, of which the coming of the railway was one of the most dramatic and life-altering, seen in the progress of his published novels. As the population boomed with the coming of the Industrial Revolution and the influx of impoverished migrant workers, so did the capital. Many of these workers, arriving from the countryside seeking work, were to find themselves living in rookeries (slum areas) where conditions for the poor were particularly brutal with inadequate sanitation and little or no running water. Also living in these slum areas were criminals, prostitutes, notable minorities such as the Jewish and Irish, as well as the working class. Such was the diversity of living in London that the poor often lived in close proximity to the richer inhabitants. Dickens talks about Covent Garden in *Little Dorrit* in which he compares the luxuriously dressed wealthy visiting the theatres while local ragged children slink and hide like rats feeding on offal and huddling together for warmth.

When walking around London it is difficult not to find Dickens' influence ever-present in every borough. In Southwark, for example, the borough has a school named after him on the very street he found sanctuary in 1824 when he moved from Camden into lodgings there. Even characters are mentioned, with Little Dorrit playground being named after his novel of the same name. All over London you quite literally walk in Charles Dickens' footsteps.

This book is by no means an academic work or a complete list of everywhere in London familiar to Dickens. In essence it is a brief snapshot of Dickens' London just over 150 years since his death in 1870. We wanted to mark the sesquicentennial in 2020; however the worldwide Covid-19 pandemic put most things on hold, including this book. Despite this many of the images were taken in 2021 when, as expected, like most of the country, London was semi-deserted, which is reflected in many of the images appearing very quiet and not quite the bustling London we knew and know again today.

London is a rapidly changing and evolving city, and we hope in years to come the images within this publication will be good points of reference for future generations of Dickens fans looking to walk in the footsteps of the inimitable Charles Dickens.

Images and introduction by Mark Davis.
Page captions by Zara Liddle.

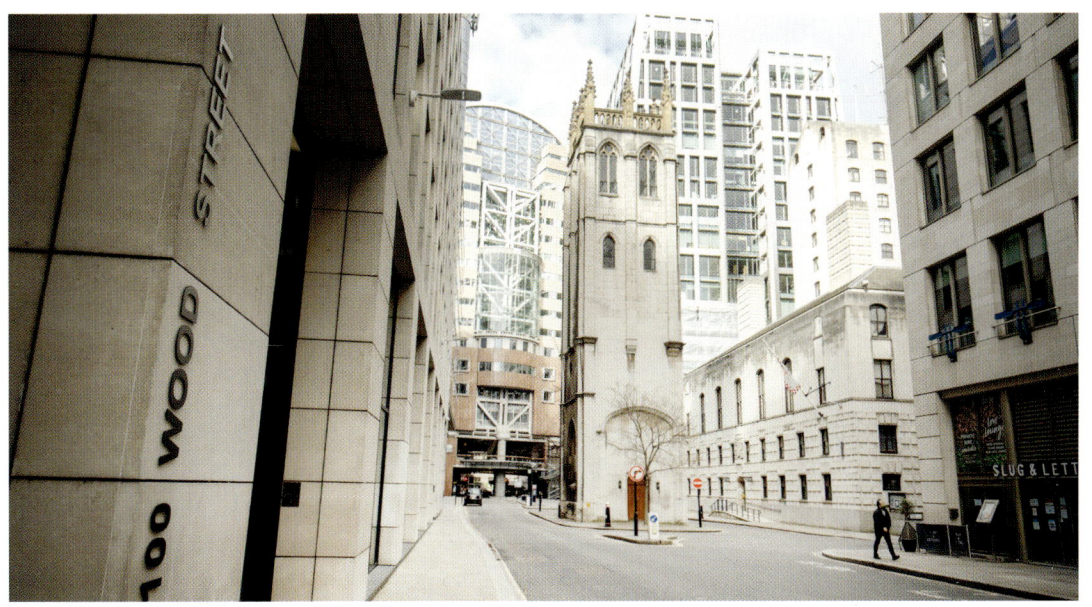

Wood Street, Cheapside

Wood Street was the location for The Compter, a debtor's prison which served as the overflow from Newgate. This jail was categorised into wings of financial wealth when it came to its inhabitants, a cruel regime which very much determined their quality of living whilst there. It was here that a twelve-year-old Charles Dickens first visited London, staying at the Cross Key's Inn after his father, John Dickens, had lost yet another job, this time in Chatham. Originally left behind to finish his school term, the young Dickens travelled alone to join his family in the capital some weeks later. Many believe Dickens used the character *Pip* in his 1861 twenty-first published novel *Great Expectations* to express his own experiences of this time. The book's description of the lonely journey *Pip* took from Kent to have tea with *Estella* mirrors Charles' own secluded commute.

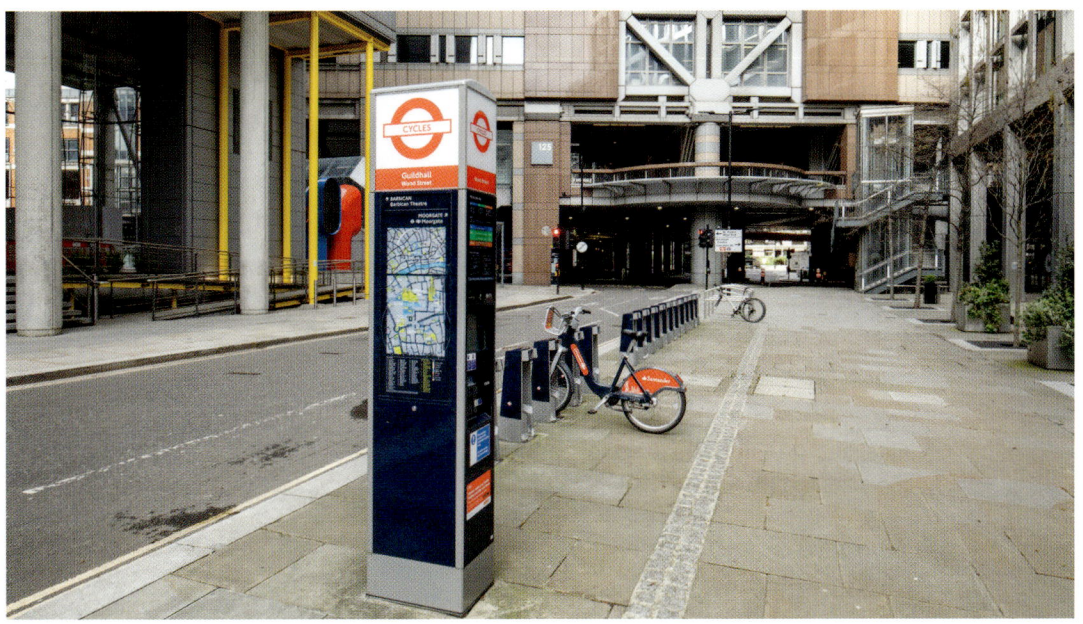

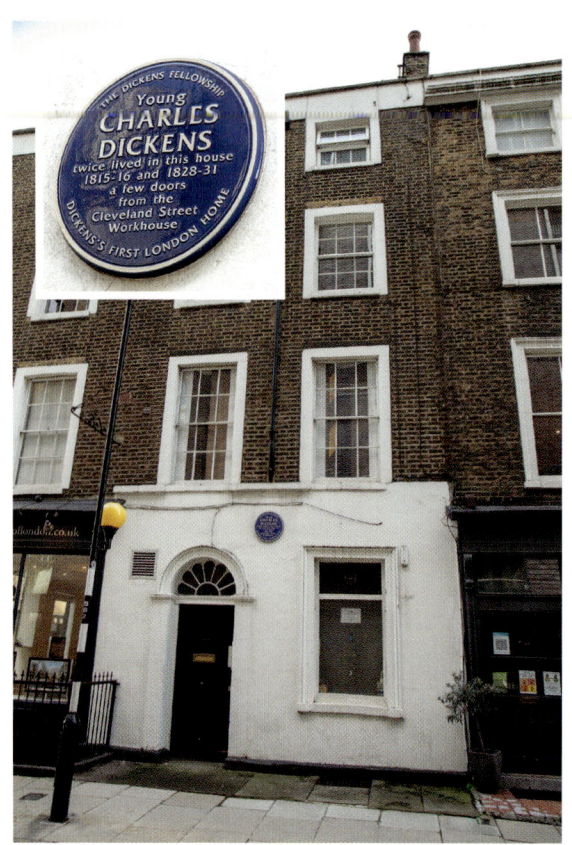

22 Cleveland Street

During numerous reassignments relating to John Dickens' role as a naval clerk, 22 Cleveland Street is the address in 1815 that the family first inhabited in London, known to Charles as Fitzroy Street. It also became a repeated dwelling for them again in 1828. Closely located was the Cleveland Street Workhouse, built between 1775 and 1778 for the care of the sick and poor. It is said by Dr Ruth Richardson in her meticulously researched book *Dickens and the Workhouse* that this workhouse was the inspiration for the impoverished and hellish settings for his 1839 full publication *Oliver Twist*.

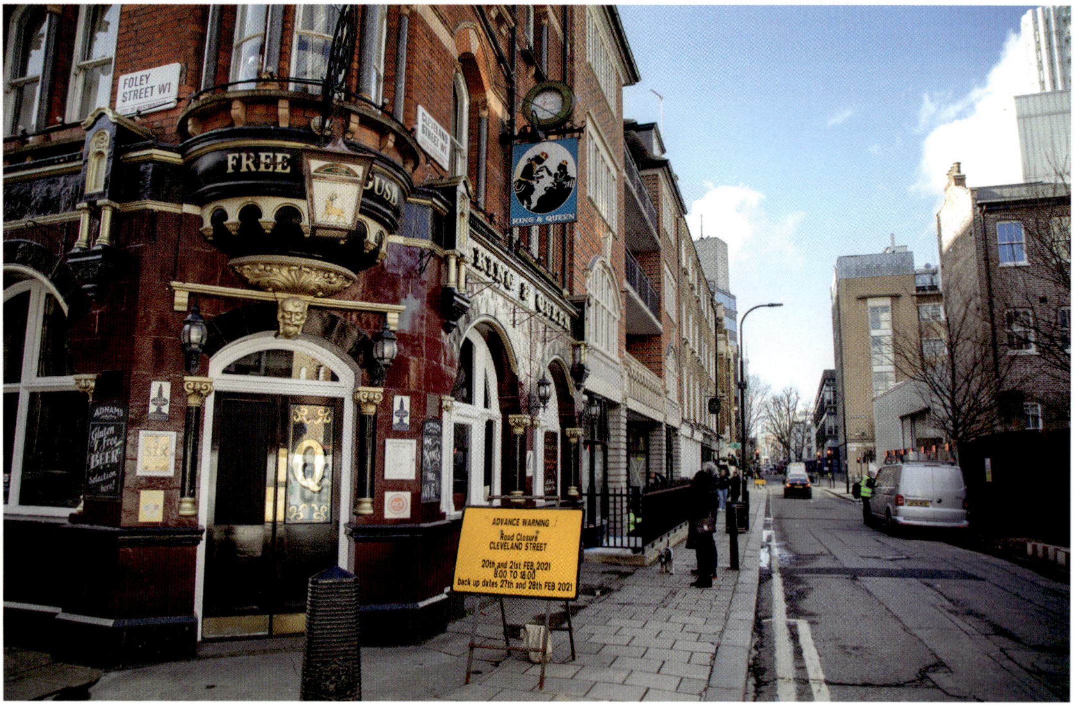

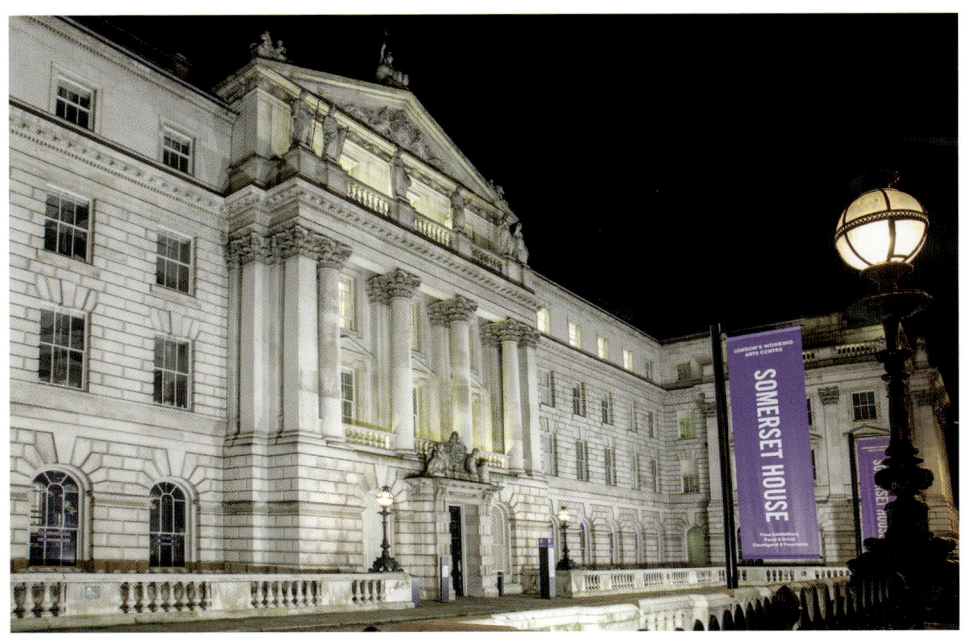

Somerset House and the British Museum

John Dickens worked as a clerk within the Naval Pay Office at Somerset House. It was through his colleague Thomas Barrow that he met and married his wife (Thomas's sister), Elizabeth, in 1809. The marriage succeeded, but John's hopes for further advancement were dashed when his father-in-law was accused of embezzlement at the company and fled the country. After a lengthy visit, the by then growing Dickens family decided to make the city a permanent home. As is now, London was the most expensive place in Britain in which to live, and John's wages did not reflect the extra expense of having to relocate to the city. It was during his father's service at Somerset House that the eighteen-year-old Charles first applied for a reader's ticket at the British Library Museum – 8 February 1830, just one day after his eighteenth birthday, as was the earliest age to meet the criteria in the eligibility.

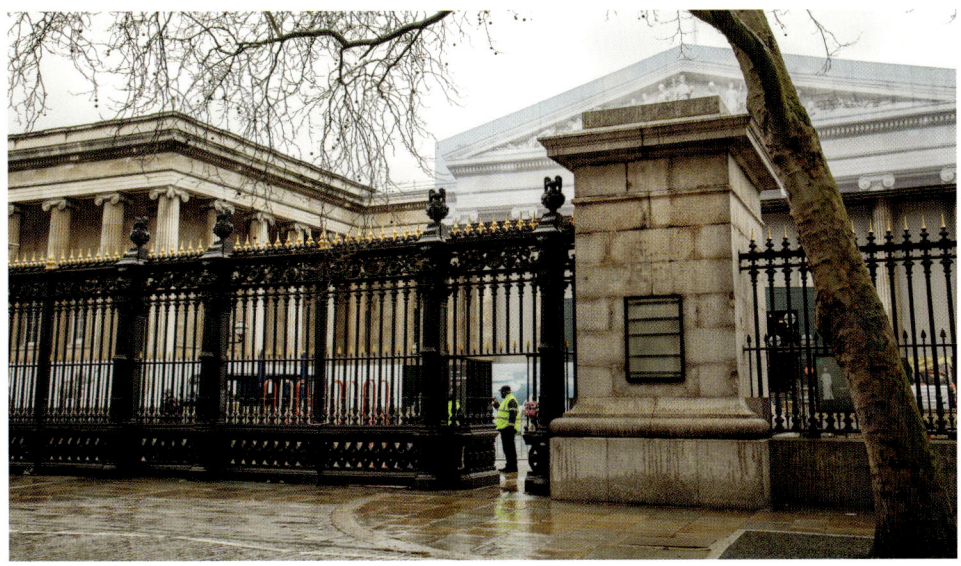

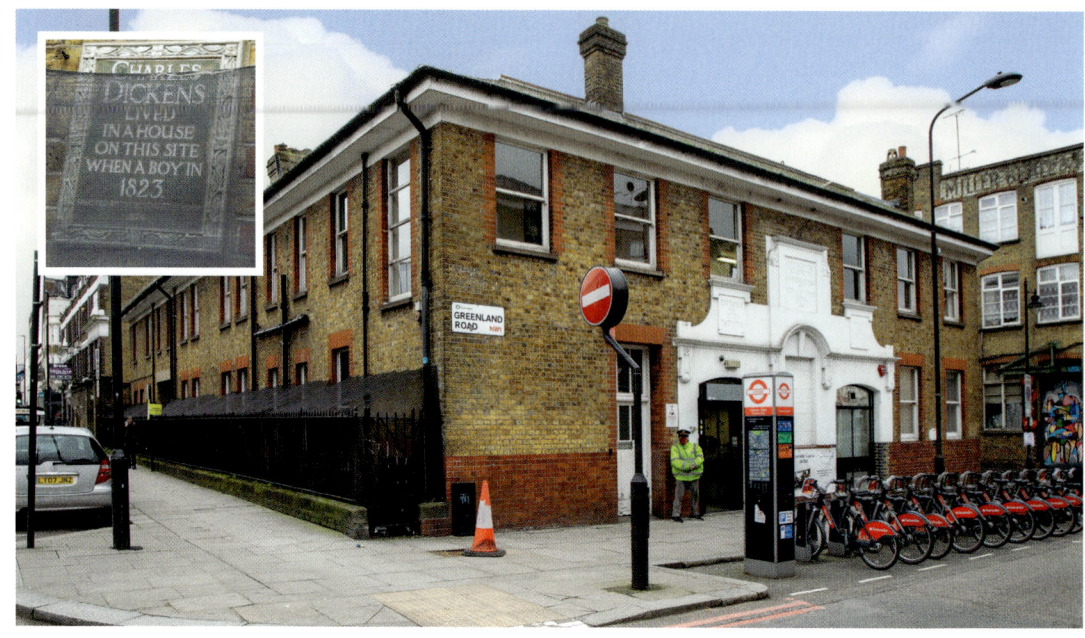

16 Bayham Street and 147 Gower Street

It was in 16 Bayham Street (the plaque is placed at No. 141 as the original house no longer exists) that the Dickens family resided in 1823. Within a year the family had moved yet again to a new address in the Fitzrovian borough of London, 4 Gower Street – now renumbered as 147 Gower Street; although newly built at the time this is the address where the childhood trauma we now know of befell a young Charles Dickens. Elizabeth's attempts to assist the family's financial woes by opening a school here had resulted in failure with her never procuring a single pupil. Unable to pay the baker John Kerr the £40 and 10 shillings he owed, John Dickens was imprisoned on 20 February 1824 at Marshalsea Debtors' Prison under the Insolvent Debtors Act of 1813.

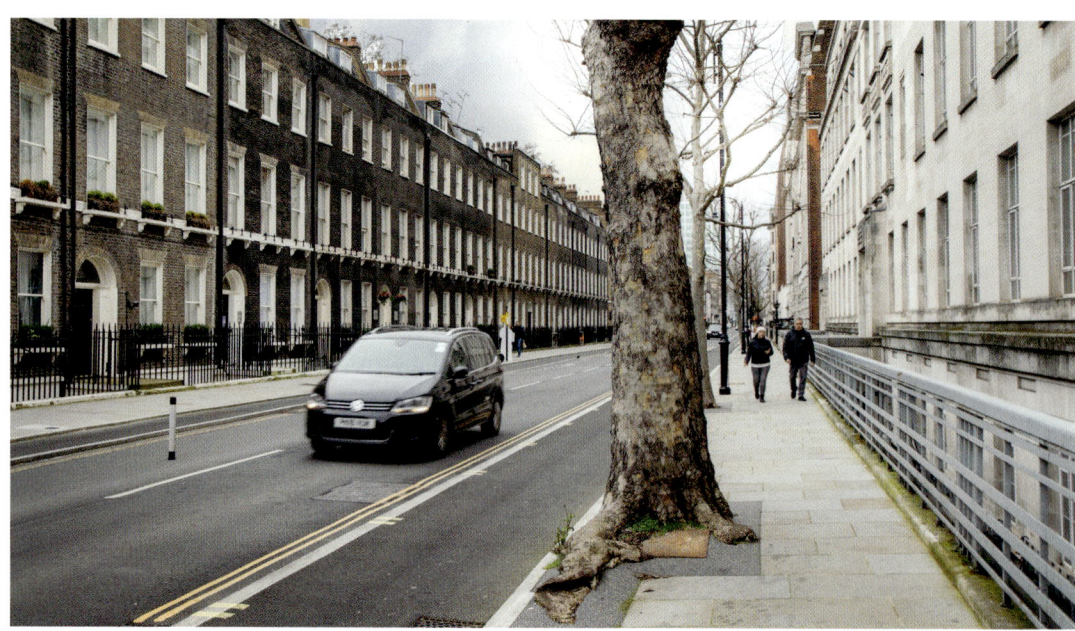

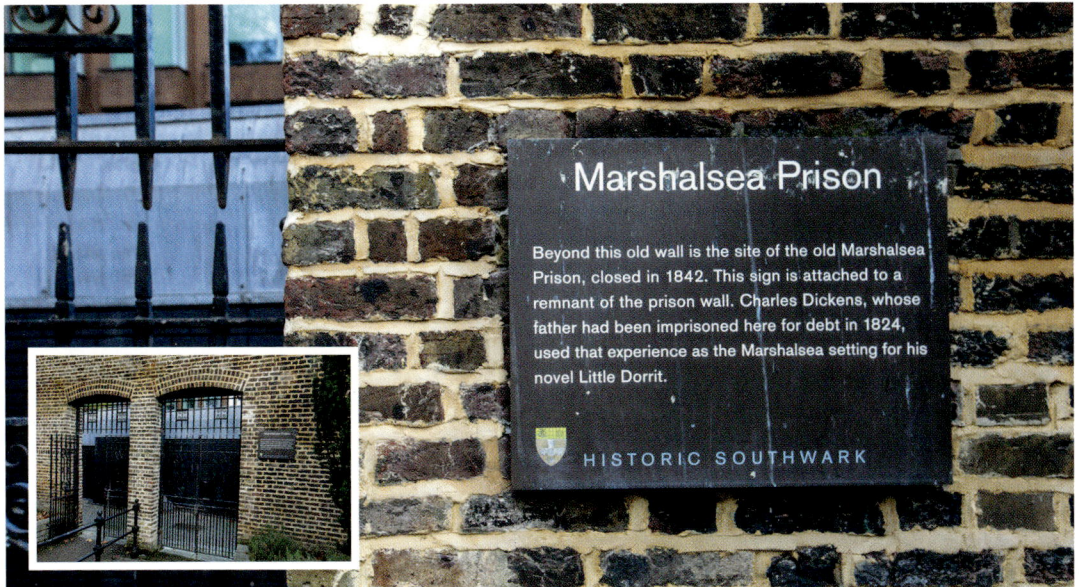

Marshalsea Debtors' Prison

Alongside the church of St George the Martyr on Borough High Street a long brick wall marking its southern boundary is all that remains of this notorious debtors' prison in Southwark. Closed in 1842, Dickens called it 'The crowning ghosts of many miserable years', recalled only by a plaque from Southwark Council. 'It's gone now,' he wrote, 'and the world is none the worse without it.' It is here inside the unpleasant and overcrowded conditions that John Dickens found himself imprisoned in 1824. The family home was given up, and the entire family, with the exception of Charles and his older sister Frances (known as Fanny), moved into John's prison cell. The churchyard grounds were used for many years as a burial place for prisoners who died in the Marshalsea and King's Bench prisons, both local debtors' jails.

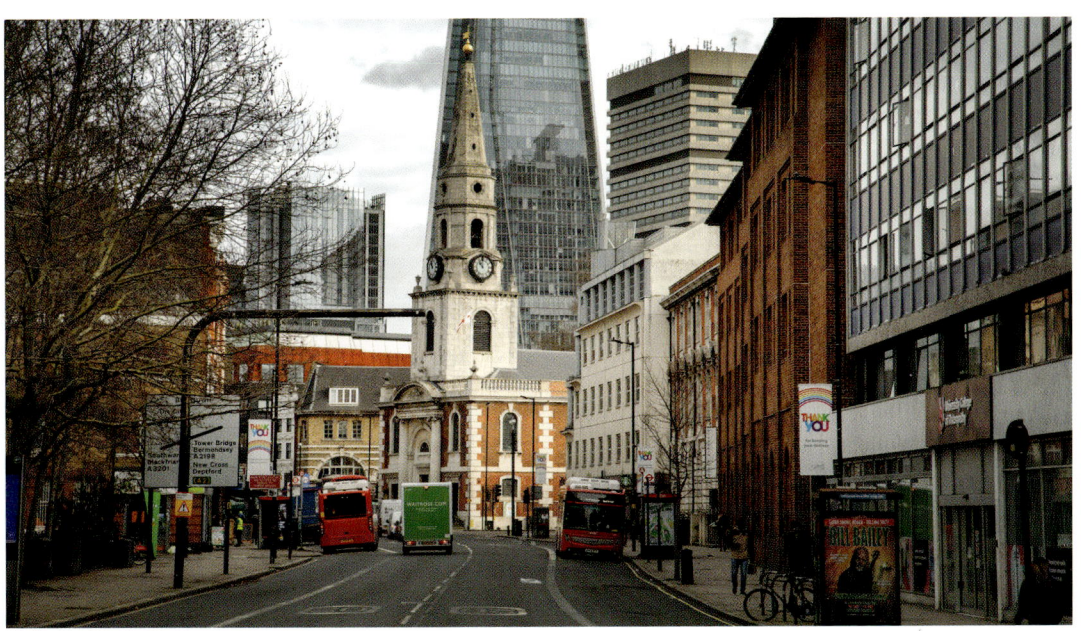

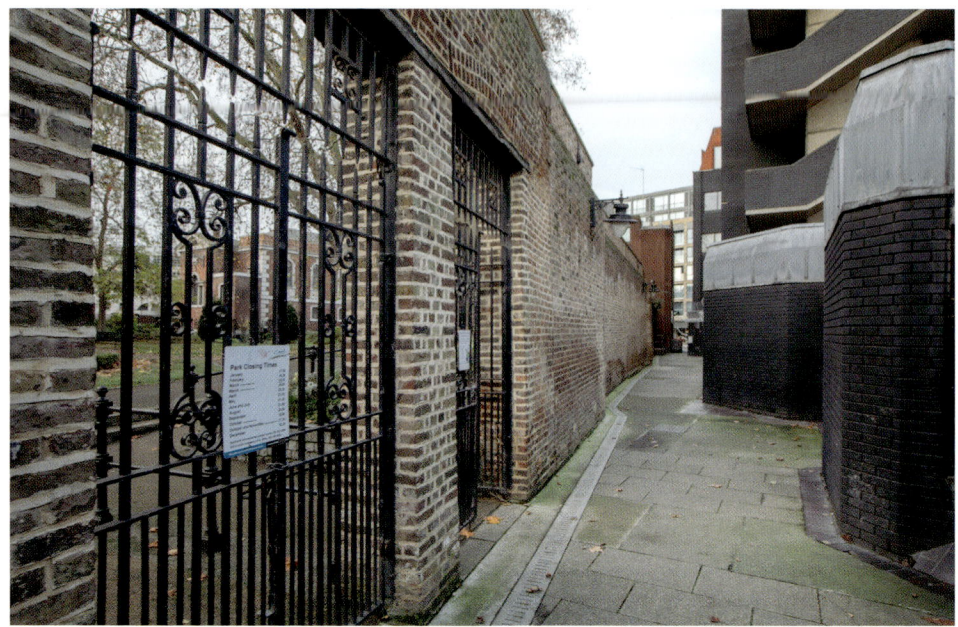

Angel Alley
Within this short path leading away from the prison gates are scribed paving flags commemorating the author's works, most notably relating to his eighteenth novel *Little Dorrit*. Originally published in serial form between 1855 and 1857, it was set almost entirely within the Marshalsea, mirroring the story of his own family's life there. The heroine of this Dickens novel, *Amy Dorrit*, was not a prisoner but a resident. She was free to earn money working and running other errands outside of the prison walls. Sadly, like Dickens' own life at the time of his father's imprisonment, although not a resident, his family were financially reliant upon the young boy's earnings.

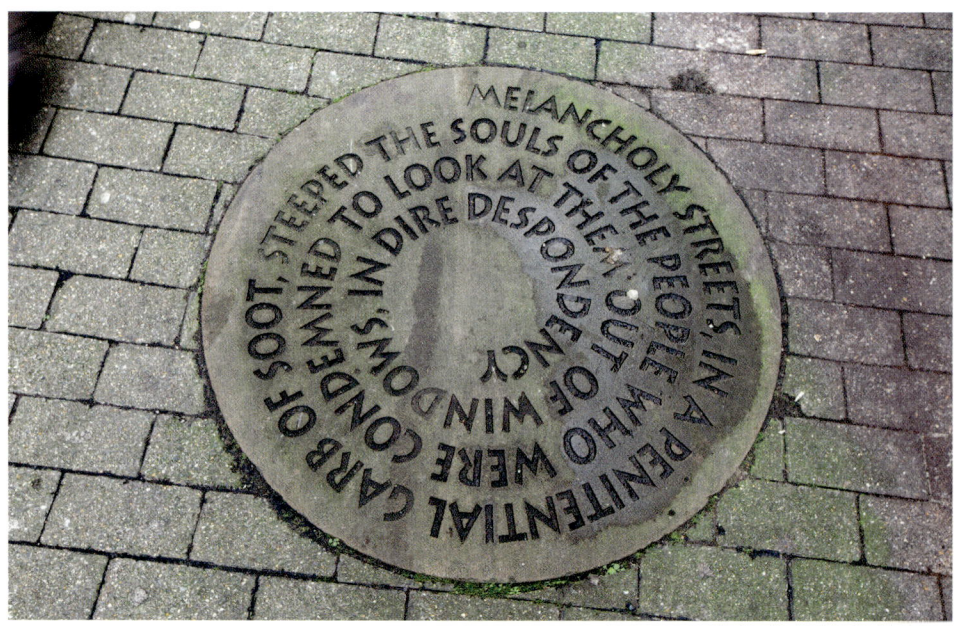

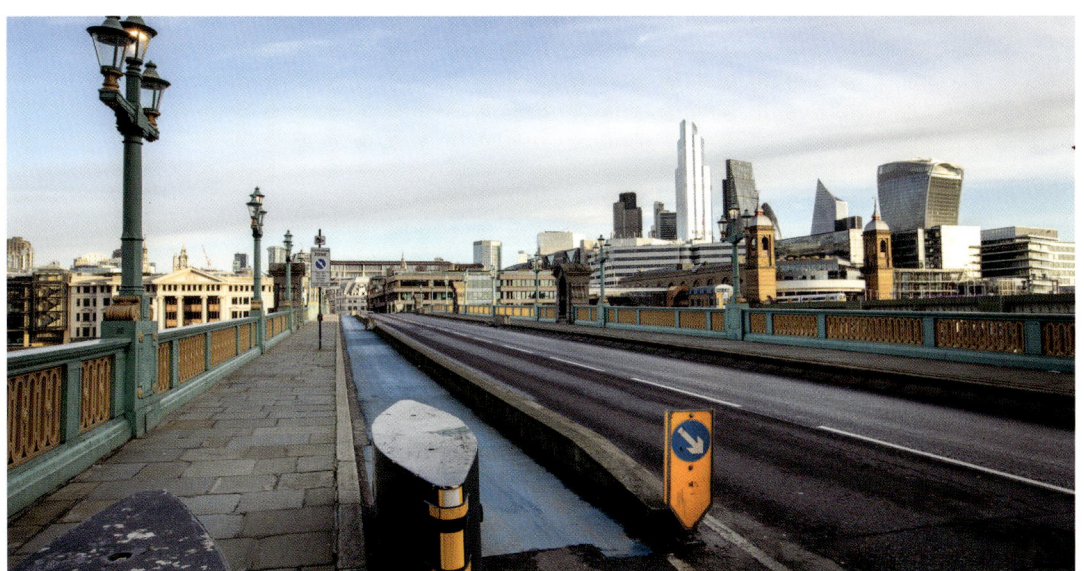

Southwark Bridge

Originally labelled as the Queen Street Bridge, the Southwark Bridge Dickens knew was designed by John Rennie and opened in 1819. It's iron structure linked the district of Southwark and the City across the River Thames. This route was taken by Charles Dickens and his sister Fanny each Sunday to reach the Marshalsea Debtors' Prison and is referenced several times in his works. It was described as 'a quiet place' by Dickens due to its toll charge to cross of one penny. The 'Iron Bridge' is featured in the first sentence of *Our Mutual Friend*, Charles Dickens' twenty-second novel, completed in 1865. Within this book the distasteful character fisherman *Gaffer Hexam* makes his living by Southwark Bridge. He uses the embankments either side as a searching point to haul dead bodies from the water to steal from their pockets. The bridge we see today was designed by Ernest George and Basil Mott and built by Sir William Arrol & Co. and opened on 6 June 1921.

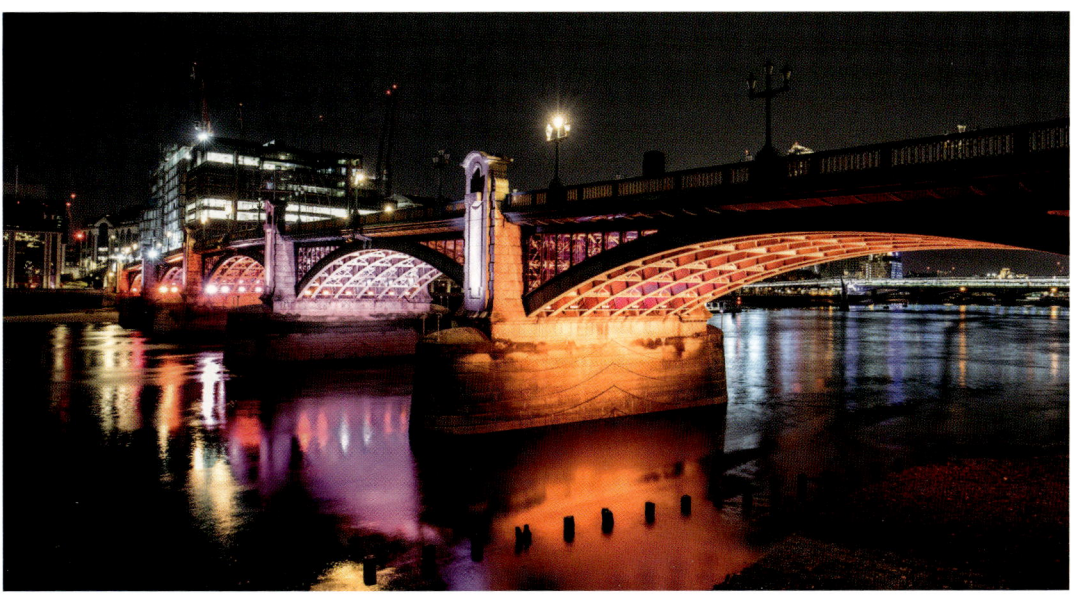

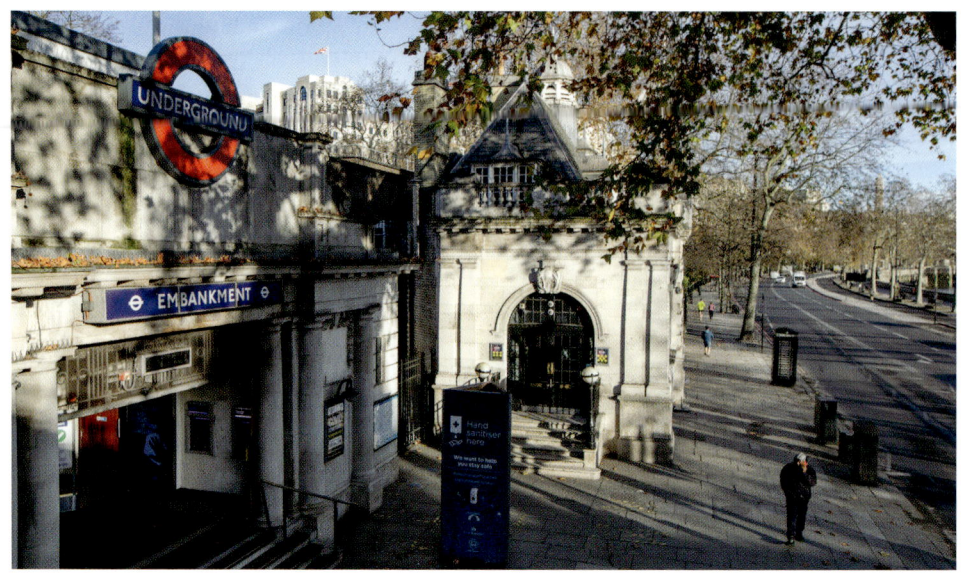

The Embankment and Warren's Blacking Factory

Originally based at 30 Hungerford Stairs, now the Embankment Station, the time Dickens spent here was miserable. His parents proposed he assist the family's finances and it led to his removal from schooling. He wrote in his biography, 'No words could paint the secret agony of my soul.' In 1824, in the rat-infested factory, twelve-year-old Dickens began his employment as a 'drudge'. Working long hours, covering pots of paste, he resentfully remained here for months after his father's release to relieve the family's expenses. It was during this time the factory moved to Chandos Place where the plaque today can be seen. The factory's supervisor was called Bob Fagin and it is his name (not personality – he wasn't supposedly all that bad) that was used as inspiration for the leader of the den of thieves in *Oliver Twist*. The location is also mentioned when *Joe Gargery* and *Wopsle* first arrive in London in his thirteenth title, *Great Expectations*.

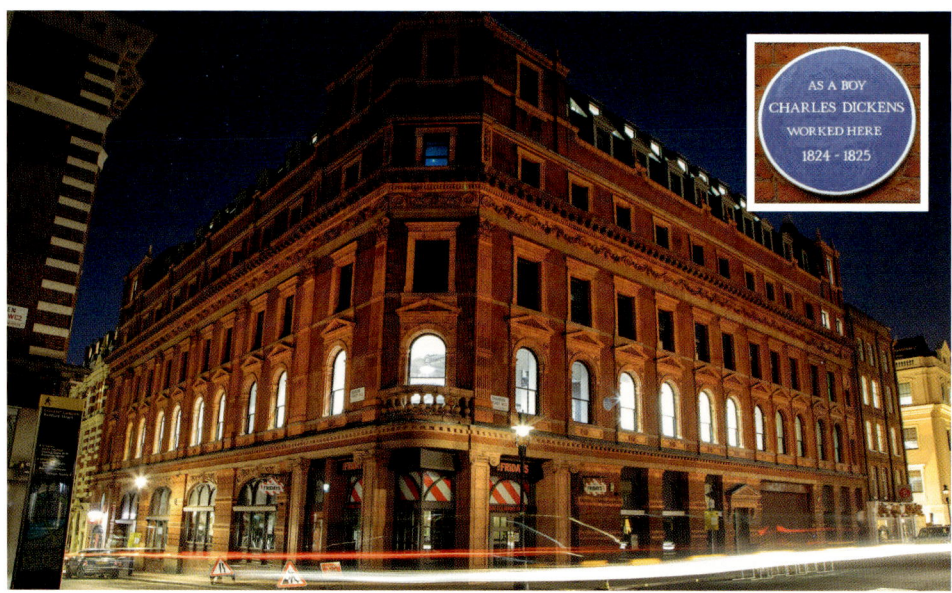

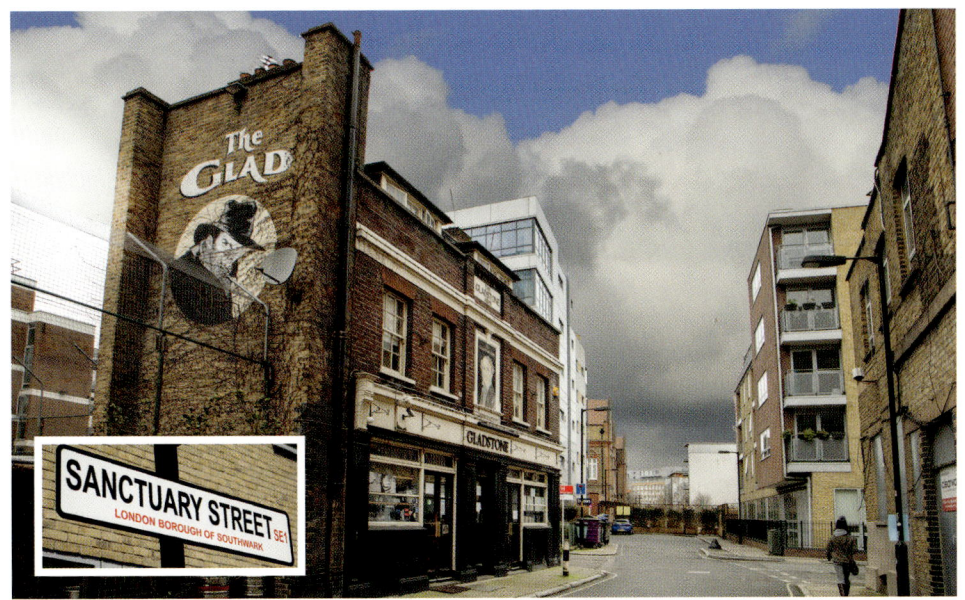

Lant Street

Named in remembrance of the Lant family and marked now by the naming of the Dickens Primary School, it is here in 1824 that twelve-year-old Charles Dickens took lodgings in the house of the Vestry Clerk of St George's Church. He was briefly placed at 37 Little College Street with a Mrs Roylance in Camden Town when his father was first imprisoned, making visiting his family in the Marshalsea a difficult and arduous journey on foot. When Charles moved to Lant Street just South of Marshalsea Road in Southwark he referred to it as 'paradise' in comparison to his spell with Mrs Roylance. Public house, The Glad has been situated here since the nineteenth century and is named after four-time former Prime Minister William Gladstone. The tavern gets a mention in Dickens' 1837 first novel *The Posthumous Papers of the Pickwick Club*, also known as *The Pickwick Papers*.

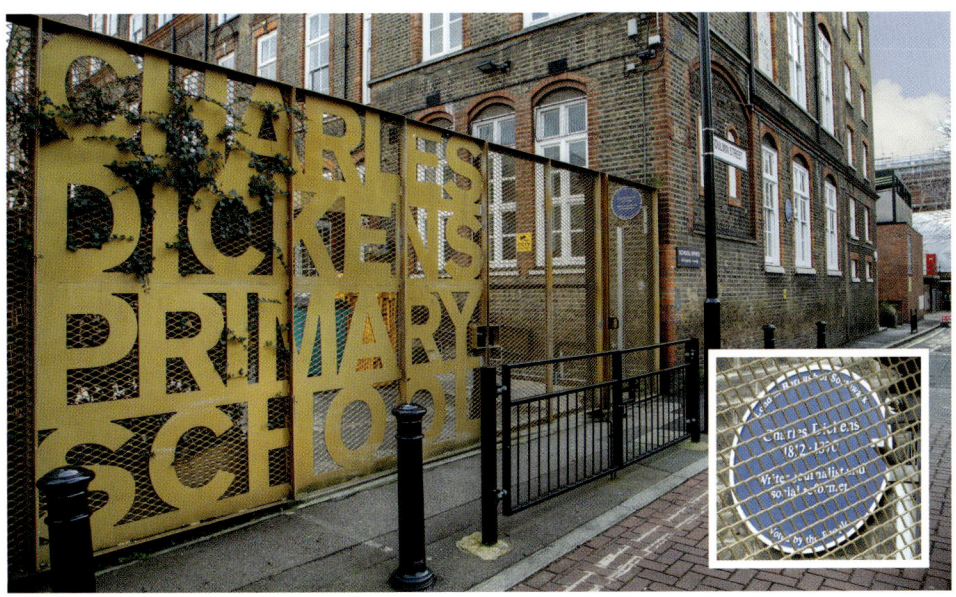

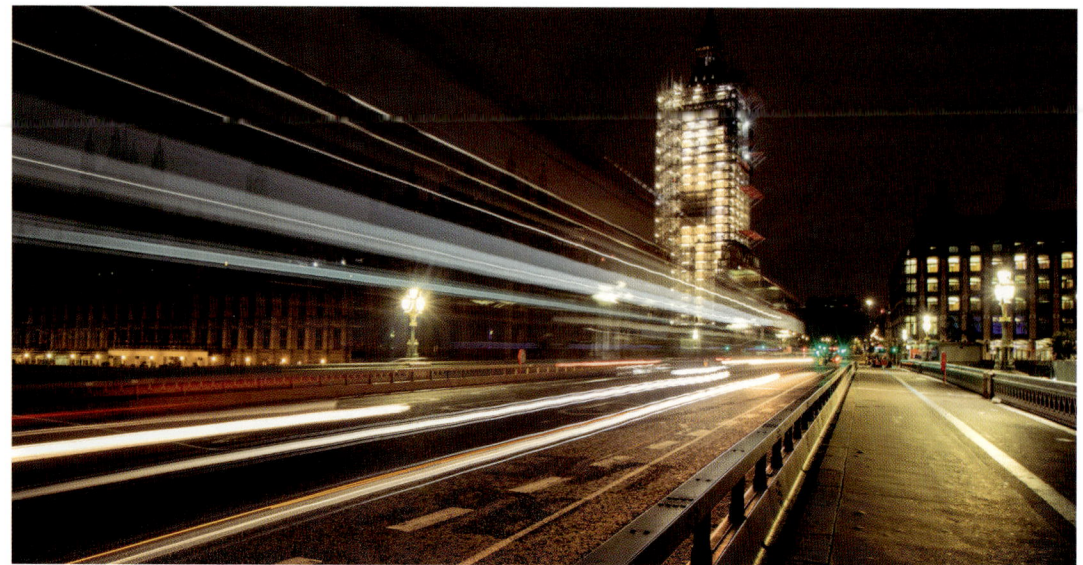

Palace of Westminster

On receipt of an inheritance of £450 from the passing of his mother, John Dickens was able to settle his debts and his family left the Marshalsea in May 1825. A few months later Charles was able to return to education at the Wellington House Academy in North London. From there he undertook an apprenticeship in a solicitor's office, before becoming a parliamentary reporter for the *Morning Chronicle* in 1833, covering the Courts of Law and the House of Commons. Whilst in this role he began a voracious program of self-improvement in retaliation to his schooling being so prematurely halted. He taught himself the Gurney system of shorthand, a process still used in the Houses of Parliament today. He refers to this talent in his lead male role of *David Copperfield*. The 1850 novel of the same title was his fourteenth published works. This character is imagined by many readers to be how Dickens may have viewed himself – born into a privileged but cruel world where a young man strives for education and opportunity to rise through the ranks of class divide. On the night of 16 October 1834, a devastating fire broke out inside the Lords Chamber and raged through the institution. The restoration and rebuild was not completed until 1868. Dickens followed the construction works with great interest.

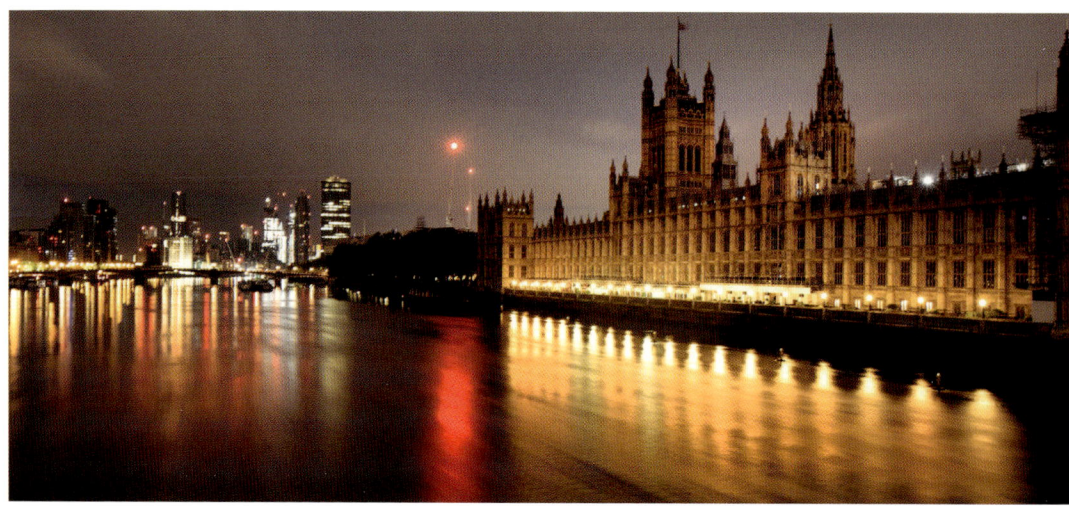

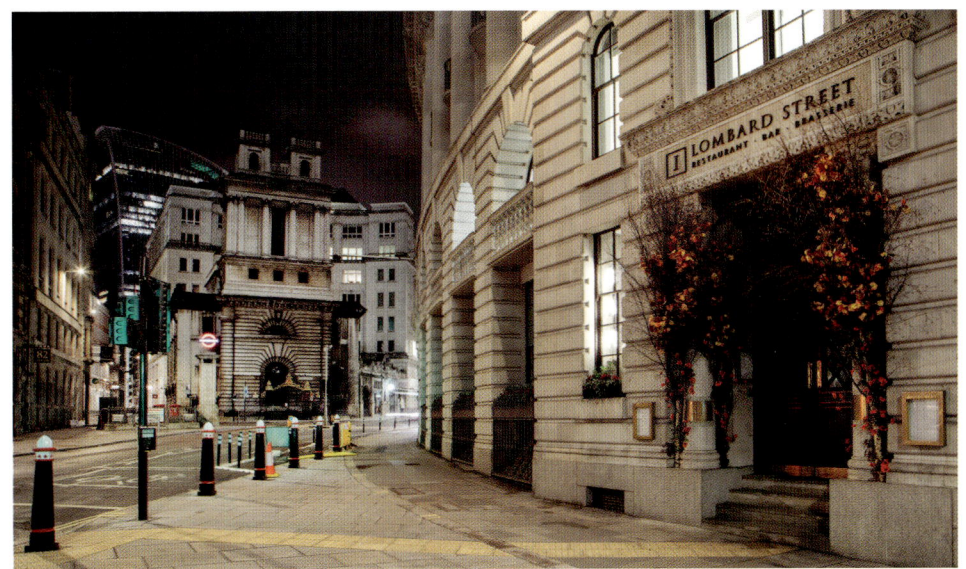

1 Lombard Street

In 1830, eighteen-year-old Dickens fell deeply in love with twenty-year-old Maria Beadnell of 1 Lombard Street. Maria's father never felt Dickens' prospects were satisfactory and attempting to end the flirtation, he sent her to finishing school in Paris. Upon her return she was much cooler towards the relationship. Defeated Dickens wrote to her: 'Our meetings of late have been little more than so many displays of heartless indifference ...' Maria married Henry Winter and in 1855 the pair had dinner with Dickens and his wife Catherine. Shocked by her 'rotund and toothless' appearance, she became the inspiration for *Dora Spenlow* in *David Copperfield* and *Flora Finching* in *Little Dorrit*. Mansion House, the official residence of the Lord Mayor of London since 1752, is referred to opulently in what is arguably Dickens' most famous work, *A Christmas Carol*, published in 1843. 'The Lord Mayor, in the stronghold of the mighty Mansion House, gave orders to his fifty cooks and butlers to keep Christmas as a Lord Mayor's Household should ...'.

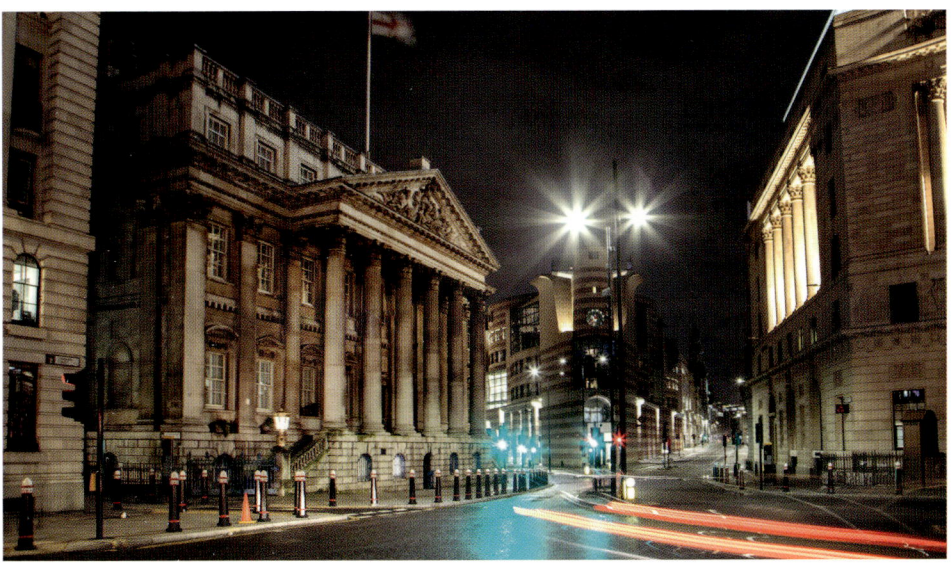

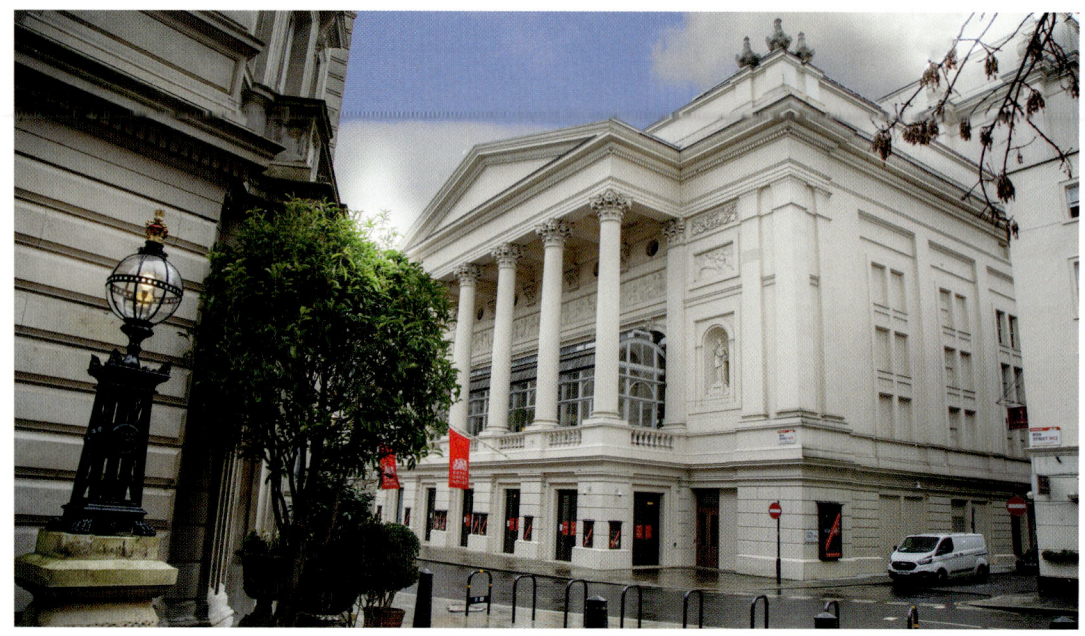

Royal Opera House and Bow Street Magistrates
The third theatre to be stood on this site, following disastrous fires in both 1808 and 1856. Dickens would've known both former buildings well and in 1832, whilst searching for his calling, he wrote to George Barclay asking to audition to act. His intention to produce a piece inspired by his love of comic Charles Matthew was cut dead when he developed a severe case of flu confining him with an inflamed face to bed. Dickens' close relationship with the law brings us to the magistrates and the inspiration in location for one of his most loved characters. The *Artful Dodger* was placed in the dock to make his plea here during the novel *Oliver Twist*.

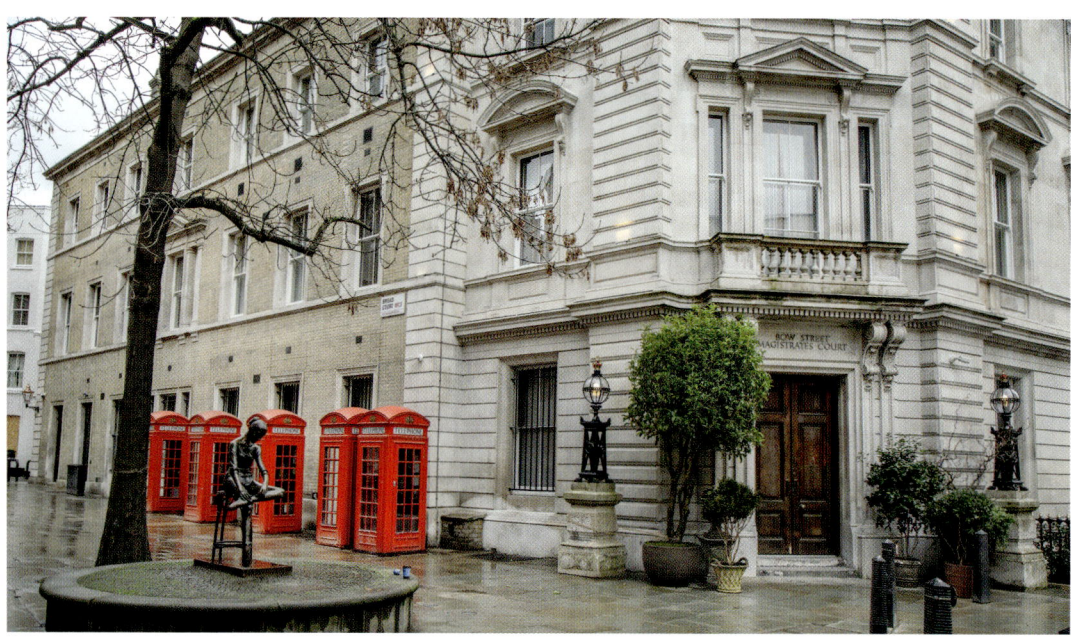

48 Doughty Street

Threatened with demolition in 1923, 48 Doughty Street was the third marital home of Charles Dickens and his wife Catherine Hogarth. It was thankfully saved from demolition by the Dickens Fellowship and the Dickens House Museum which was opened in 1925. Following the bicentenary of the author's birth in 2012 and a heritage grant from The National Lottery, No. 49 was also acquired, and they set about a magnificent refurbishment to delicately turn the museum into a replica of the Dickens home to be enjoyed by today's Dickensian devotee. Notably it now houses a large collection of the family's memorabilia and Dickens' personal manuscripts and artefacts. His chair and desk sit proudly on display, as does the only known existing item of clothing worn by Dickens – his court suit and sword, which he wore when he presented to the Prince of Wales in 1870.

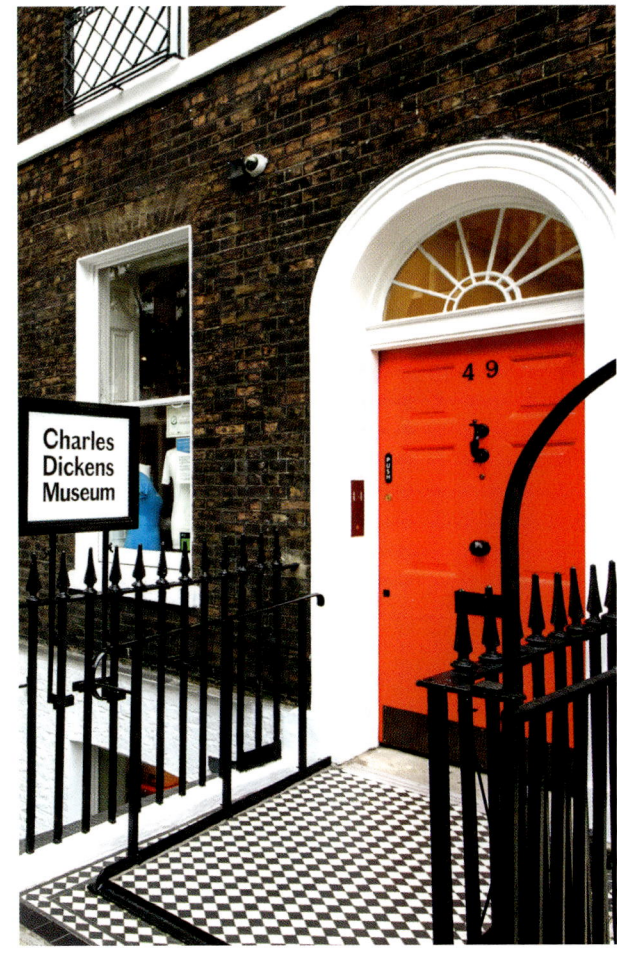

Following his first well-paid set of literary successes in 1837 the author took out an £80 per annum tenancy. Reflecting his rise in finances and social standing he moved his family to this tree-lined Georgian square.

The newlyweds moved here with two-month-old baby Charles, and Catherine gave birth to Kate and Mary in quick succession soon after. Whilst only a short lease of two and a half years was completed the home holds great personal and professional importance for the author; he was certainly very productive whilst at its residence. His written output was staggering considering his newly appointed position as editor of the literary magazine Bentley's *Miscellany*. Unbelievably he completed *The Pickwick Papers, Oliver Twist, Nicholas Nickleby*, not to mention the writing and overseeing of four small plays whilst setting out the beginnings *of Barnaby Rudge* whilst here.

Not all events were happy ones in this twelve-roomed dwelling though, and in true Dickens style suffering was just around the corner. At around 3 p.m. on Sunday 7 May 1837 Dickens' beloved sister-in-law Mary Hogarth died unexpectedly. She had fallen ill after a theatre trip to see *Is She His Wife?* As wasn't unusual for a younger sibling, she lived with the young married couple and was undoubtably close to her brother-in-law. The relationship has been questioned by some and admired by others, but it cannot be argued that her death had a profound effect on the author.

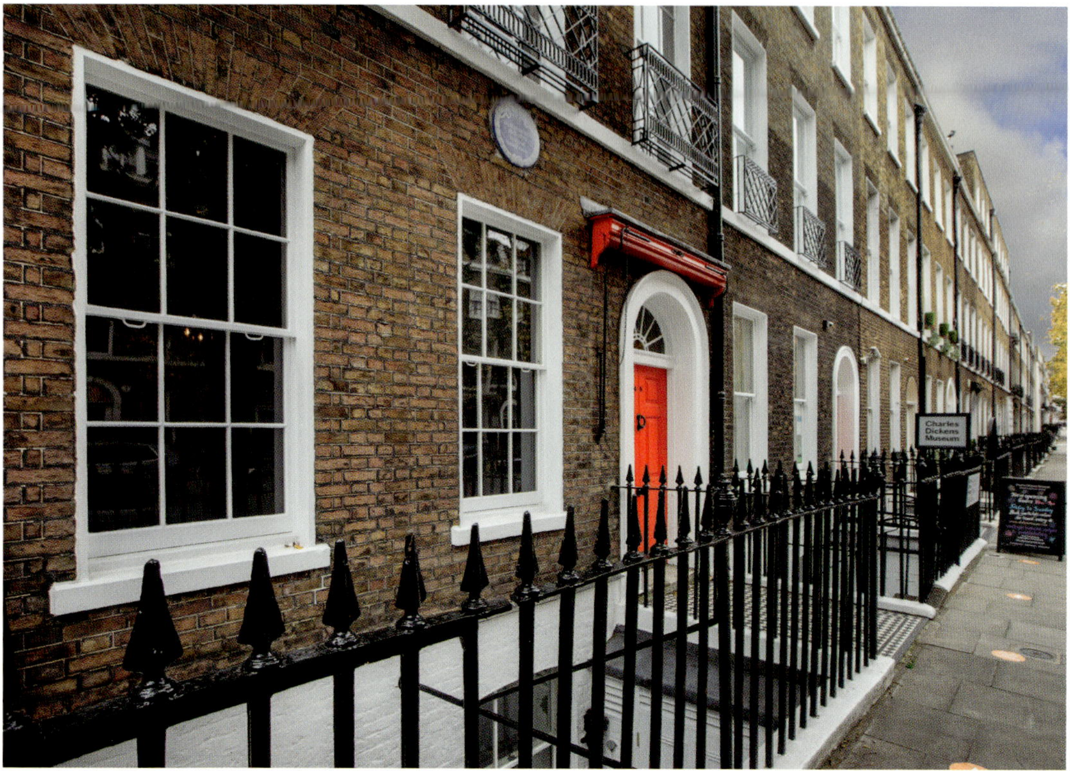

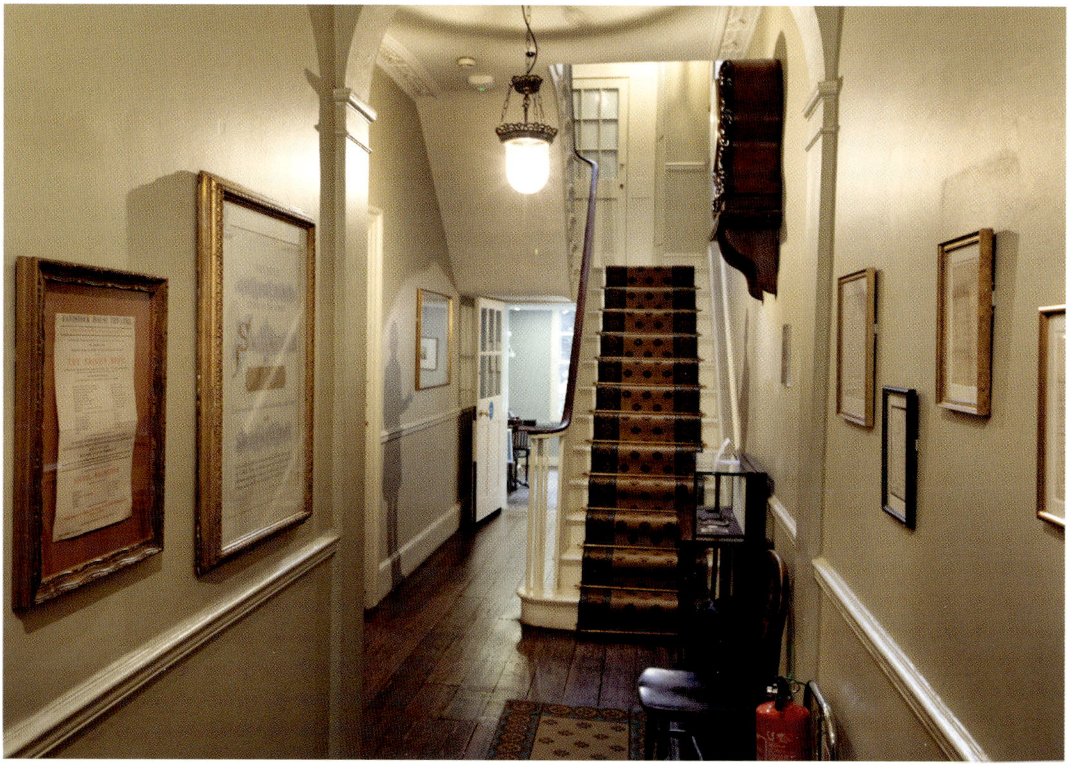

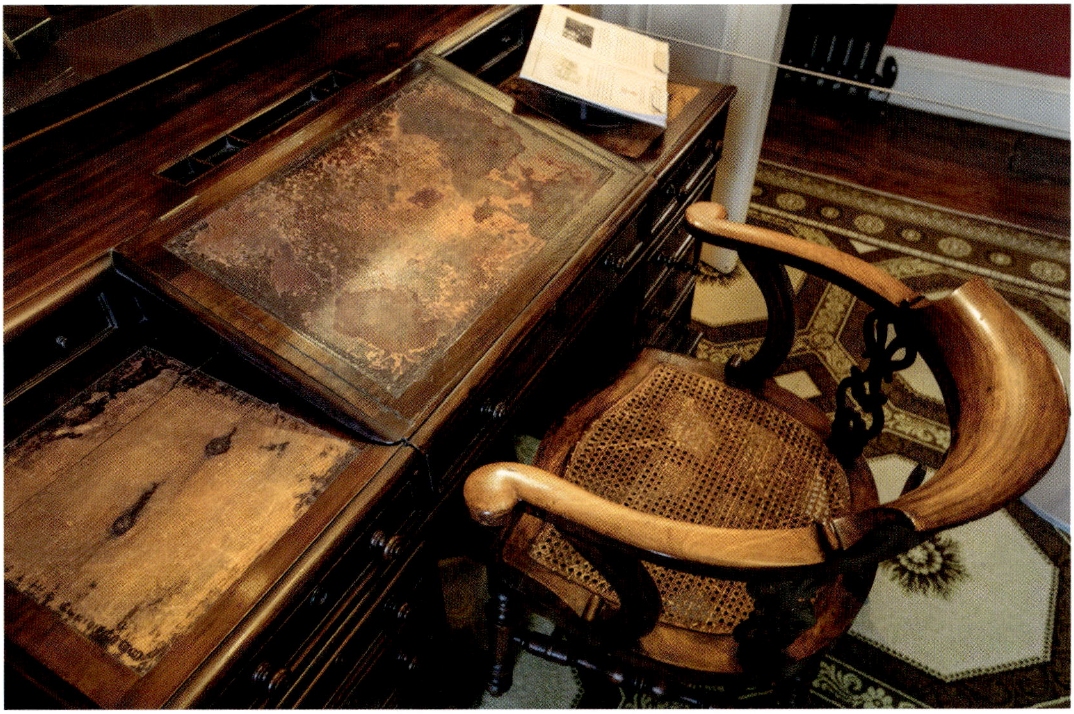

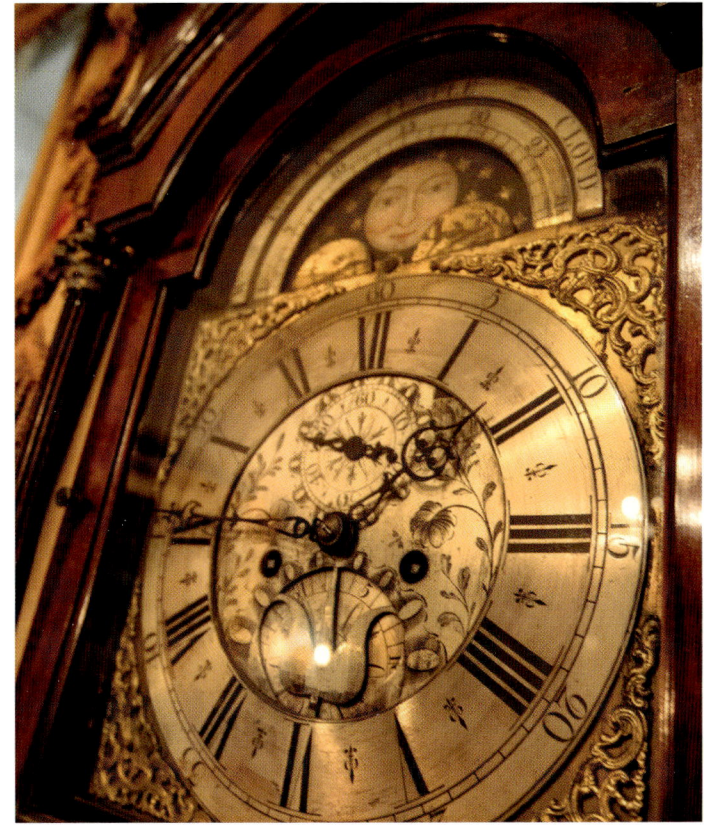

Despite a doctor being called she died in his arms, and he took a ring from her stilling finger to wear upon his own for the rest of his days. Drowning in grief he stopped writing for a considerable amount of time also; something he failed to do when his own child had died. He later used her memory to inspire such characters as *Little Nell* in *The Old Curiosity Shop*, *Rose Maylie* in *Oliver Twist*, *Kate Nickleby* in *Nicholas Nickleby*, and *Agnes Wickfield* in *David Copperfield*. She fixed forever his ideal of what a woman should be – a girl. She had died at exactly the age at which some have the opinion after his grief for Mary that for him a woman was, at her most perfect: she never grew fat, dull, tired or tedious.

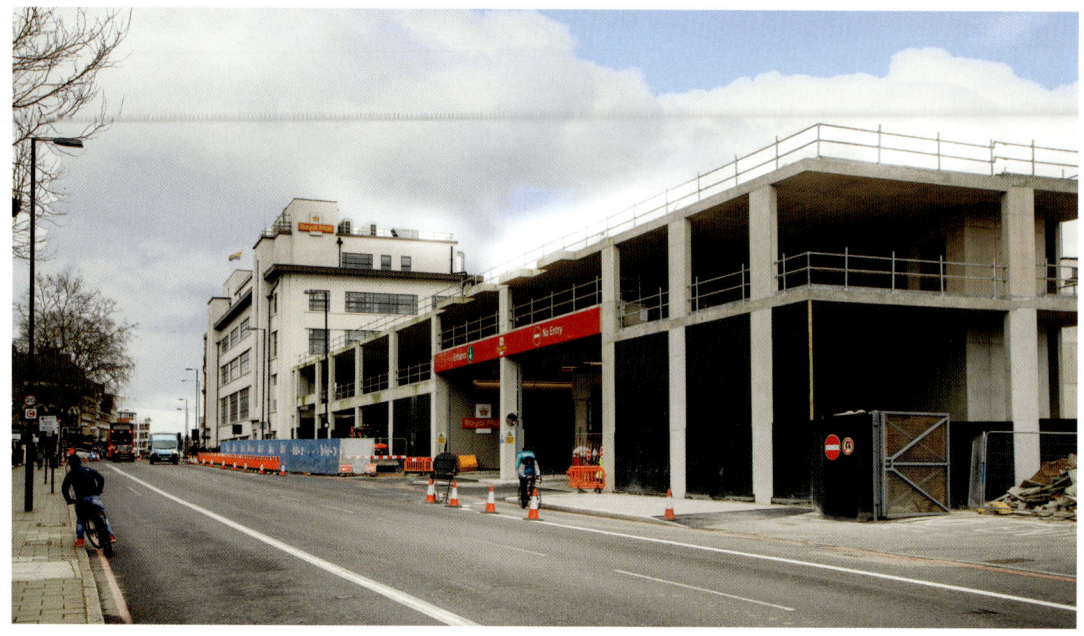

Mount Pleasant Sorting Office and Clerkenwell

A short walk from his home in Doughty Street, Dickens made Mount Pleasant the ironic home of the *Smallweed family* in *Bleak House*. A dangerous part of London in Dickens' lifetime, this site was known as a dumping ground for cinders and refuse. Close by, between 1794 and 1877 the brutal Coldbath Fields Prison, also known as the Middlesex House of Correction, was a domineering feature to the area, housing criminals and miscreants. *Mr Bumble* from *Oliver Twist* is invited here to the Clerkenwell sessions where he is warned of its notoriety and characters. His response: 'If there is any trouble to be had ... they shall have it with me.'

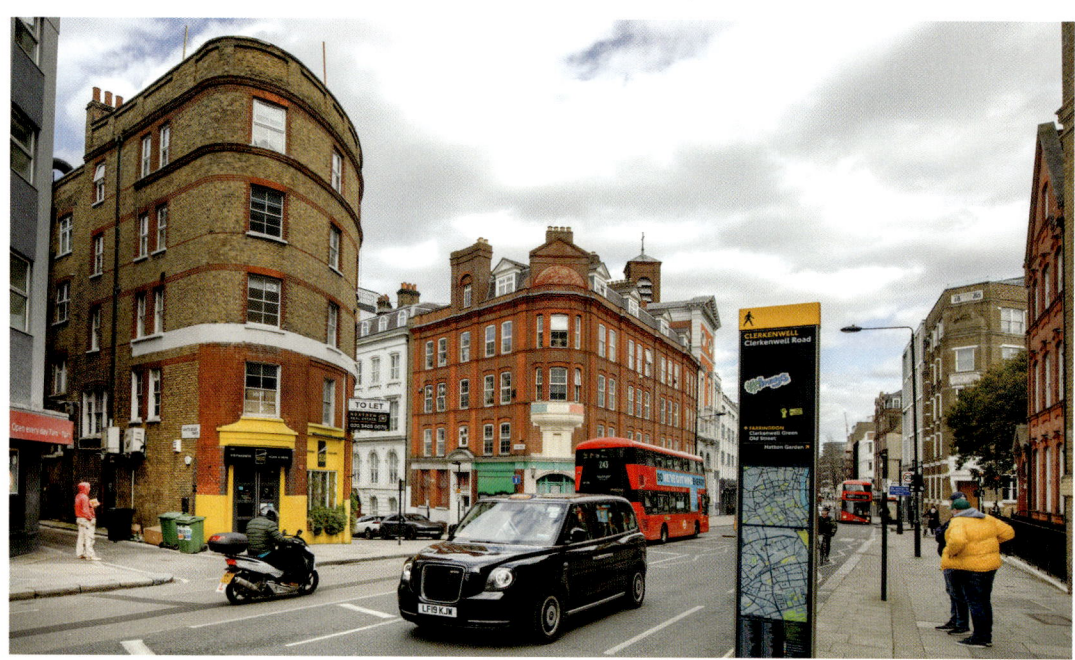

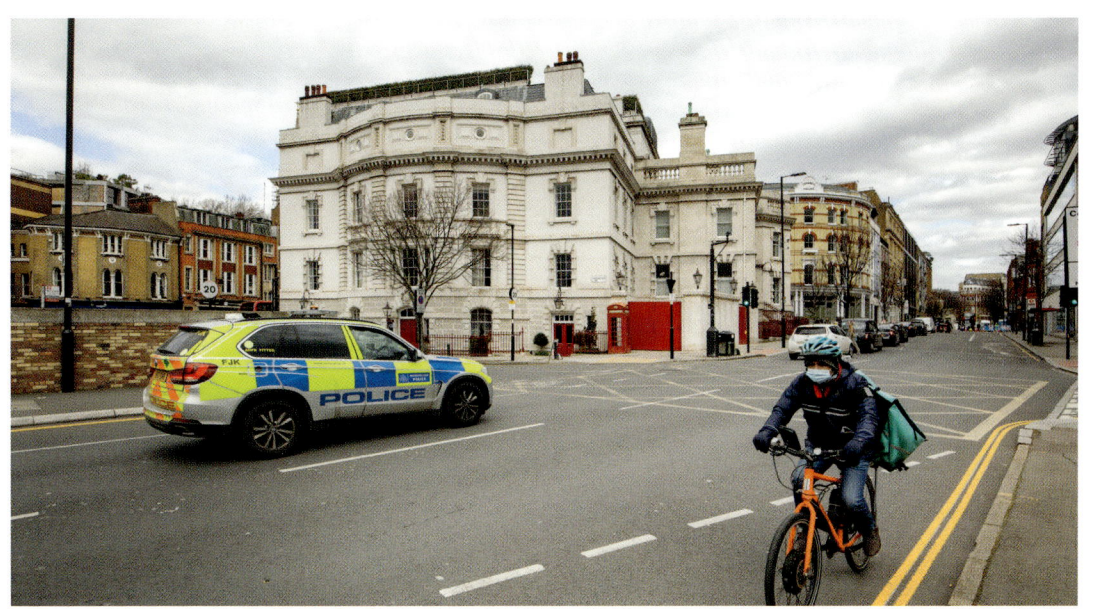

Clerkenwell Green and the Old Middlesex Sessions House

Heavily referenced as an impoverished location in the serial *The Parish Boy's Progress*, which later became the much-loved novel *Oliver Twist*, Clerkenwell Green was the setting for where *Fagin's* gang of young pickpockets practised their trade. Also, it is only a short distance from Saffron Hill, which is thought to be the spot the band of young thieves were housed together under the watchful eye of their greedy leader. As a cub reporter in the nearby Old Middlesex Sessions House, Dickens chose this intimidating structure as the location for little Oliver to stand trial accused of stealing a pocket watch. The sessions were also paid a visit by *Mr Bumble the Beadle* from the same title. A cruel but undoubted nitwit, he provides some comic relief during his scene: 'The Clerkenwell Sessions have brought it upon themselves, ma'am,' replied Mr Bumble; 'and if the Clerkenwell Sessions find that they come off rather worse than they expected, the Clerkenwell Sessions have only themselves to thank.'

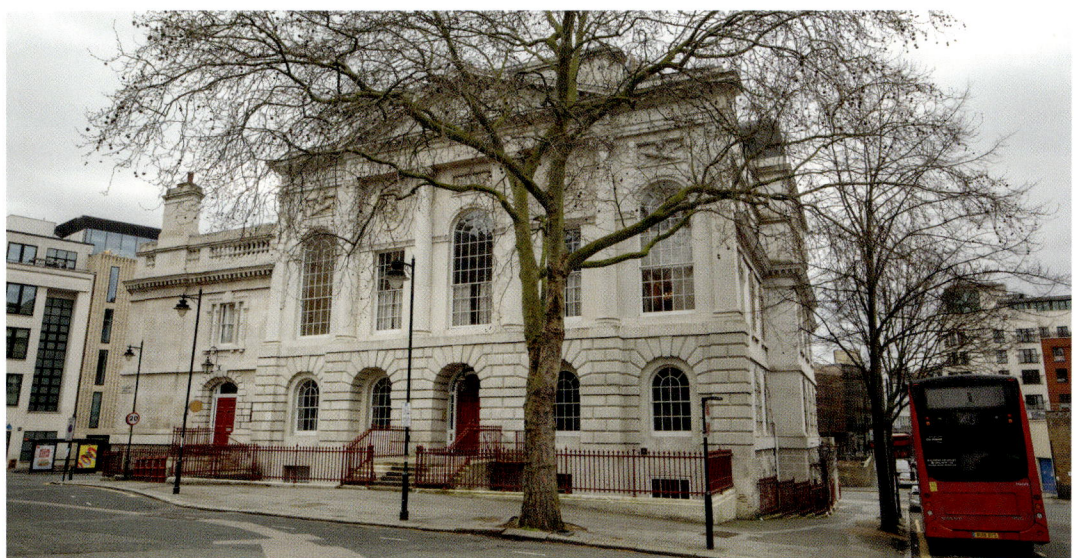

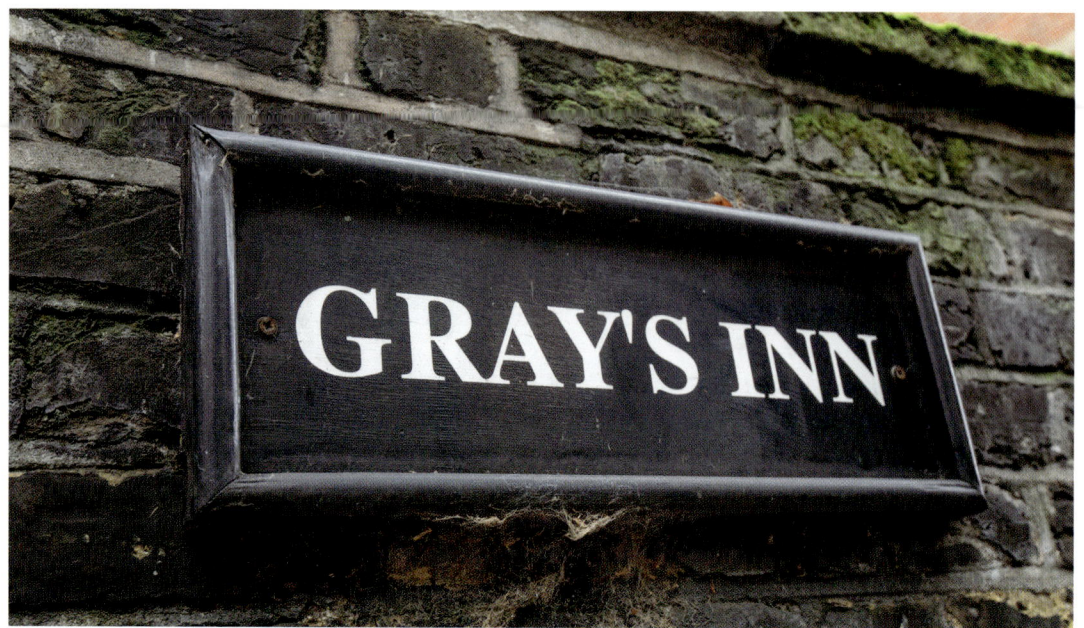

Gray's Inn

Although no official blue plaque can be seen at 1 South Square, it is here at Gray's Inn, located in Holborn, that a fifteen-year-old Dickens began work as a junior solicitor's clerk. He described the offices of Ellis and Blackmore as 'one of the most depressing institutions in brick and mortar known to the children of men'. Inns such as these were professional associations for barristers and judges, providing both offices and accommodation to legal professionals. Gray's Inn is one of four Inns of Court within London. Gray's has been established since the early fifteenth century.

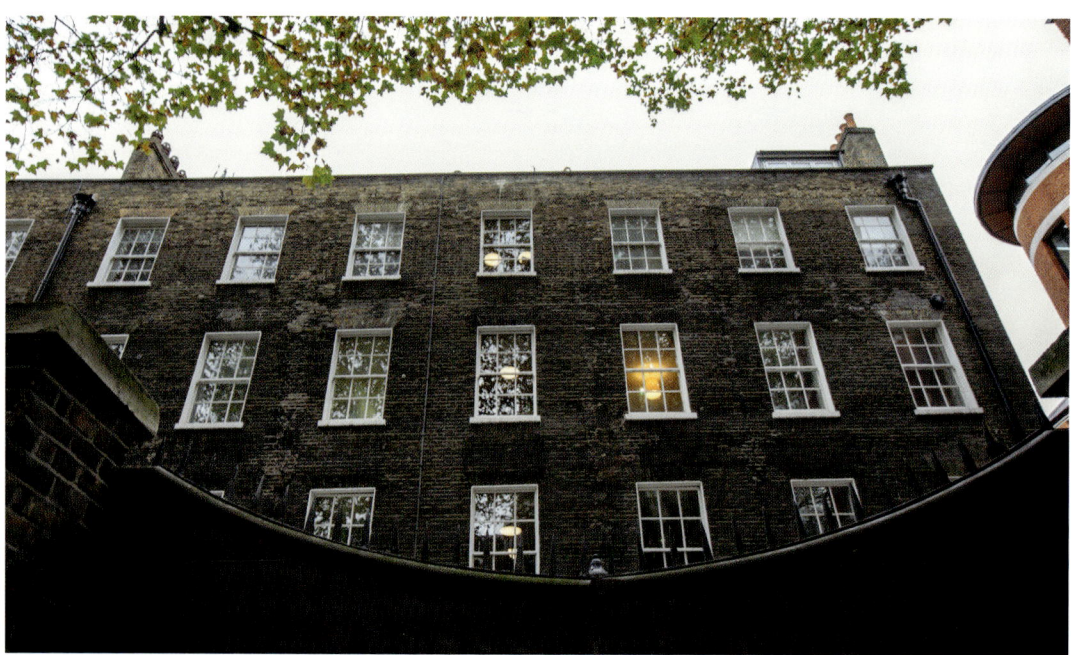

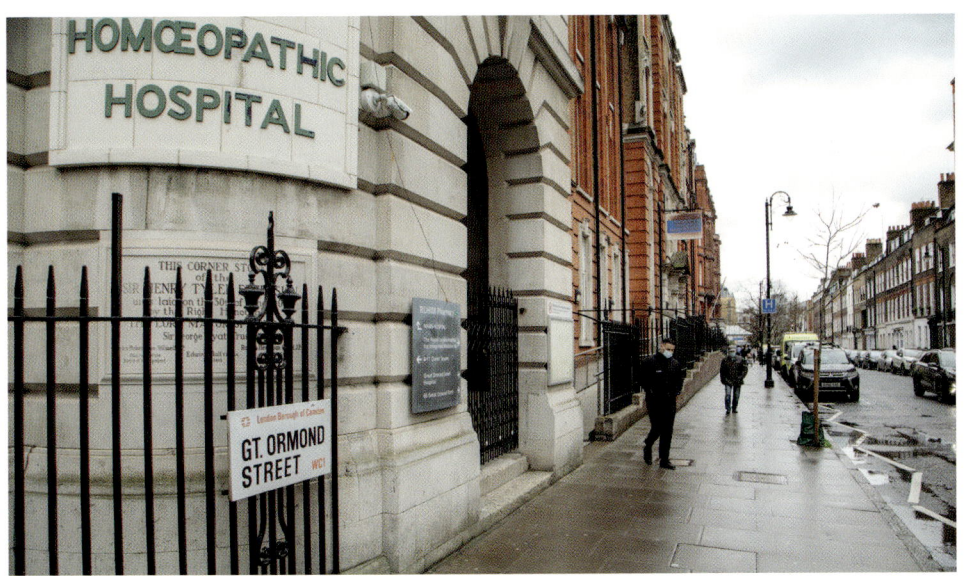

Great Ormond Street Children's Hospital

Great Ormand Street was opened in 1852. Dickens, appalled by child mortality rates of the time, became an unusual but dedicated supporter of the hospital. More than likely reminded of his own impoverished upbringing and sensitivity towards his surroundings, he appeared to be truly pained by the thought of children suffering. Dickens also featured an advertisement for the hospital in *Our Mutual Friend*. The orphan boy *Johnny Higden* is brought to 'the Children's Hospital' terminally ill with tuberculosis and cared for properly for the first and only time in his life at 'a place where there are none but children; a place set up on purpose for sick children; where the good doctors and nurses pass their lives with children, talk to none but children, touch none but children, comfort and cure none but children'. In 1994 a memorial was unveiled to Dickens in the hospital chapel in the presence of several of his great-grandchildren.

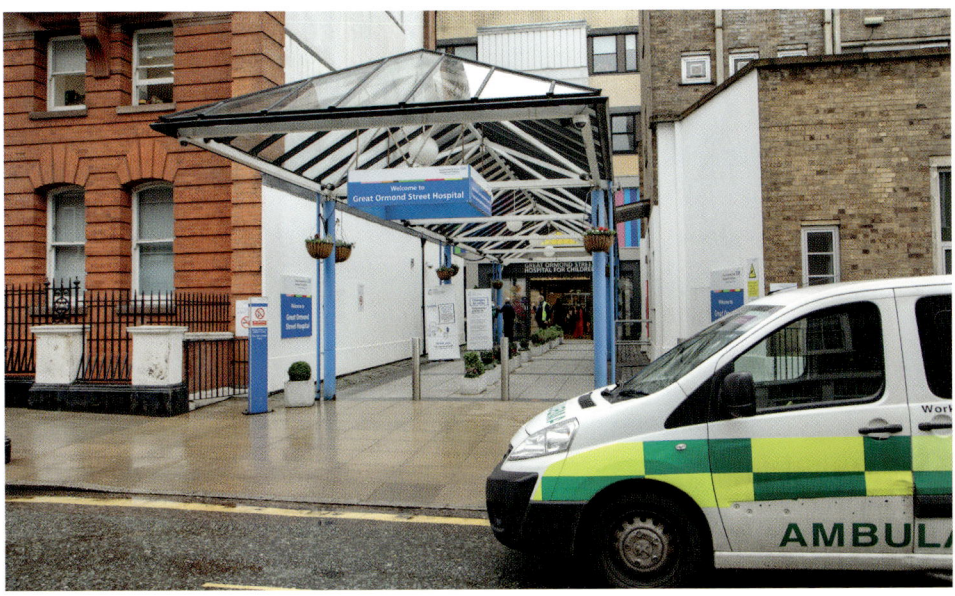

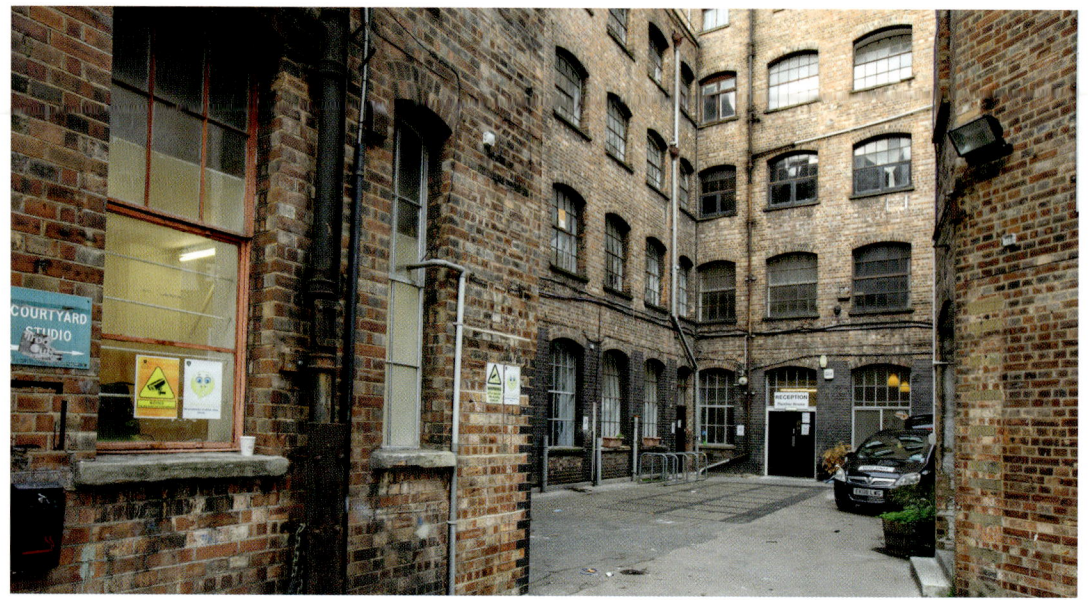

Holborn Union Workhouse

Situated on the site since 1746, Holborn Union Workhouse was the view from the window when our young author worked as a junior clerk. He watched the comings and goings daily, and the people he saw were arguably his inspiration for a long list of heroic and villainous characters – from the down on their luck to those revelling in positions of power over them. Dickens seemed to have a strong opinion about what was morally right and wrong when it came to social classing versus financial circumstance. Many years later in 1850 he wrote 'Walk in a Workhouse' as an article for his own magazine, *Household Words*. His plight to shed light on the atrocities of poverty and injustice were never far from his heart throughout his life.

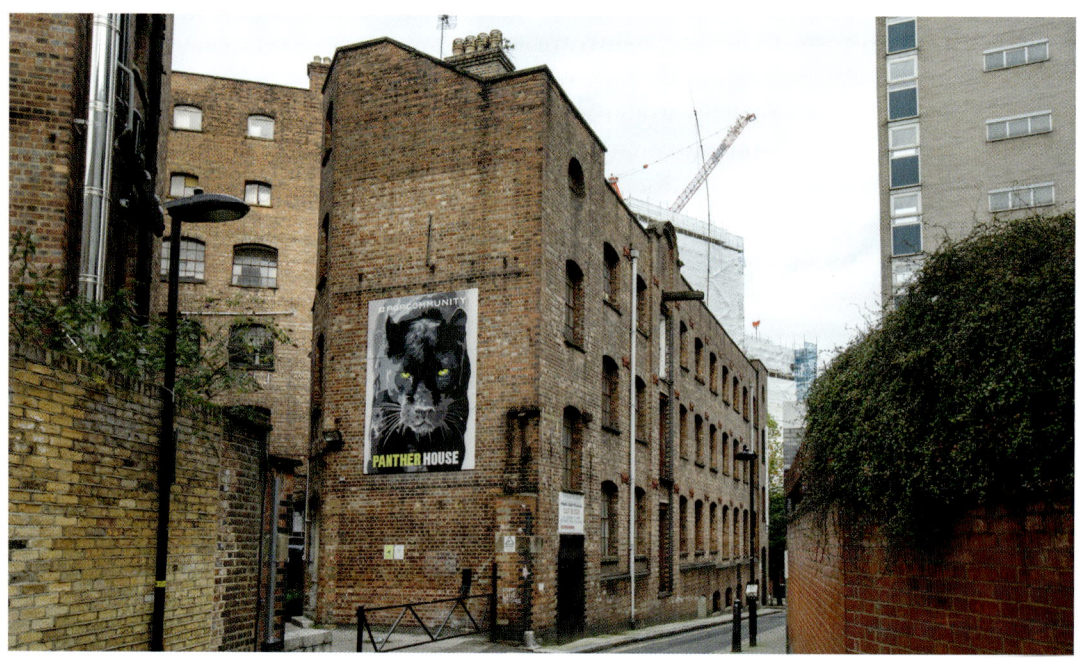

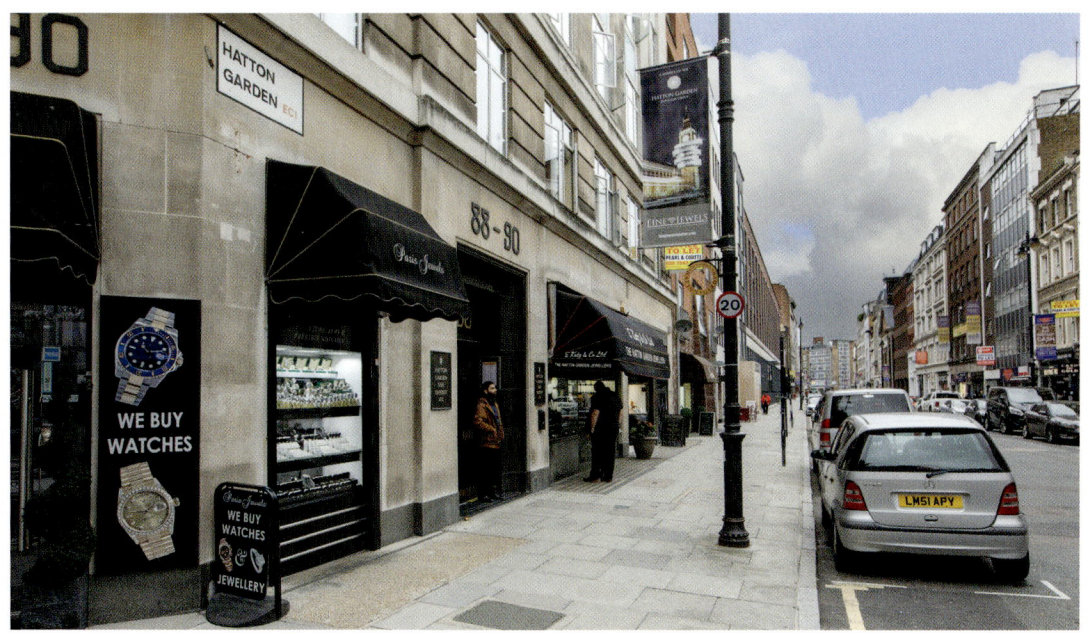

Hatton Gardens

The home of diamond dealers and lavish spending in today's world, Hatton Garden was an entirely different experience in Dickensian times. It is here at No. 54 Hatton Garden that Dickens brings us to the police courthouse where *Oliver Twist* is presided over by *Mr Fang*. This ferocious character has a genuine inspiration by the name of Mr A. S. Laing, a feared but infamous judge in whom our author had taken a great interest. Dickens' request to meet the man resulted in an angry outburst by his superiors and Laing eventually being removed from his post – possibly his intention all along considering his feelings on the dubious rulings he dealt out.

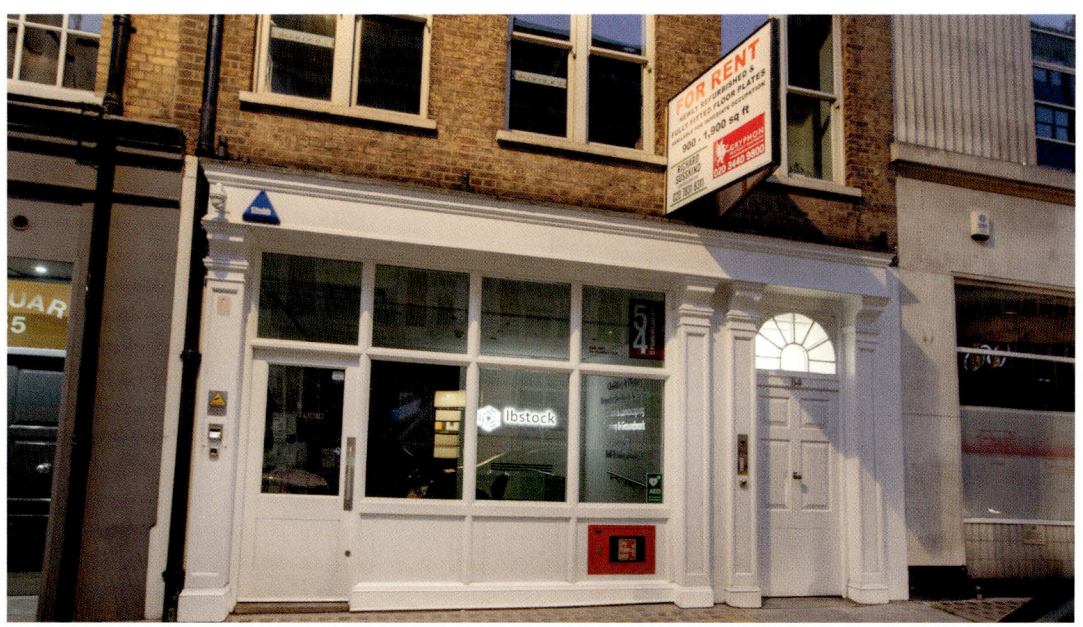

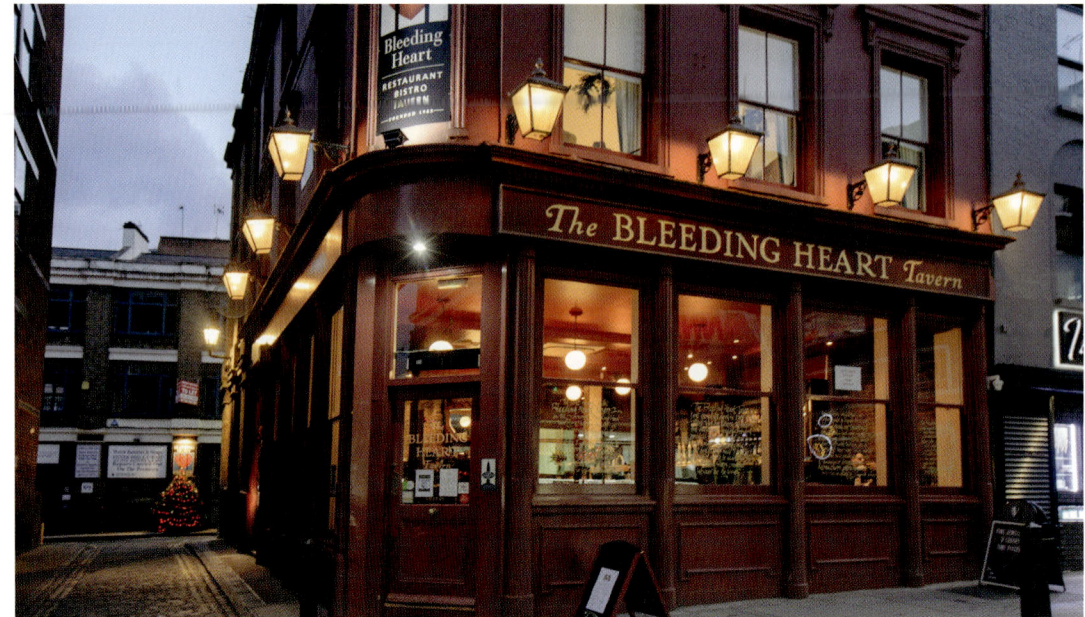

Bleeding Heart Yard

The site is named after the murder of Lady Elizabeth Hatton. It is said that her body was found here in 1626 with her heart still pumping blood onto the cobbles. Dickens described Bleeding Heart Yard as 'a place much changed in feature and in fortune, yet with some relish of ancient greatness about it. It was inhabited by poor people, who set up their rest among its faded glories, as Arabs of the desert pitch their tents among the fallen stones of the Pyramids; but there was a family sentimental feeling prevalent in the Yard, that it had a character.' Home of hardship but good spirit, he made it the home of the *Plornish family* who helped lift the fortunes of the heroine *Amy Dorrit* in *Little Dorrit*.

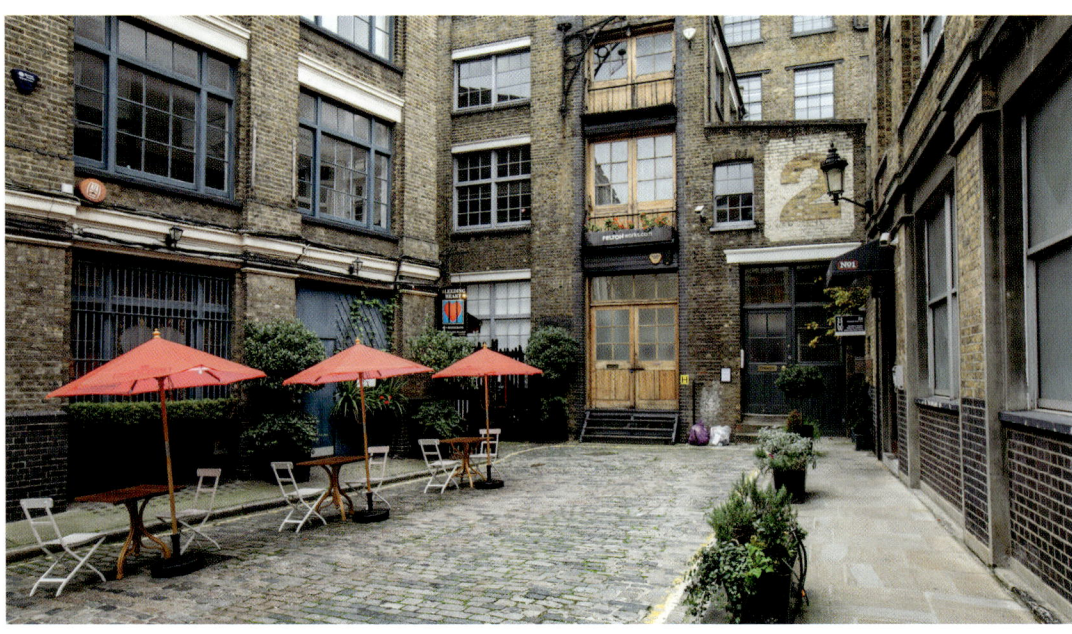

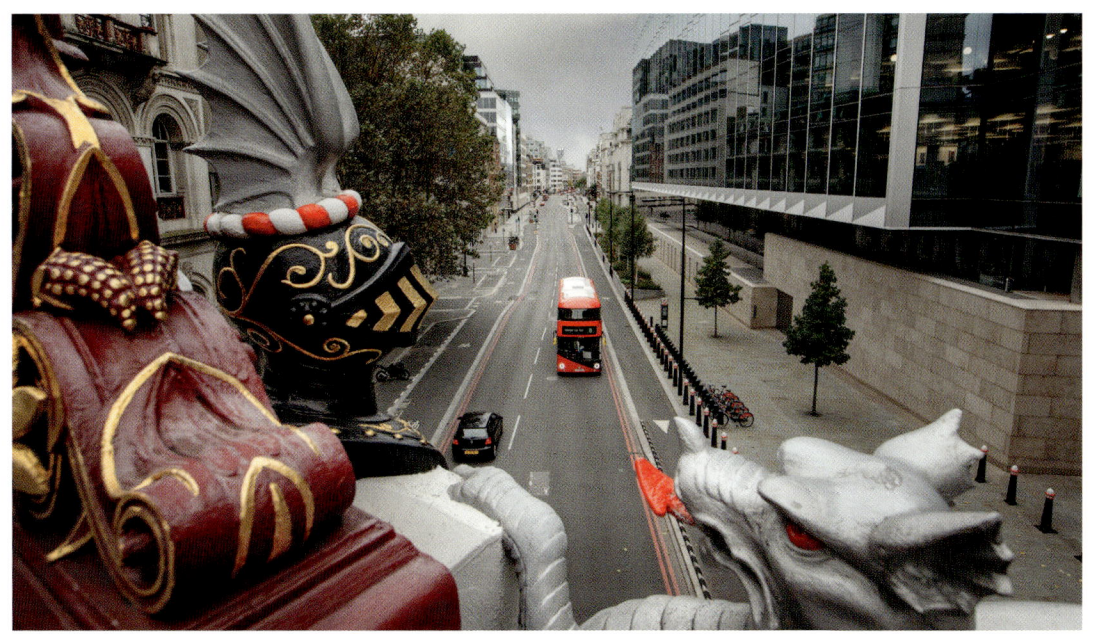

Holborn Viaduct and Tavern

Developed between 1863 and 1869, Holborn Viaduct is 1,400 feet long, 80 feet wide and became the first fly-over in central London. It claimed both Saffron Hill and an area known as Field Lane when workers began to make way for its vast structure. This location had been among the inspirations that led our author to pen the beginnings of *A Christmas Carol*. Still on this site remains The Viaduct Tavern, one of the last remaining examples of a gin palace in London. It is rumoured to have been used as overflow due to its underground cells for the local debtor's prisons. Opposite can be seen the Old Bailey Courthouse and during Dickensian times, the actively in use execution gallows.

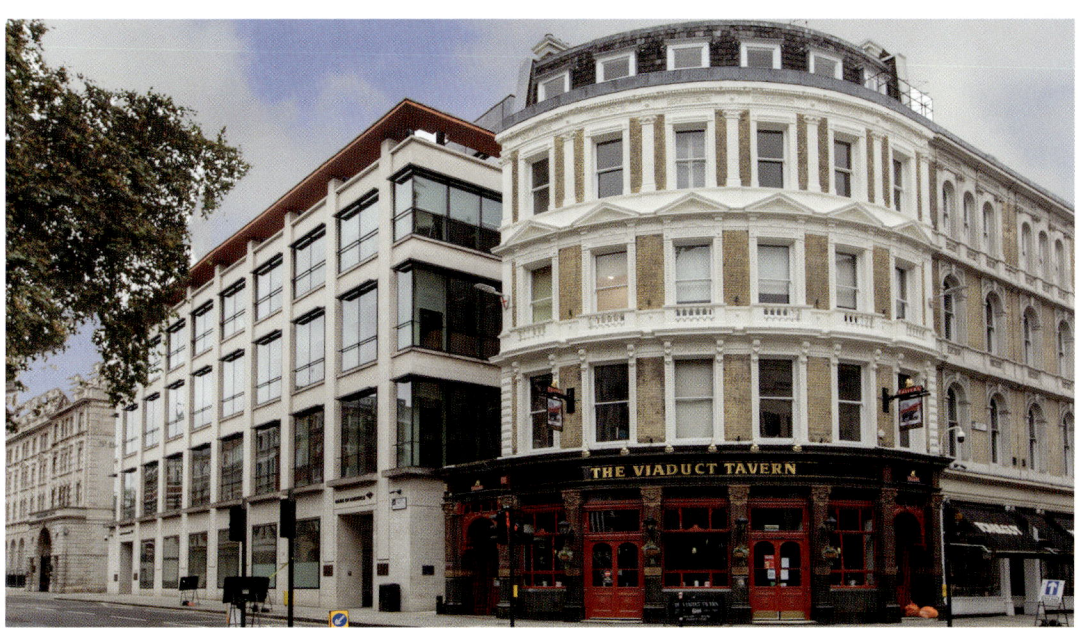

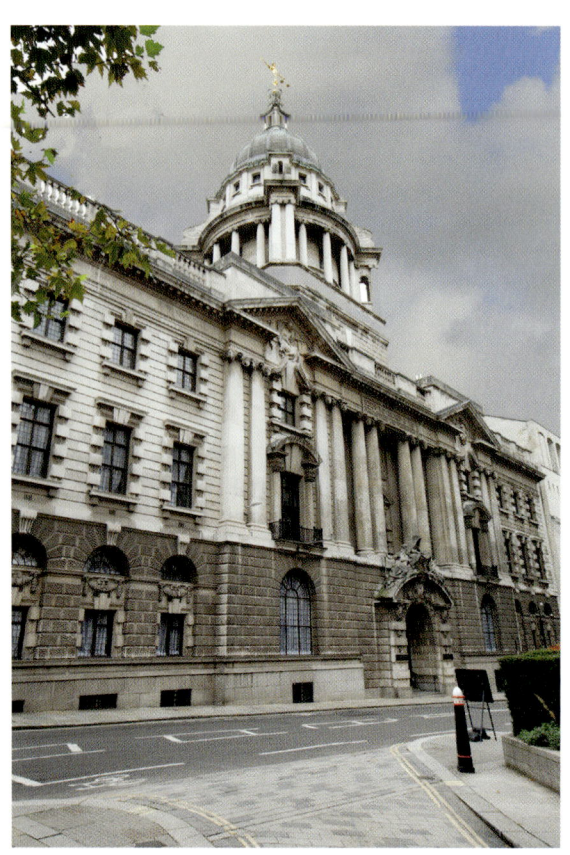

Old Bailey

During his time as a young reporter Dickens was a regular at the Old Bailey and his experiences there feature within his works. It is said the character of *Abel Magwitch* in *Great Expectations* is based upon the true trial of convicted thief Thomas Knight who was also deported to New South Wales. Like his fictional counterpart both, although forbidden, returned to England. Set in the 1780s, *A Tale of Two Cities* depicts the trial of Frenchman *Darnay*, of which he is acquitted for passing information between France and England. This piece may have been somewhat satirical for our author as entering this institution most often resulted in a fast-tracked departure to the grave.

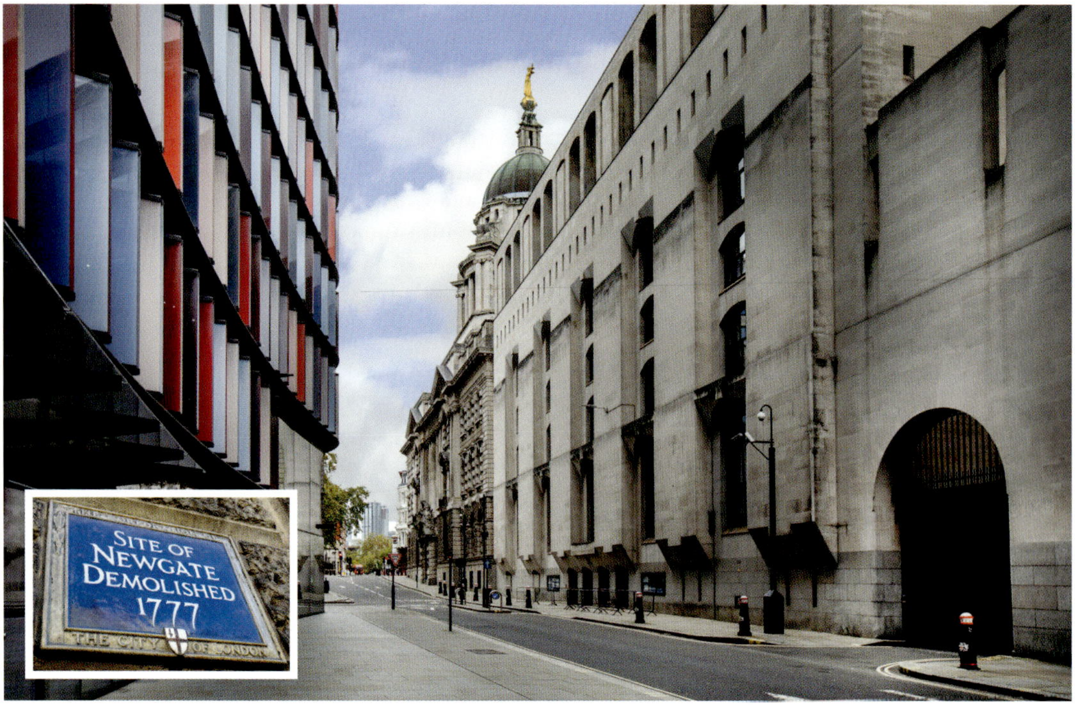

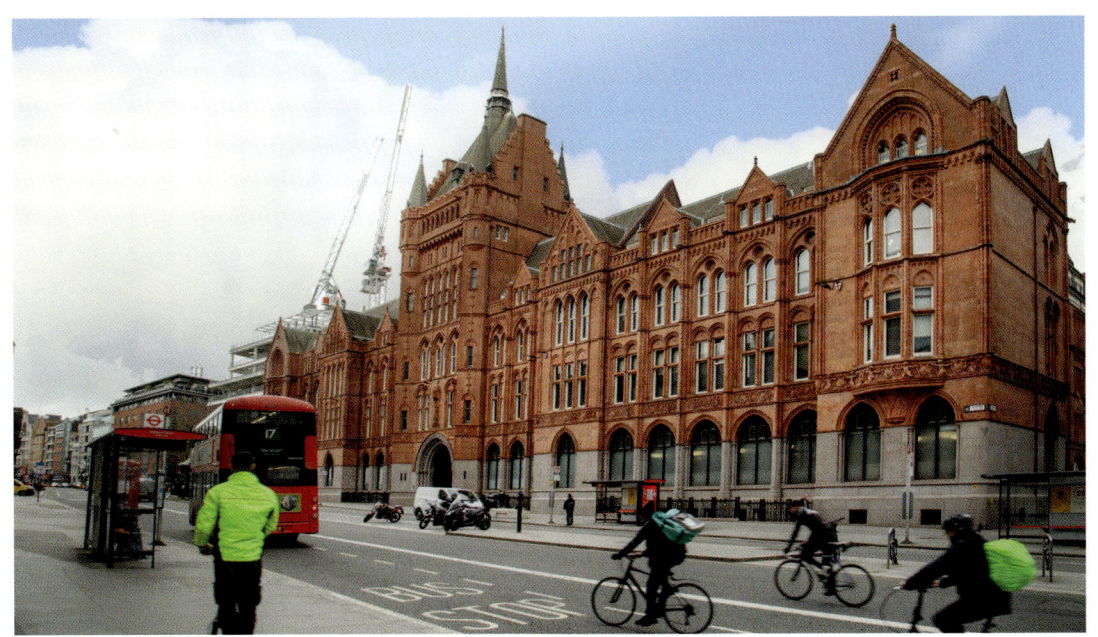

Furnival's Inn

Founded in around 1383, Furnival's Inn was a boarding facility for the Clerks of Chancery. Dickens rented rooms here between 1834 and 1837, spending his first year of marriage to Catherine Hogarth within its walls. It is here he began penning *The Pickwick Papers* and describes his character *John Westlock* in his eighth published novel *Martin Chuzzlewit* as a tenant of the inn. In the book *Westlock* describes the site as 'a shady, quiet place, echoing to the footsteps of the stragglers who have business there; and rather monotonous and gloomy on summer evenings ... there are snug chambers in those Inns where the bachelors live, and, for the desolate fellows they pretend to be, it is quite surprising how well they get on'.

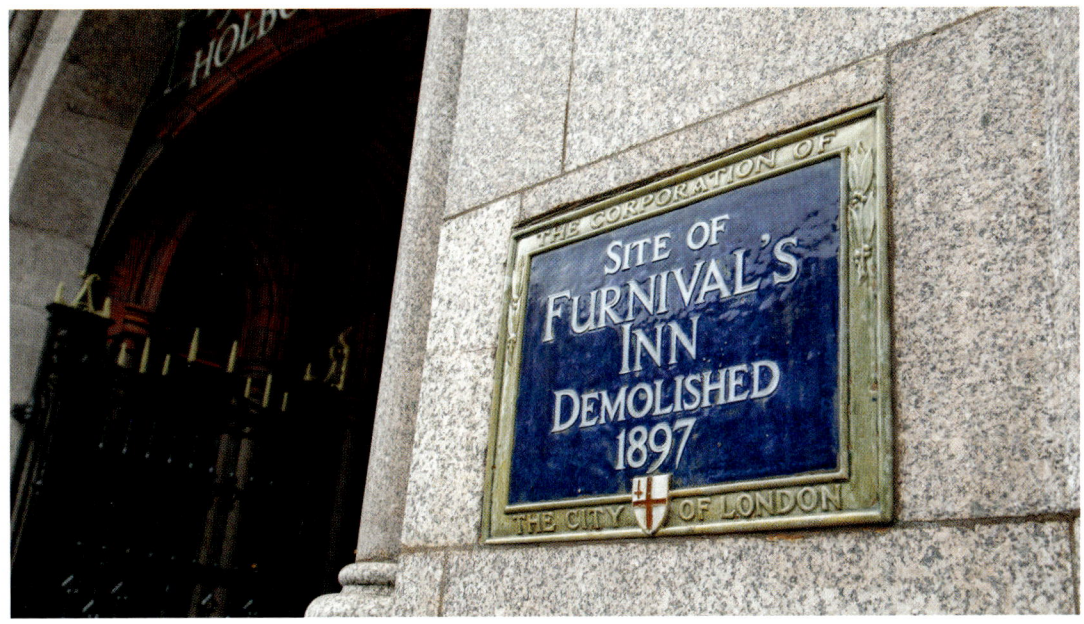

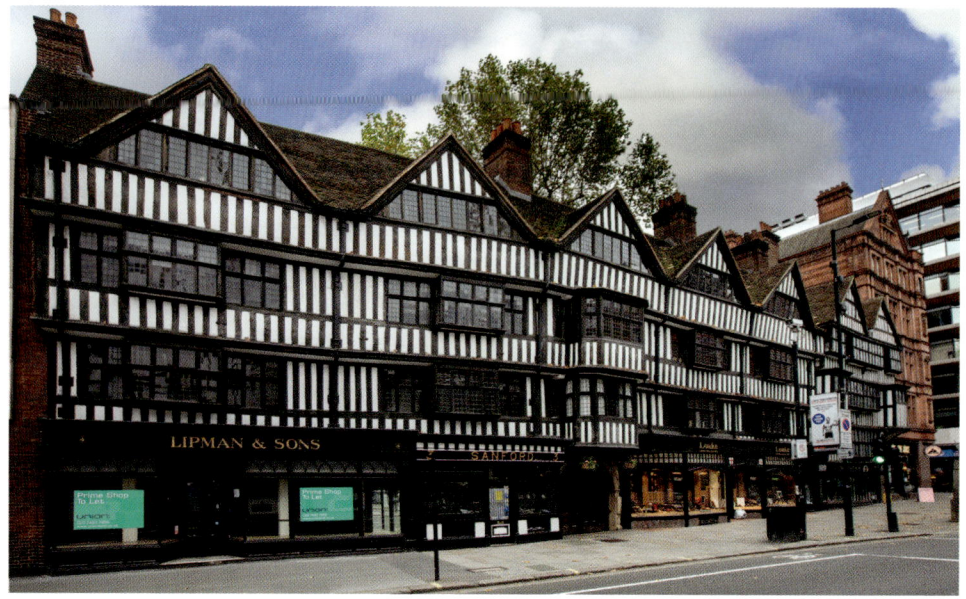

Staple Inn

One of just a handful of Tudor timber-framed buildings left in the country, Staple Inn predeceases the plague, fires and bombs. Dating from 1576, its lattice windows and angled gables have had some restoration, but it is very much the exquisite relic our author would have known. Its quaint exterior finds itself being affectionately described by Dickens as having characteristics of a standstill age. In his final 1870 novel *The Mystery of Edwin Drood* he explains that it is a relief from the 'clashing streets of London' and that 'it imparts to the relieved pedestrian the sensation of having put cotton wool in his ears and velvet soles on his boots'.

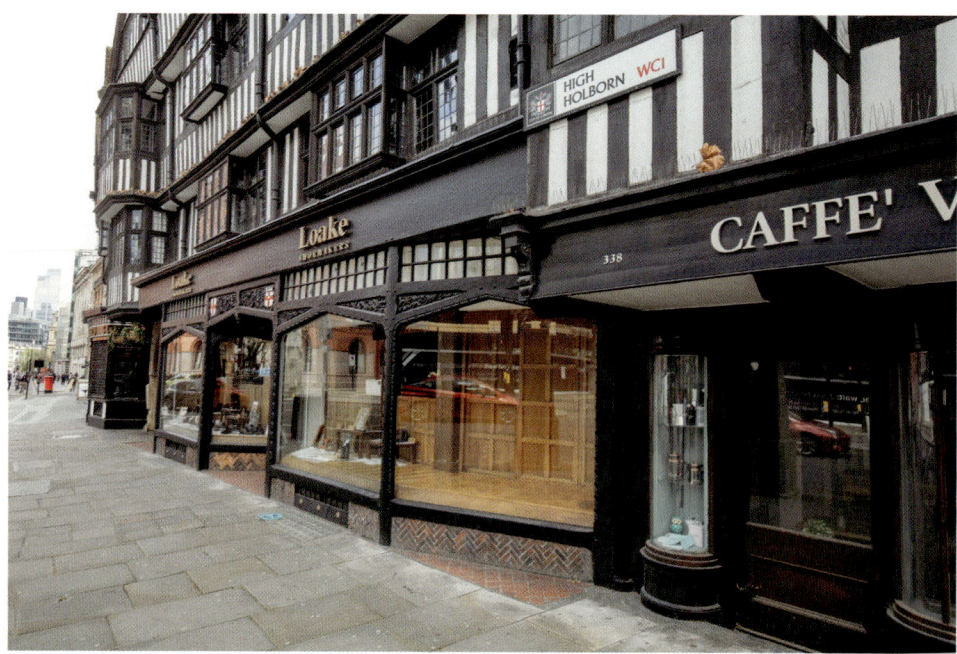

Saracen's Head Inn
This watering hole dates back to the Middle Ages and was long used as a coach house inn frequented by Samuel Pepys. It was demolished during the construction on the Holborn Viaduct. Dickens featured it in his 1839 third novel *The Adventures of Nicholas Nickleby*. It is said to be the scene where *Nicholas* and his uncle waited for the Yorkshire schoolmaster *Wackford Squeers* of Dotheboys Hall. Along with his illustrator Hablot Knight Browne, Dickens had visited some of these notorious northern institutions. The character of *Squeers* was modelled on a real headmaster, William Shaw. He had been convicted of criminal negligence when two of his pupils were found so injured they were blind at Bowes Academy in Greta Bridge.

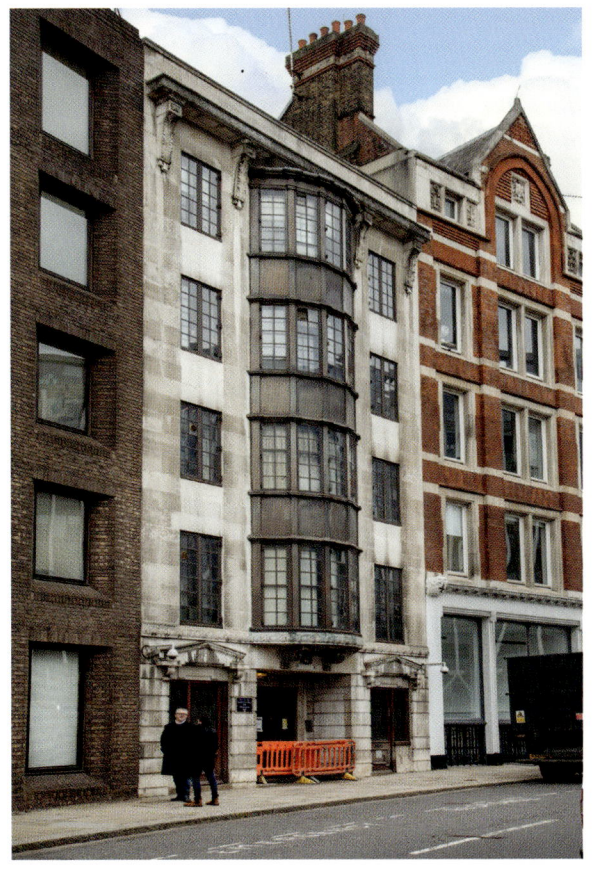

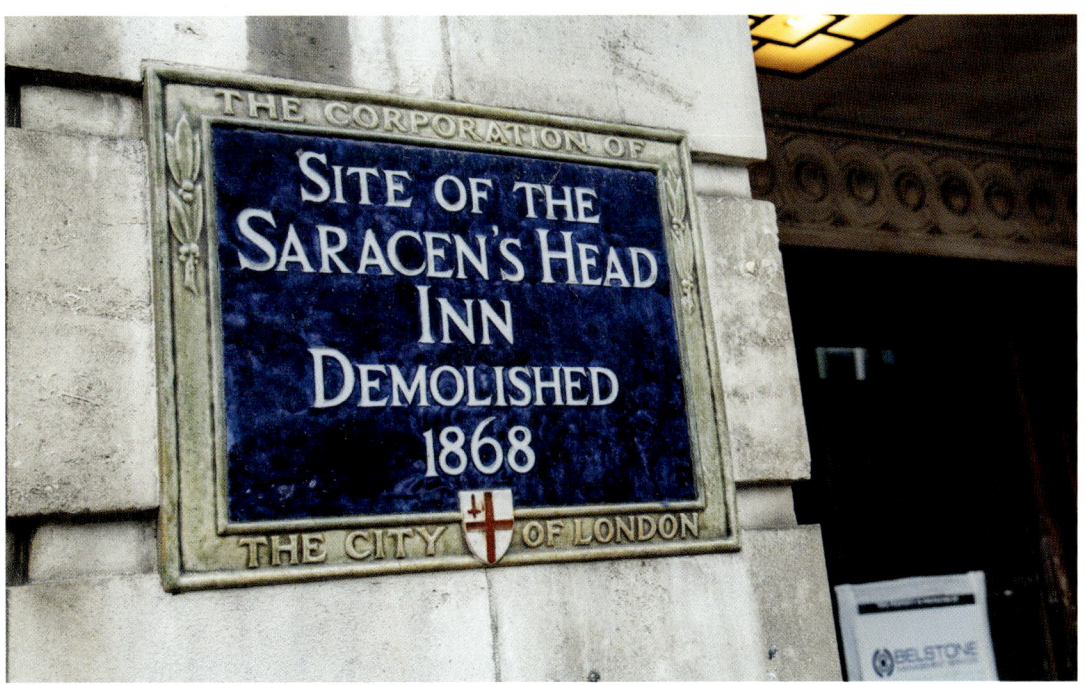

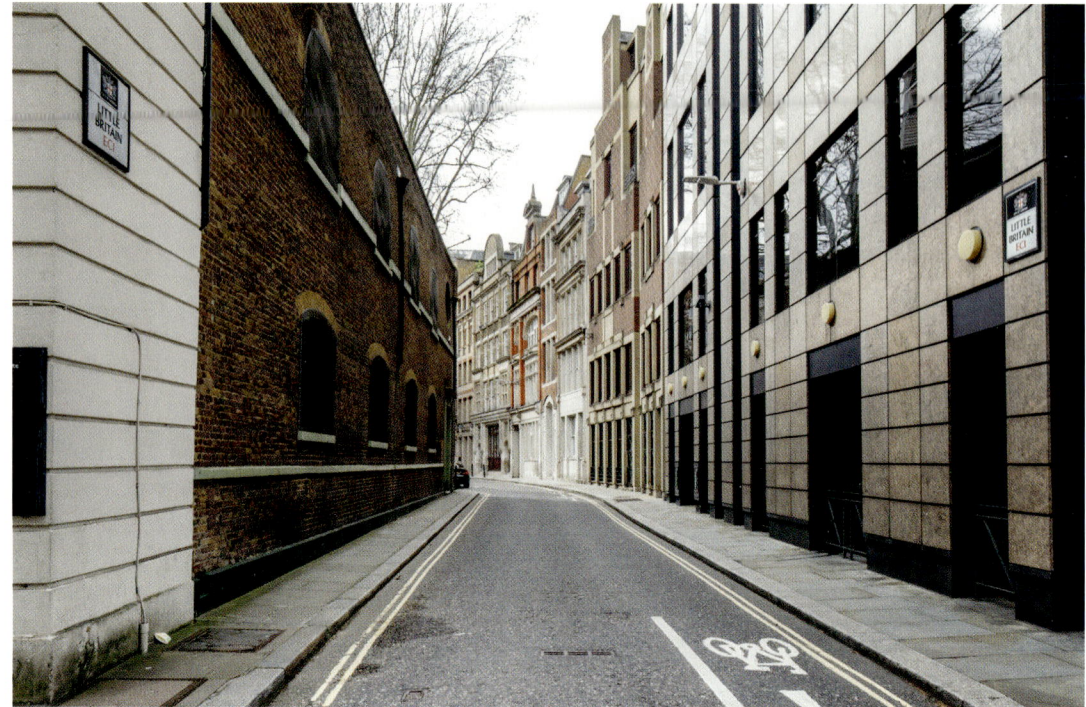

Little Britain
This street running from St Martin's Le Grand to West Smithfield features heavily in *Great Expectations* as a 'gloomy street' and the address of *Mr Jagger's* office. It is also mentioned during the infamous passage to include the novel's title upon *Pip's* meticulous narration: 'From Little Britain I went, with my check in my pocket, to Miss Skiffins's brother, the accountant; and Miss Skiffins's brother, the accountant, going straight to Clarriker's and bringing Clarriker to me, I had the great satisfaction of concluding that arrangement. It was the only good thing I had done, and the only completed thing I had done, since I was first apprised of my great expectations.'

St Paul's Cathedral

With its impressive height and ornate domes, St Paul's Cathedral is a familiar backdrop to any cinematography depicting Dickens' works, although it was in 1852 whilst attending the funeral of the Duke of Wellington that Dickens professed his disdain for the opulent setting. He described the affair to be laced with ostentatious pomp and the ceremony to be appalling and excessive. He vowed his funeral to be a simple and private event in a small site in Kent. Unfortunately, his wishes weren't followed when his biographer, John Forster, and the Dean of Westminster, Arthur Penrhyn Stanley, orchestrated a national mourning and burial in Poets' Corner, Westminster Abbey. Many believe they did this to gain on their own infamy.

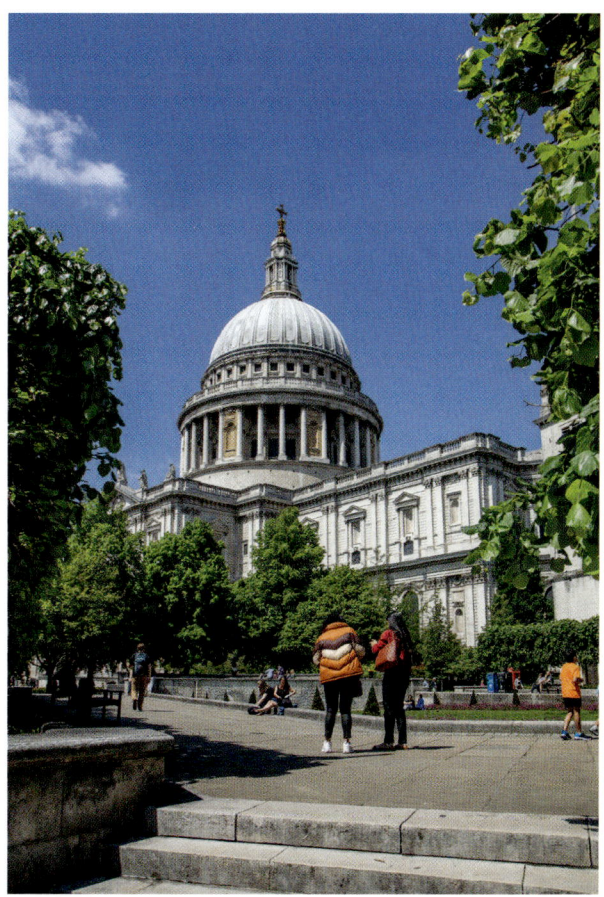

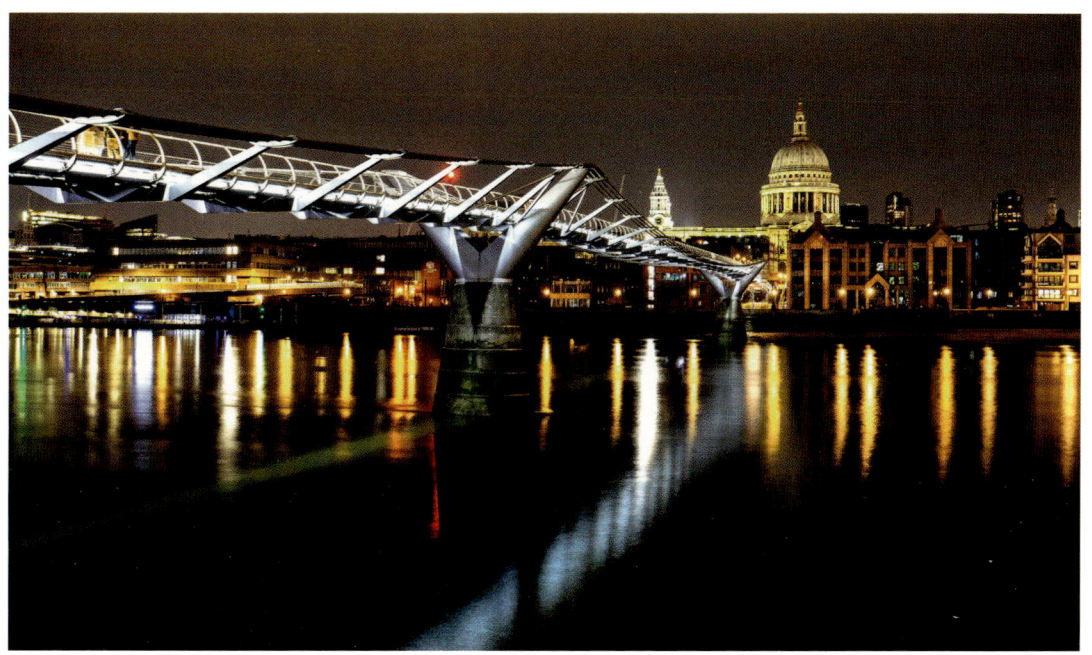

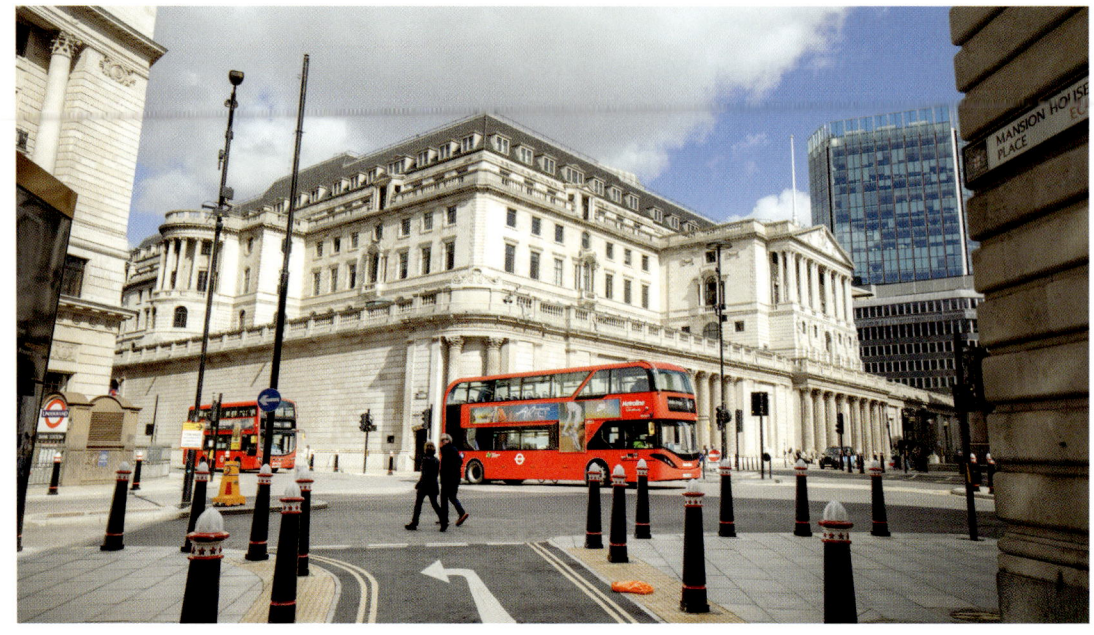

The Bank of England and the Royal Exchange

The area of Cornhill inspired Dickens to write his seventh novel which was published in 1843. *A Christmas Carol* is without doubt his most famous work, delighting many generations. Being the city of London's main financial hub, today it houses the Bank of England. The Royal Exchange, known then as 'The Change', was the centre of commerce in Dickensian times also. It is here that *Scrooge* overhears associates speaking badly of someone ... to later find out, that someone is him. It is also the place the '*Ghost of Christmas Yet to Come*' first drags him to show him of his miserly ways.

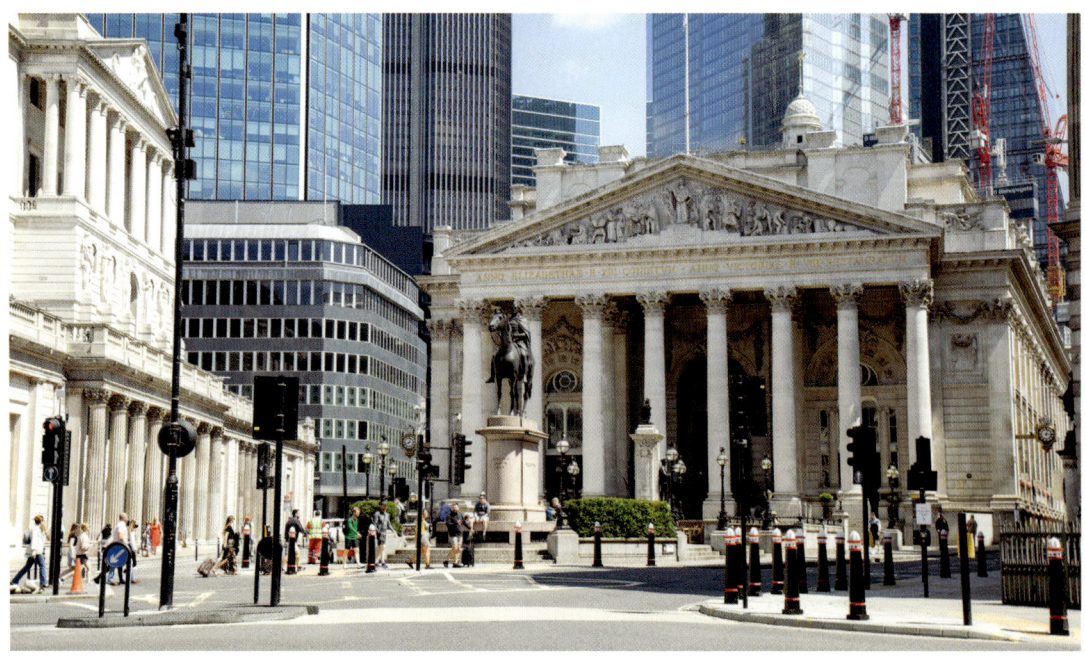

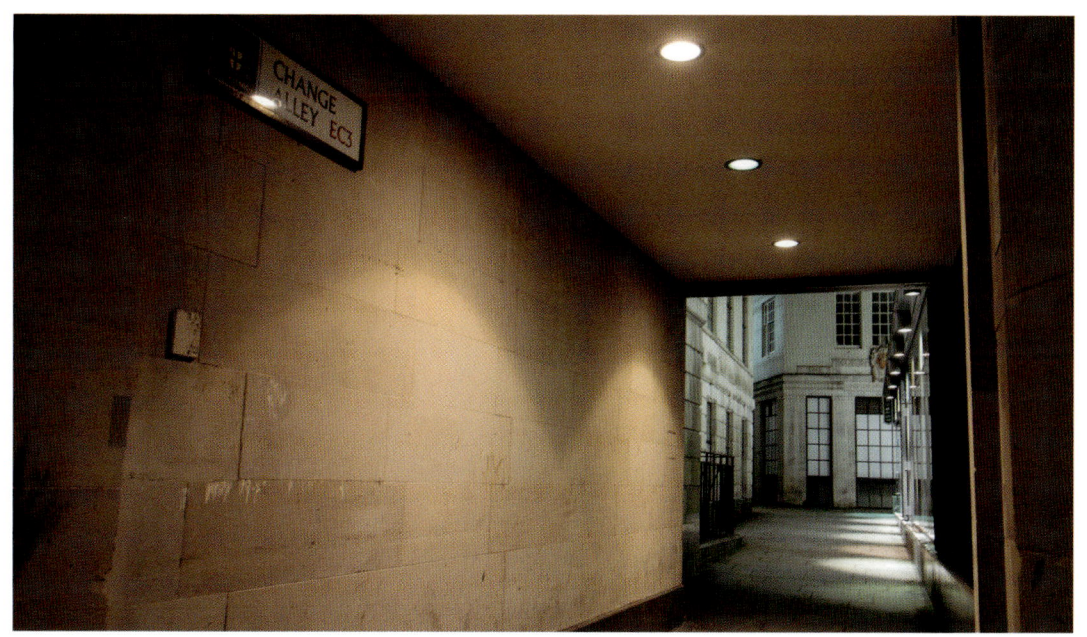

Change Alley and Bakers Chop House
Change Alley, linking the financial quarter surrounding Cornhill, was known to Dickens to be frequented by wealthy traders from all over the City. Garraway's Coffee House, which was unfortunately destroyed by fire in 1748, is referenced numerous times by our author despite his predeceasing it by many years. Bakers Chop House narrowly escaped this fate and still trades here today. Change Alley is where *Nadget* spies over Jonas in the novel *Martin Chuzzlewit* and also where *Samuel Pickwick* writes his Chops and tomato sauce letter to *Martin Bardell*.

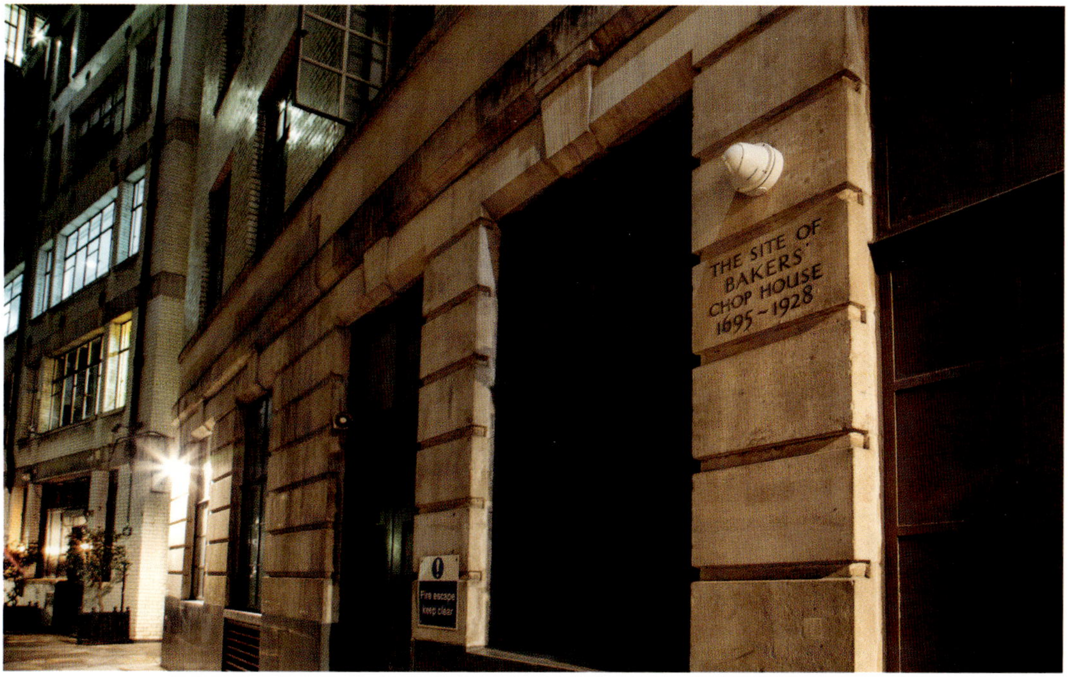

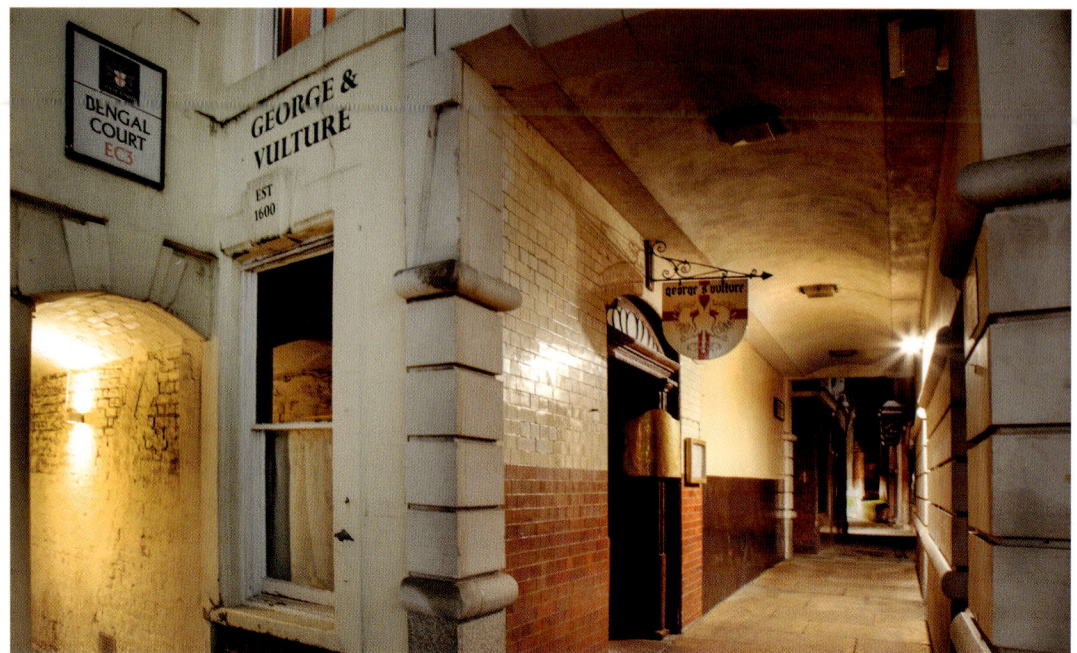

The George & Vulture
Frequented often by the author, the George & Vulture in St Michael's Alley quite rightly featured heavily in Dickens' works. It is in fact mentioned over twenty times in *The Pickwick Papers* alone as he chose it as the headquarters for The City Pickwick Club – *Mr Pickwick* and *Sam Weller* chose to take board in the tavern's lodging rooms upstairs, affectionately naming it 'The Wulture' throughout much of their dialogue. Watched over closely by the large white marble bust of the Victorian writer, the tavern is still a special place for the Dickens family. It hosts his descendants to this day at Christmas each year in commemoration of our author's spirit of the festive season.

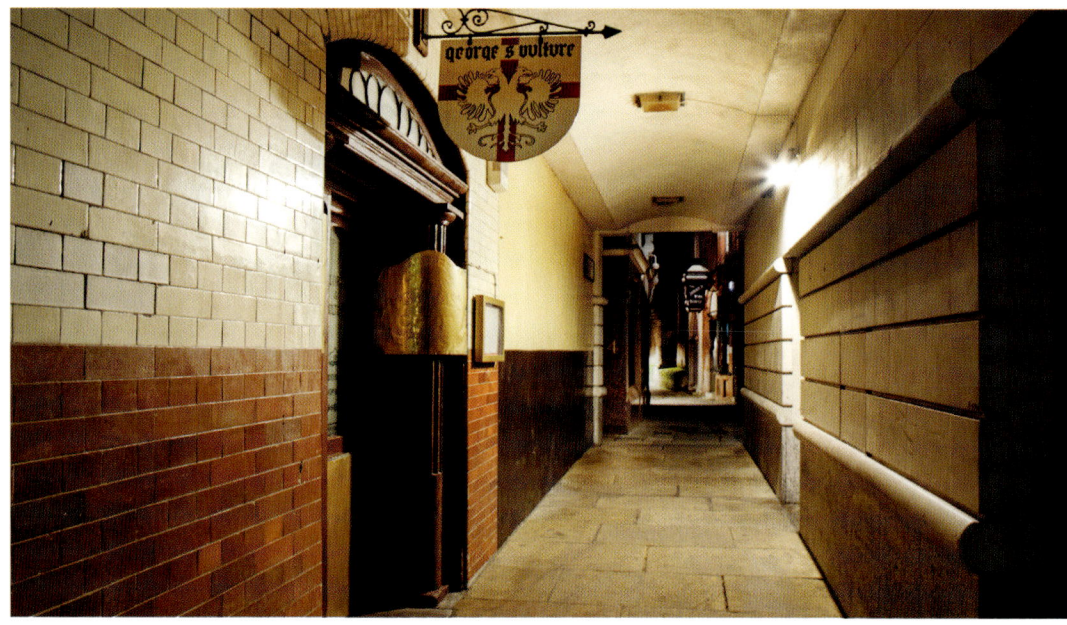

Jamaica Wine House

Known locally as 'The Jampot', the Jamaica Wine House was opened in 1652 and was the first coffee shop in London. Another victim of the Great Fire of London, it was rebuilt in 1885 by architect Banister Fletcher in Gothic detailing to match the churchyard opposite. Grade II listed, it reopened after restoration in 2009 as a public house. It is said Dickens used the shop's internal ornate features as inspiration for his descriptions of *Scrooge's* office in *A Christmas Carol*. It is worth noting the dark historic background the shop, as it was heavily involved in the sugar plantations and slave trade. It is where those in opposition of slave trade abolishment would meet to plot their halt to the bill. It begs the question if Dickens was creating a link between his cruel and miserly character and the dirty origin of the businesses' gain?

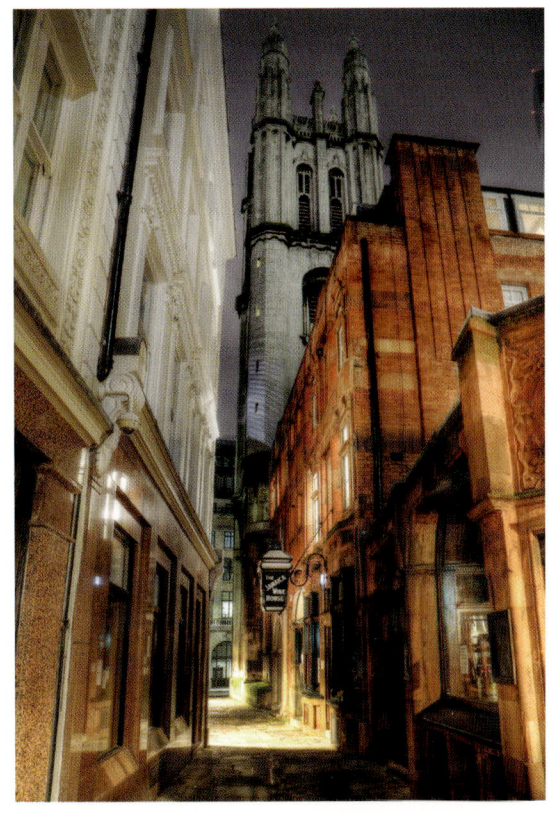

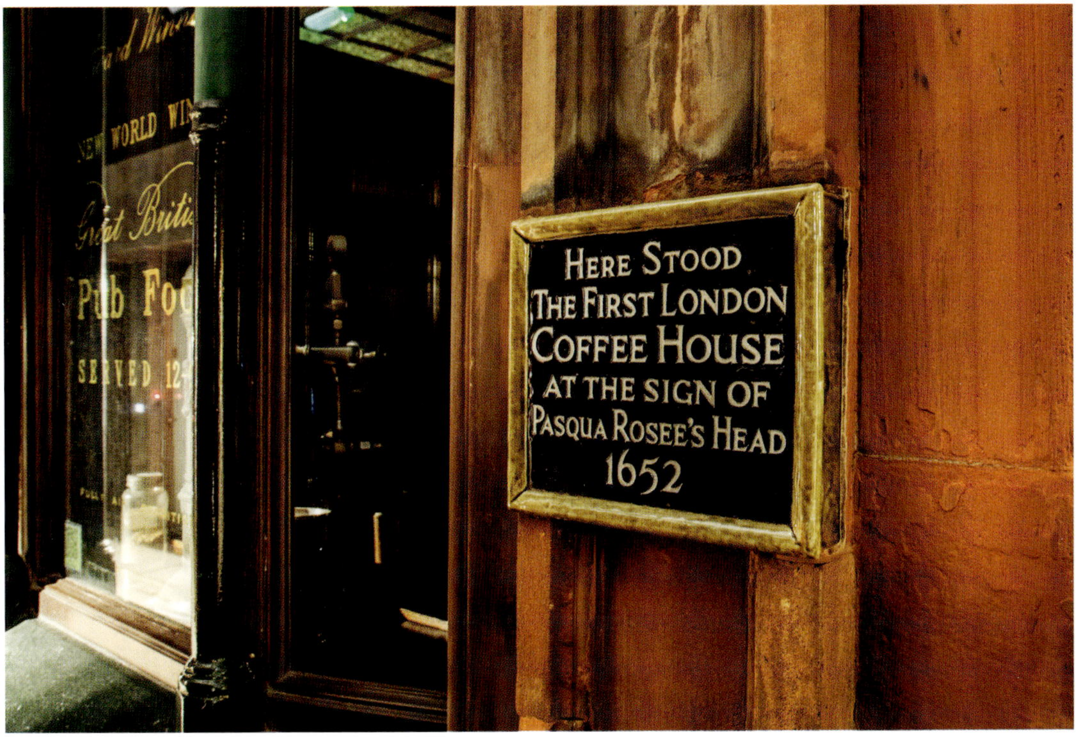

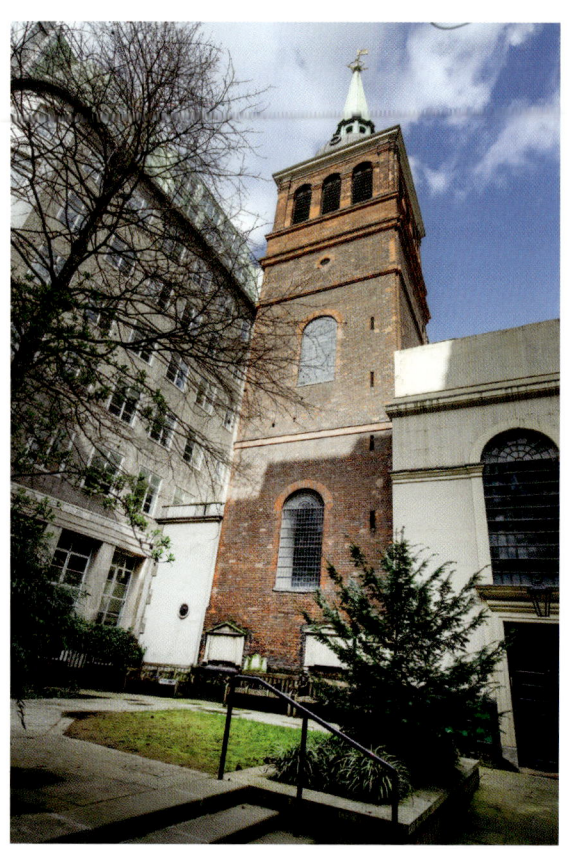

St Peter's Churchyard

Dickens refers to this churchyard in *Our Mutual Friend*. When *Lizzie Hexam* meets *Bradley Headstone* he begins to describe the graves as 'conveniently and healthily elevated above the living'. More notably, this is the nearest churchyard to The Exchange, causing many to believe it to be the setting Dickens chose for *Jacob Marley* to be buried and *Scrooge* being shown his unvisited and unremarkable headstone by the '*Ghost of Christmas Yet to Come*'. Running parallel of the alley which held Dickens' most frequented taverns, it is safe to assume he passed this way often. He found it to be curious in nature, so much so to bother to describe it as 'walled in by houses'.

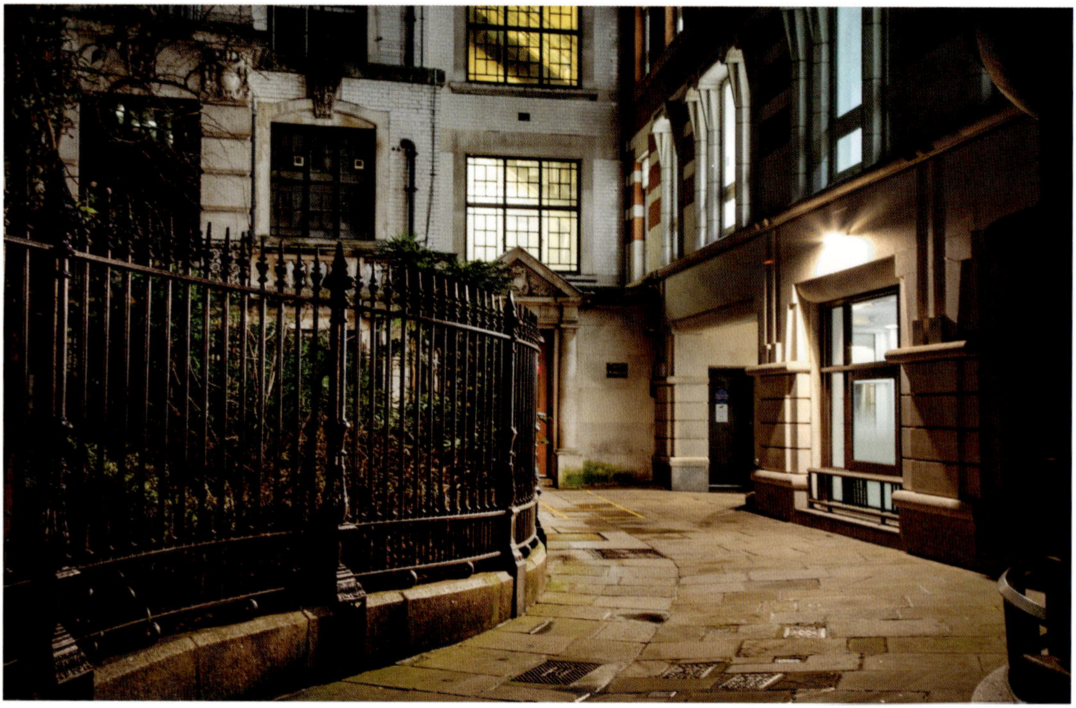

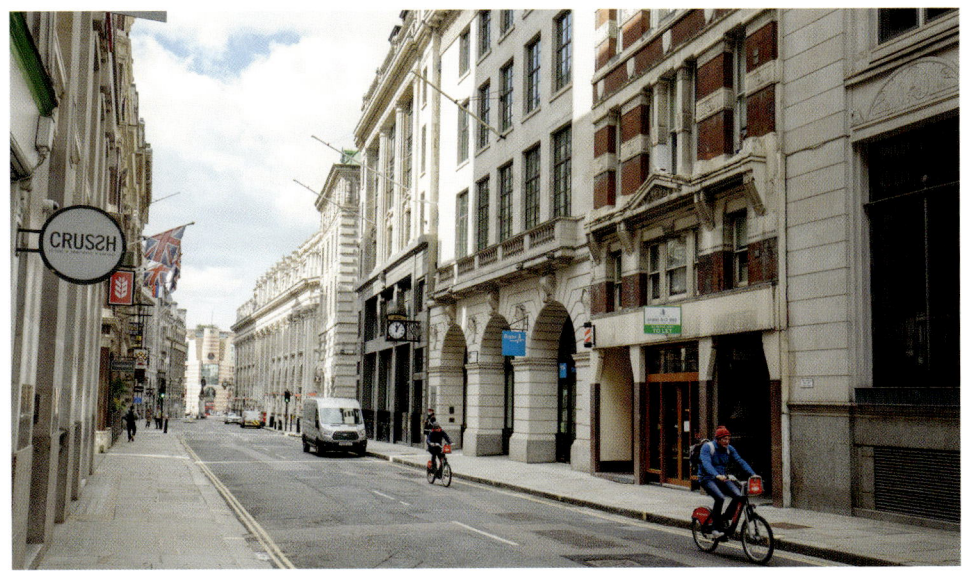

Cornhill

The street of Cornhill runs directly through the financial centre of the City. It is referenced by Dickens in *A Christmas Carol* when *Scrooge* closes the counting house for the day and begrudgingly dismisses his downtrodden clerk *Bob Cratchit* for the evening. The following scene is a much-loved favourite of most Dickensian enthusiasts: 'The office was closed in a twinkling, and the clerk, with the long ends of his white comforter dangling below his waist (for he boasted no great-coat), went down a slide on Cornhill, at the end of a lane of boys, twenty times, in honour of its being Christmas-eve, and then ran home to Camden Town as hard as he could pelt, to play at blindman's-buff.' Interestingly, the address of the impoverished *Cratchit* is Bayham Street, where our author resided in 1823 when his own family was suffering financial hardship.

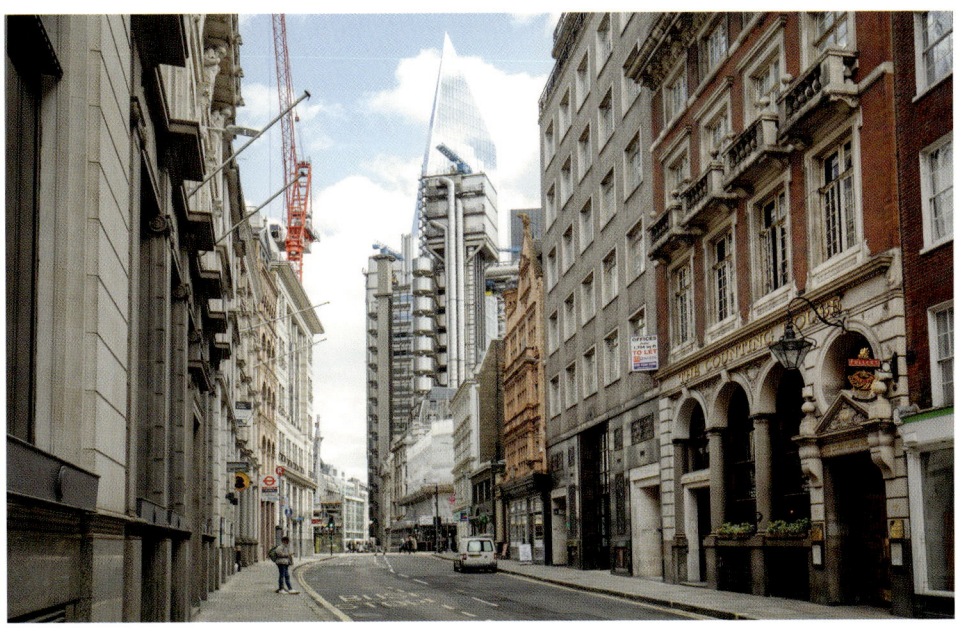

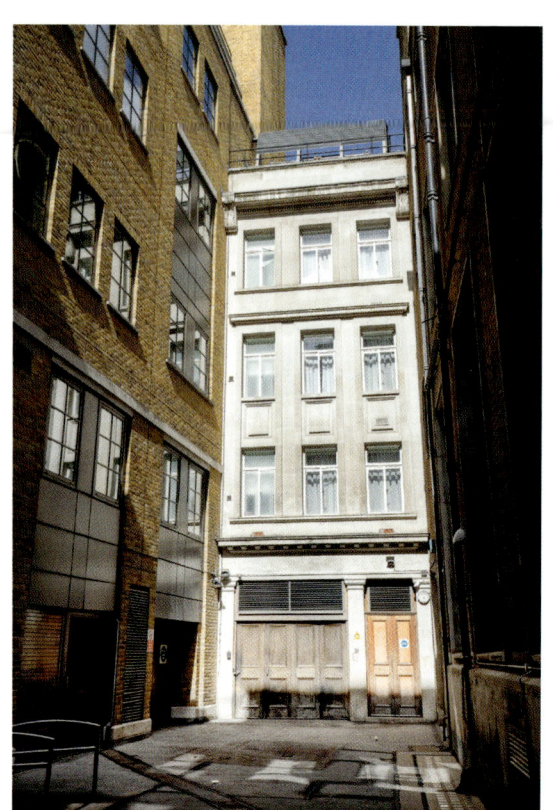

Newman's Court

Known to be an area for pawning items of value and the loaning of monies, Newman's Court is the putative location of *Ebenezer's* counting house. Although Dickens never quite gives a specific address, many feel this to be the most likely spot from his descriptions. He writes of the shop's courtyard setting, facing 'the ancient tower of a church'. Newman's Court itself is shadowed directly under St Michael's bell tower. Research into the inspiration for *Scrooge's* tight-fisted character has uncovered many worthy opponents. A favourite *for many* is John Elwes. Born into privilege in 1714, he inherited a large wealth at an early age. Despite his good fortune he was notorious for refusing to spend absolutely anything. He ate dead rats and pigeons found in London's dirty streets and was often mistaken for a beggar due to his appearance. He thought nothing of taking coins from strangers who took pity on him and climbed into bed under his leaking roof every night before dark set in to save on candles.

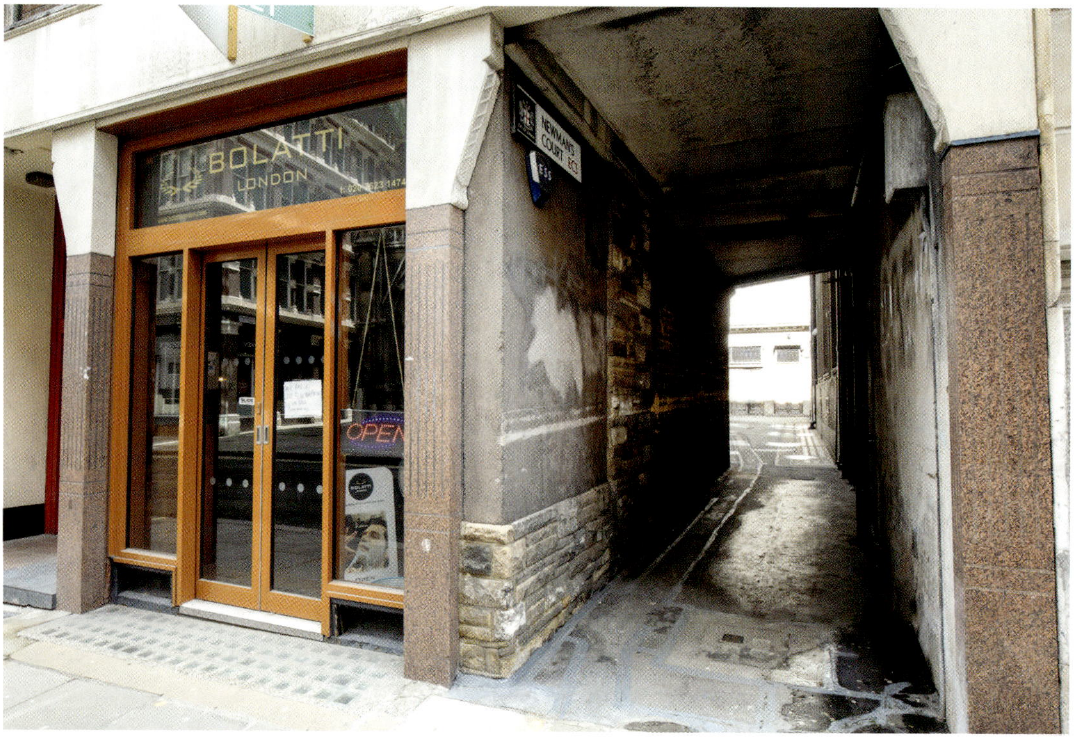

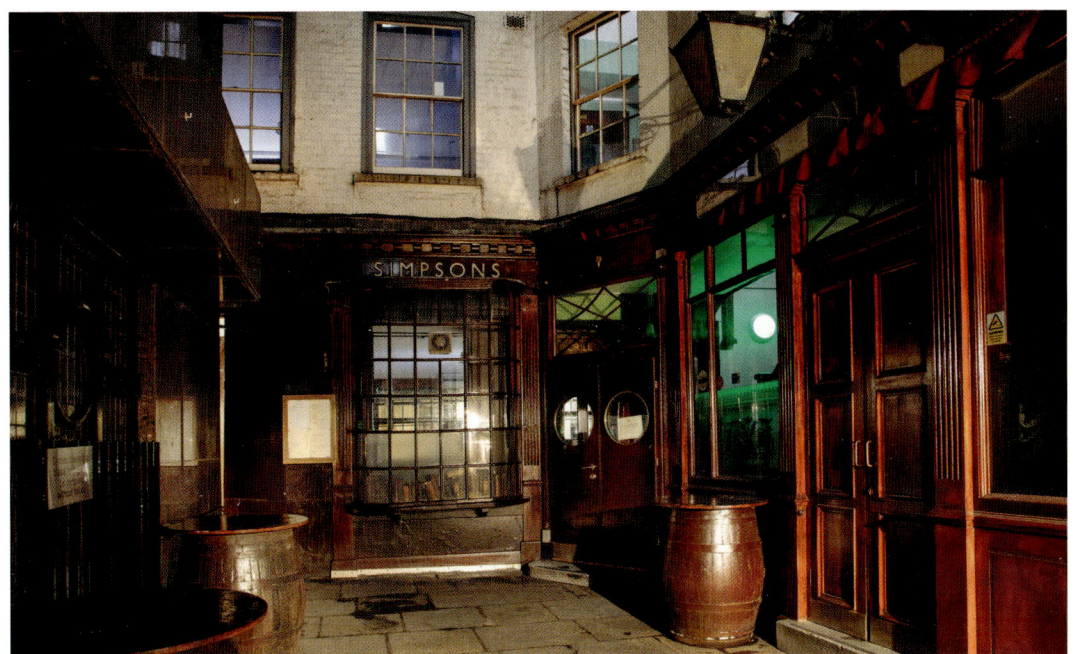

Simpson's Tavern

The oldest surviving chop house in London, originally built in 1757, the Simpson's Tavern, although never formally named, is believed to be the place *Scrooge* dined Christmas Eve, taking 'his melancholy dinner in his usual melancholy tavern'. Formerly known as Ball Yard, the site was renamed in nineteenth century as Ball Court. The public house was already eighty years old when Dickens penned *A Christmas Carol*. Simpson's Tavern is set in what was formerly a large part of the City's food trading area at Cornhill; a place where merchants would strike deals over a pint. Named literally as a hill where corn was sold, it links with nearby Bread Street, Poultry, Honey Lane, and Milk Street, revealing aspects of the area's origins.

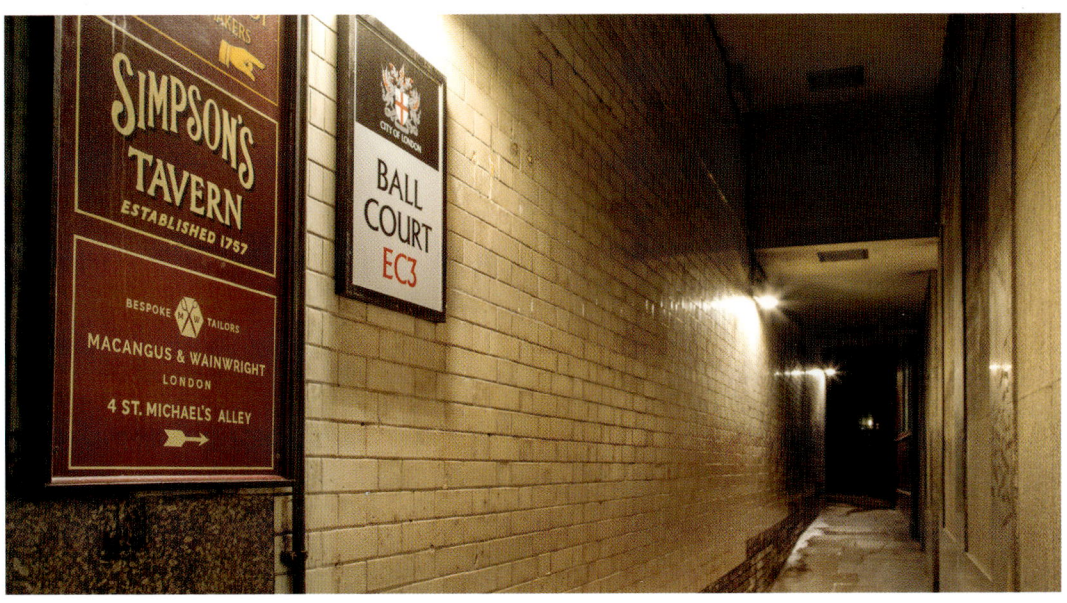

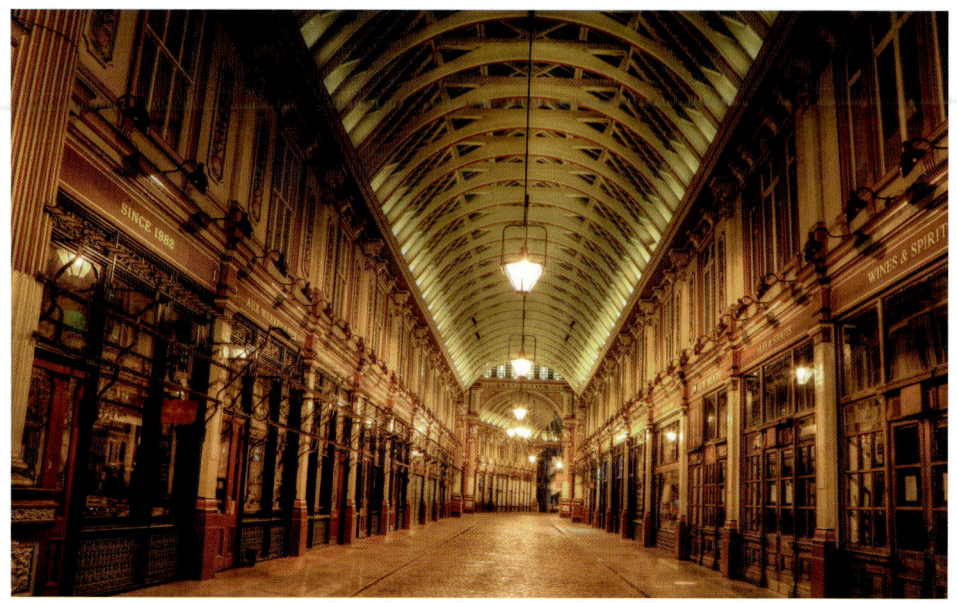

Leadenhall Market

This ornate and Gothic structure was constructed in 1888 by Horace Jones who also designed Tower Bridge, so this building would not have been known to Dickens. Despite this there has been a market on this site since 1377 and was London's go-to for purchases of all things fowl and poultry related. When *Ebeneezer Scrooge* awakens a changed man on Christmas morning he sends a young boy here to fetch a plump turkey to be delivered to the *Cratchits* via a costly carriage. Leadenhall is also famed for the tale of a lucky gander named Old Tom, a brave goose who evaded his Christmas fate in 1797 and was affectionately adopted by the stallholders. Old Tom lived unscathed and by all accounts very much loved as an infamous attraction in the market for an incredible thirty-seven years. He is commemorated in statue form perched above Poultry near Bank Junction.

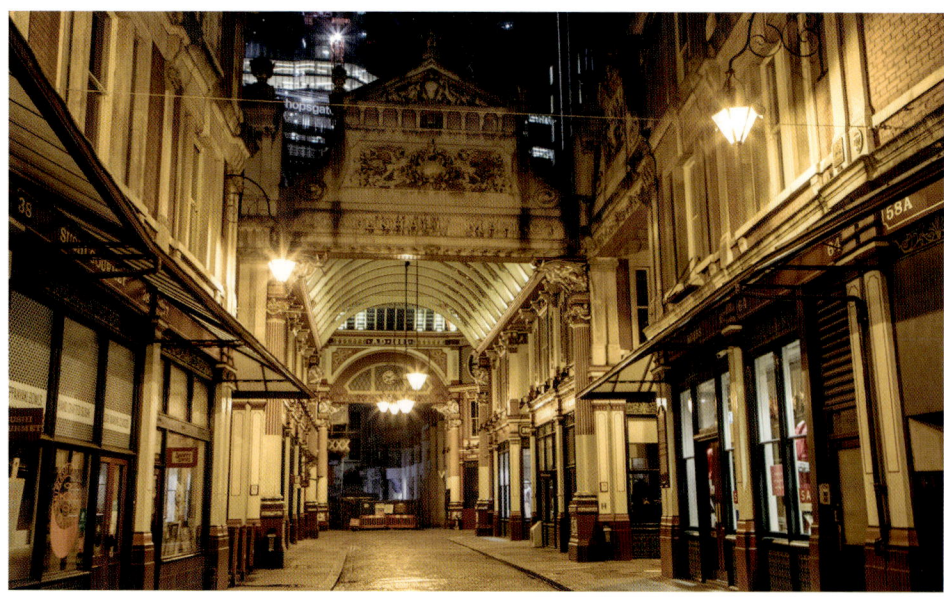

The Monument

Constructed between 1671 and 1677, this is The Monument to the Great Fire of London. It stands 202 feet high and is 202 feet away from Pudding Lane, which was where the fire started in 1666. It is the tallest isolated stone column in the world. The Monument features heavily in Dickens' *The Life and Adventures of Martin Chuzzlewit*, his 1844 publication. He uses it for the location of Todgers' Commercial Boarding House, which was where *Pecksniff* and his daughters stayed. Here is where he chooses *Tom Pinch* to find his bearings after getting lost in the city. Upon approaching the attendant for directions, he witnesses a couple paying him their 'tanner' to be let inside a 'dark little door'. The attendant proceeds to sit and chuckle to himself that 'They don't know what a many steps there is! It's worth twice the money to stop here.' The are 311 steps to The Monument's viewing gallery. The site is arguably worth the effort though.

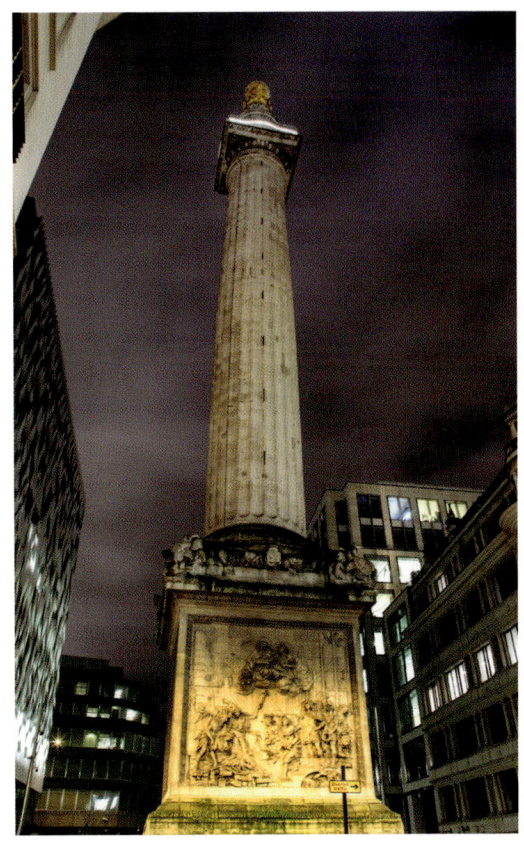

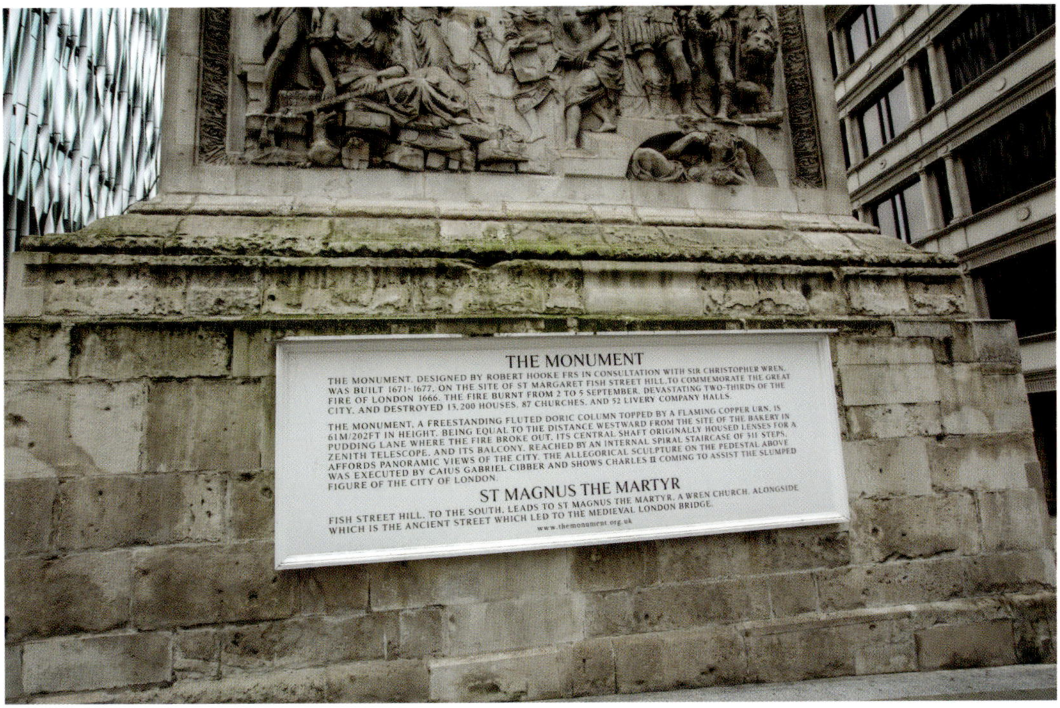

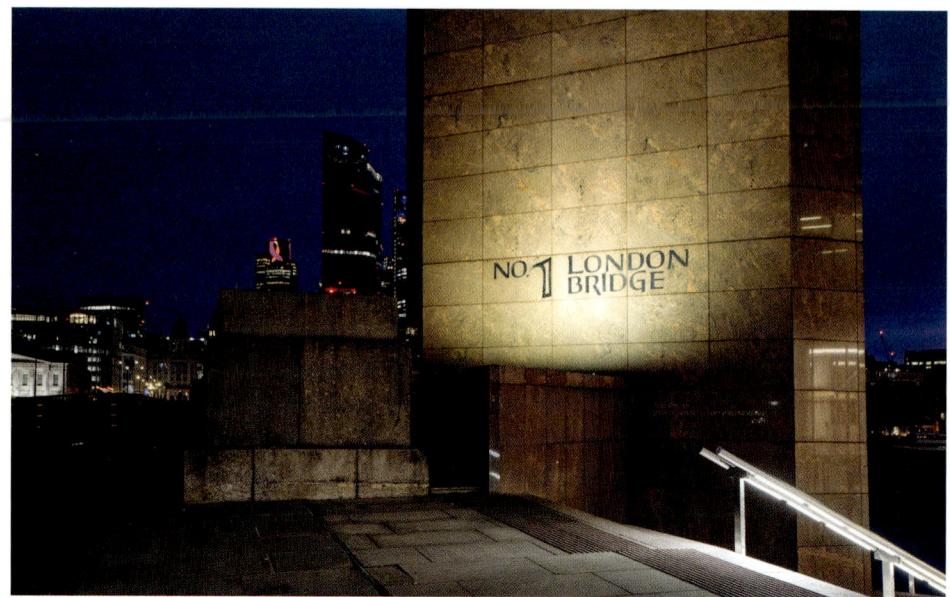

London Bridge

Originally built by the Romans sometime around AD 43 (although rebuilt many times), London Bridge is one of the most mentioned locations in Dickens' novels. He uses it when describing contemplation time taken by his main character in *David Copperfield*. *Pip* crossed it in great despair, having recently learned that *Estella* was betrothed to oafish *Bentley Drummle* in *Great Expectations*. It is also the site of one of his most well-known scenes when *Nancy* risks her life to meet *Rose* and *Mr Brownlow* in an attempt to save little *Oliver* in the beloved novel *Oliver Twist*. London Bridge always held a great importance to Dickens. As a young journalist he had seen many a gruesome sight here whilst following the Thames River Police for his latest scoop. The waters below London Bridge hold some very dark history and inspired his writing of an essay called 'Down With the Tide', which includes reports of suicide, water thieves and murder.

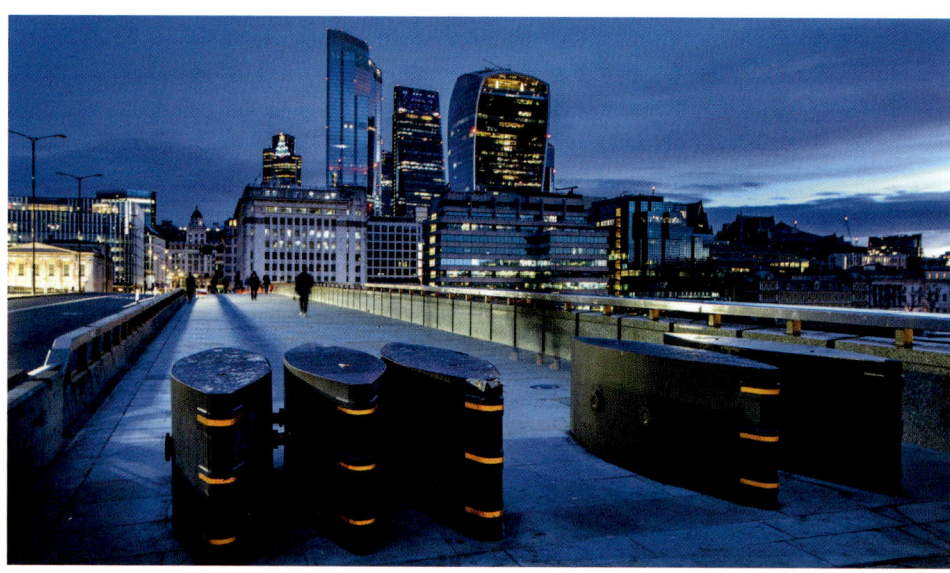

Nancy's Steps

This small surviving section of the 1831 London Bridge designed by John Rennie would have been familiar to our author during his regular jaunts through the city. Whilst the location and wording of the plaque is a lie within itself (The 1838 book *Oliver Twist* portrays that *Sykes* murdered his prostitute girlfriend in their shared room using a heavy club), this hidden gem situated under the steps off London Bridge is a beautiful tribute to *Nancy's* act of bravery. Believed to have been erected in 2020, this heritage-style plaque is a new addition of which City Bridge Trust deny any knowledge of its origin. The wall once held a wooden square sign with the same wording; this has since disappeared, thought to be stolen, sometime in 2016. *Nancy's* maternal instinct towards young *Twist* and defiant act of betrayal towards the band of thieves she classes as family make way for a Dickens classic ending – good conquering all. Little *Oliver* advances his way forward in a safe and loving environment whilst the villains of the piece receive a 'short, sharp drop'.

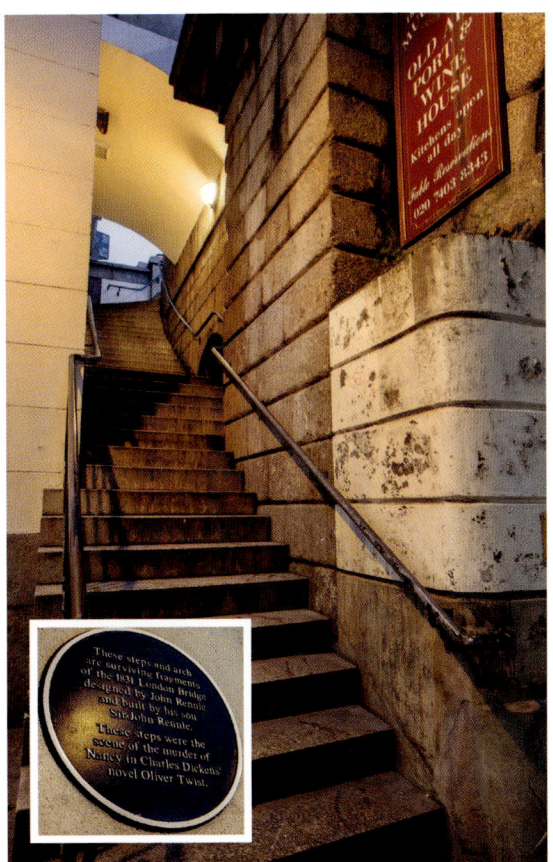

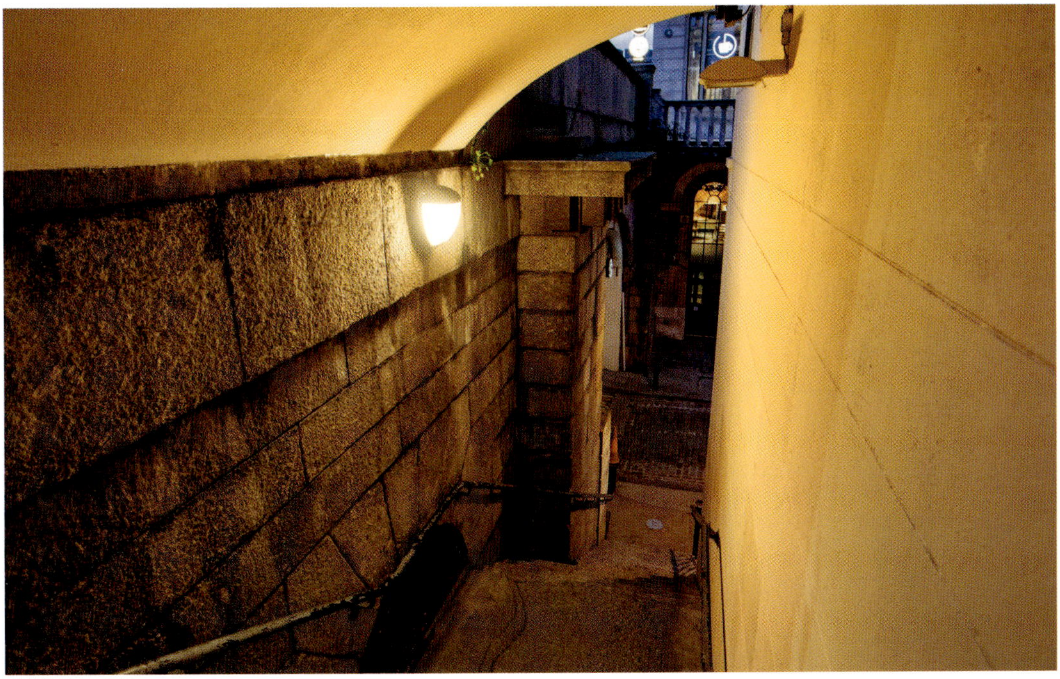

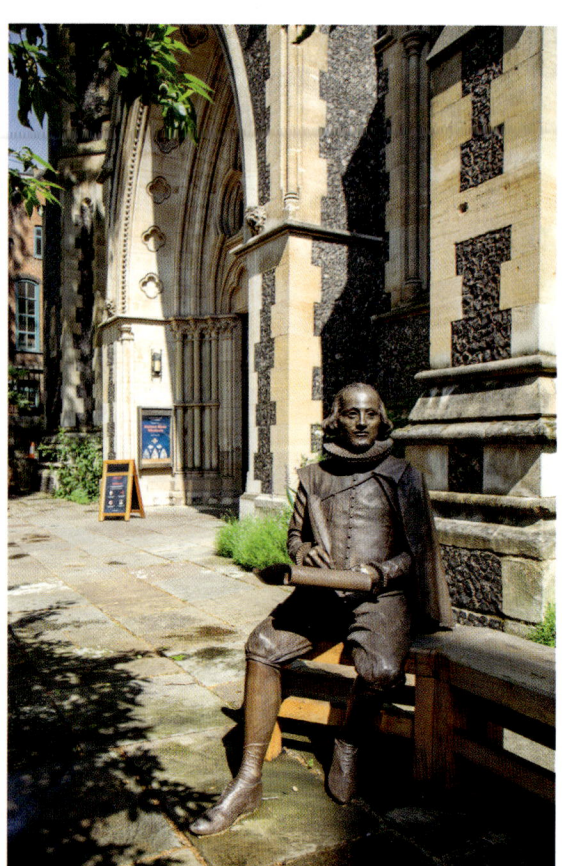

Southwark Cathedral

Having been a place of Christian worship for over 1,000 years, Southwark Cathedral, located at the steps to London Bridge, was the local church to Dickens, Shakespeare and John Harvard. They will have known it as St Savior's, as it changed its name in 1905 when it became a cathedral. Admittedly unknowledgeable, Dickens wrote an essay, 'City of London Churches', in *The Uncommercial Traveller* where he confesses he is 'profoundly ignorant' of the names of 'at least nine-tenths' of London's churches. He was a regular here though and was particularly fond of visiting the tomb of John Gower, known as the first English poet. Dickens attended a bell-ringing practice here in 1869 and subsequently published an account of his observations in *All Year Round*, his personal literary magazine. He wrote 'we shrink back as from a blow, from the stunning clash of sound with which he greets us'. The bells of the church had been recast in 1734 creating one of the loudest peals in England.

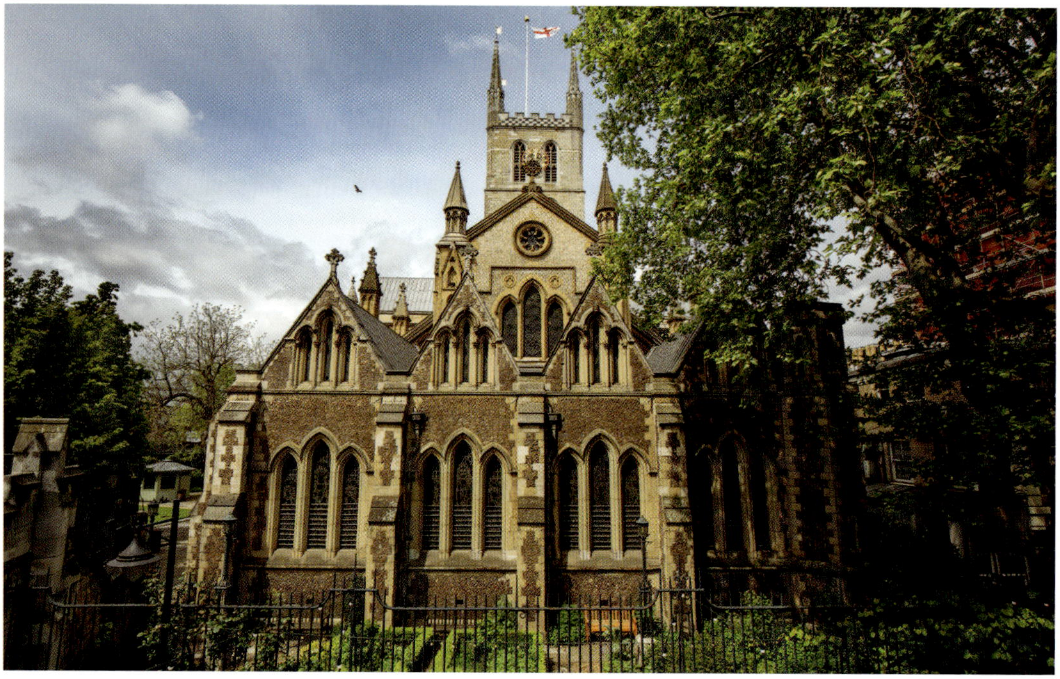

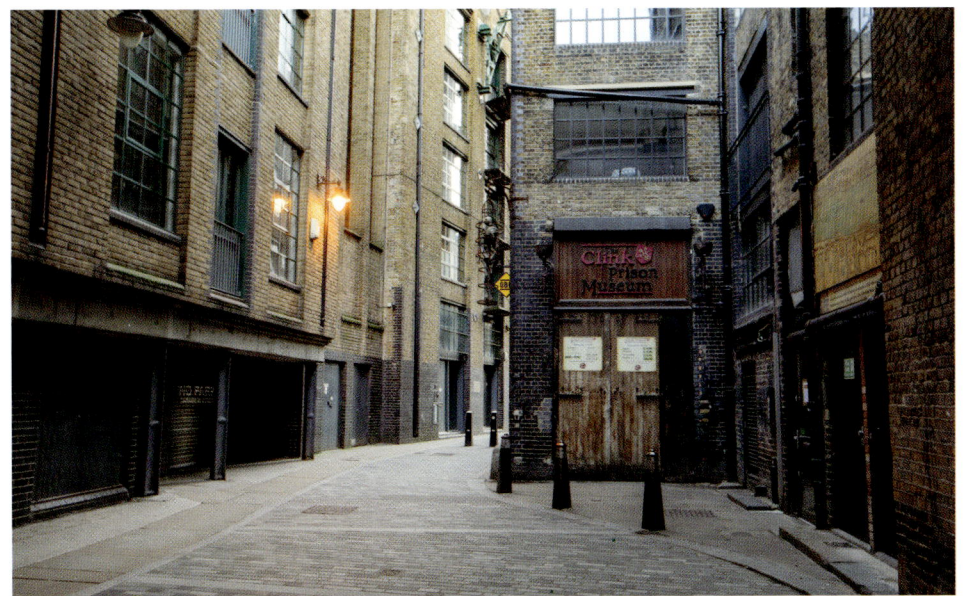

The Clink
Dating back to 1144, The Clink Museum sits on the original site of the infamous Clink Prison named after the sinister sound of being clad in iron restraints. The prison was renowned for its cramped and poor living conditions. Controlled by the Bishop of Westminster, it served as a place of reform and execution for those committing offences in Bankside and nearby brothels. In 1849, along with over 30,000 other spectators, Dickens witnessed the double hanging of the murderers the Mannings. He was so appalled by the event he wrote to *The Times* ordering for the abolishment of public hangings due to their barbaric and inhumane nature. Burnt down during rioting in 1780, our author uses this as his inspiration for his theme for *Barnaby Rudge*, his novel of 1841.

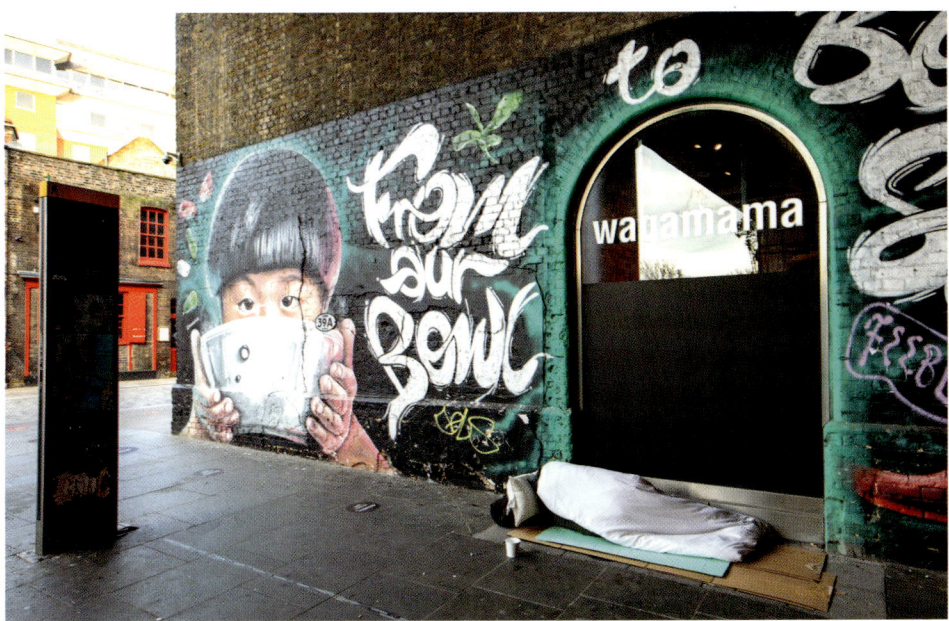

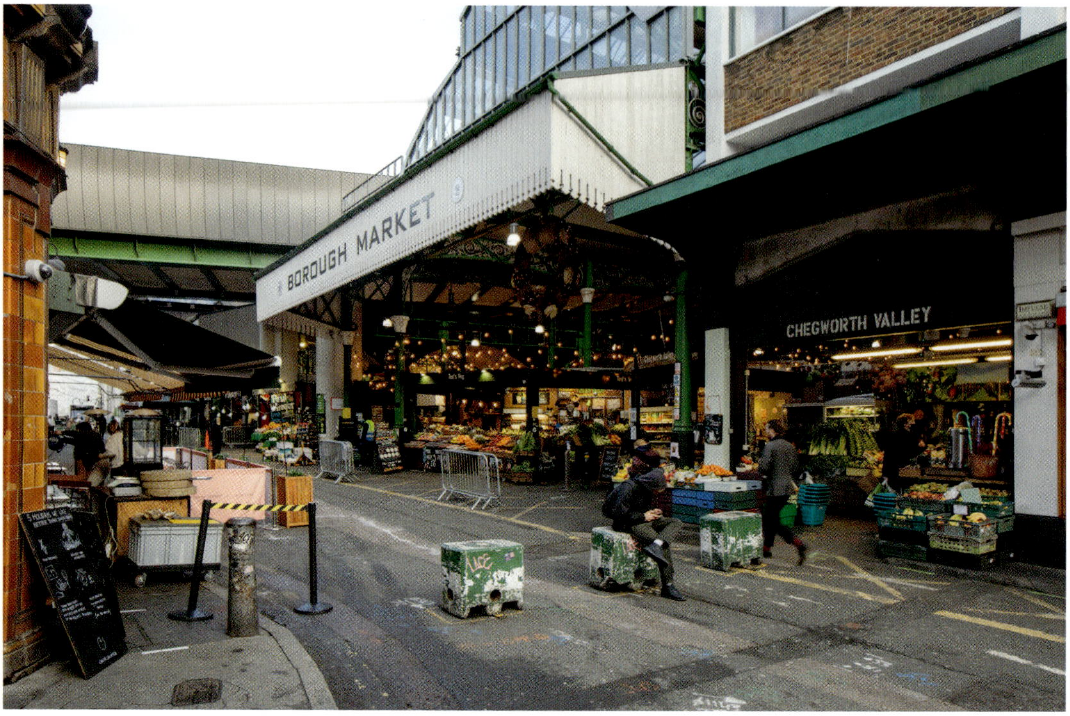

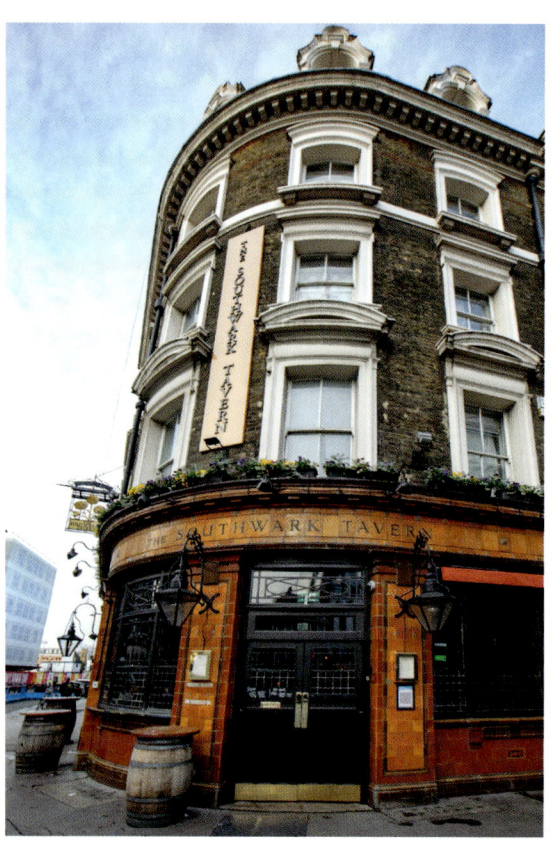

Borough Market and Southwark Tavern
Believed to be the oldest continuously operating urban farmers' market in the world, Borough Market makes an appearance in *The Pickwick Papers* when a very drunk *Bob Sawyer* attempts to find his way back to his lodgings and 'double knocks at the door of the Borough Market Office' and takes 'short naps on the steps … under the firm impression he lived there and had forgotten the key'. The Southwark Tavern has long claimed to have held overflow from the prisons, although actual records are scarce. This theory isn't as far-fetched as it may seem though: the inn was central to many of the debtors' jails in Dickensian times and its basement holds actual cell structures. Dickens also mentions the tavern during a lengthy description of a celebration in *The Mystery of Edwin Drood*.

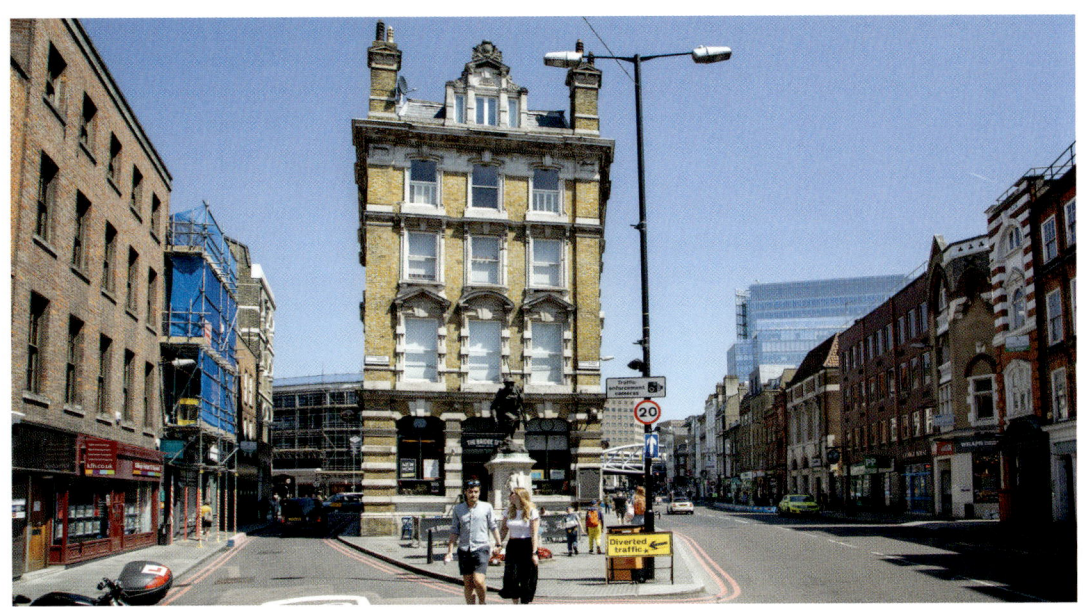

Borough High Street

One of the oldest roads in London, Borough High Street was popular for its many inns serving the convenience of travellers coming in from Kent and Surrey. Because London Bridge closed its gates of an evening, it was also a favourable spot for board and lodgings for those trapped south of the river of a night. Much of the action in *Little Dorrit* focuses in and around here and the street gets a mention in *The Pickwick Papers* when the tale by the little old man is regaled to *Samuel Pickwick* and *Sam Wells* in the Magpie and Stump tavern. There has been a tavern called The Blue Eyed Maid on Borough High Street since the seventeenth century, although not always thought to be on this site. This pub gets a mention in *Little Dorrit* as well as *A Tale of Two Cities* and *The Uncommercial Traveller* by our author.

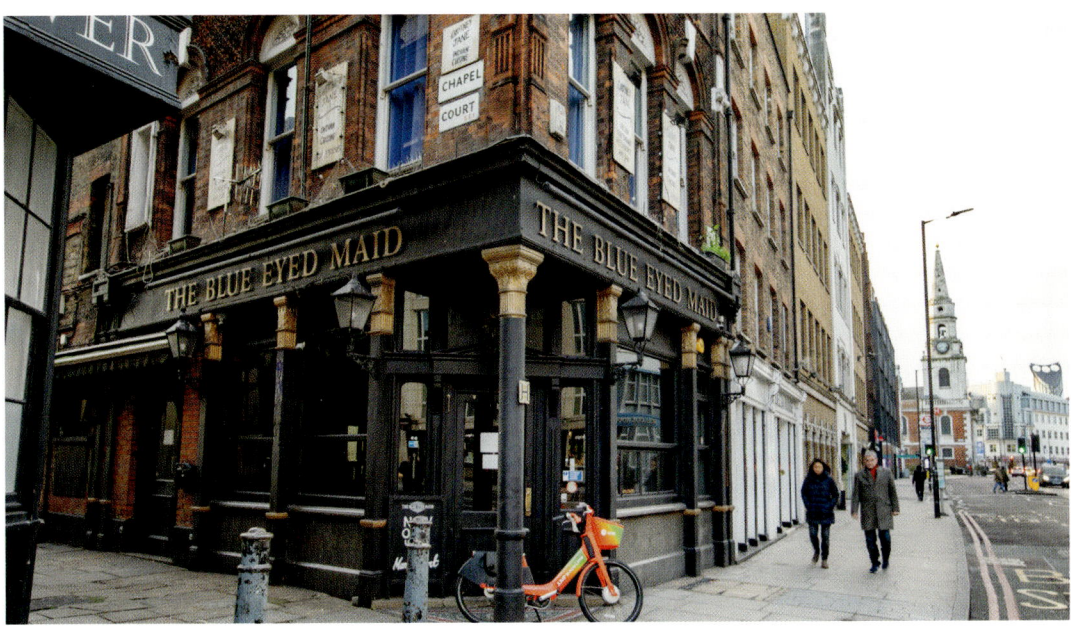

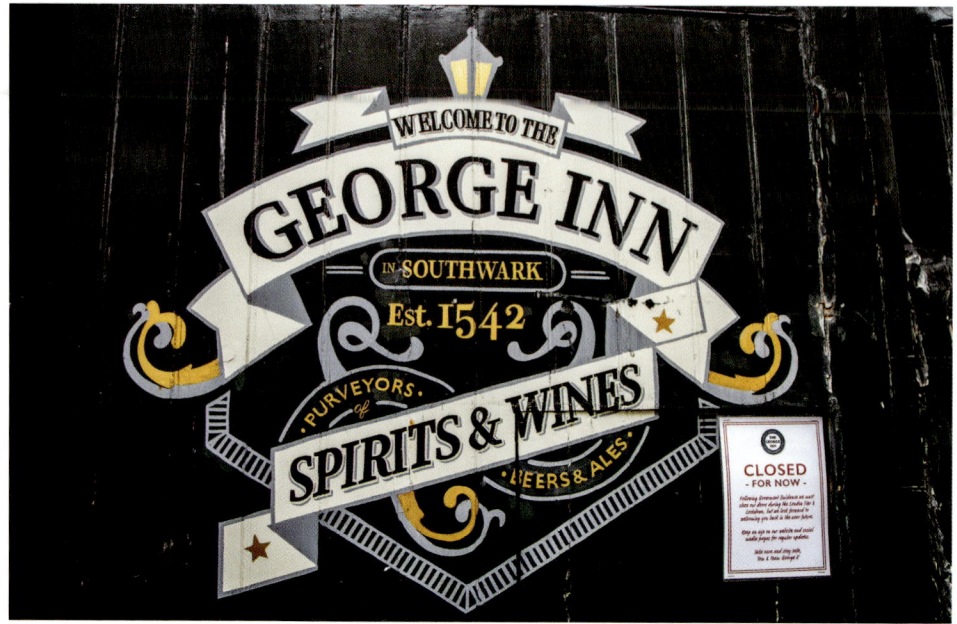

The George Inn

One of two surviving coaching inns in London, The George Inn (formerly known as The George and Dragon) is the oldest public house in the area and includes the only viewing gallery. It was rebuilt in 1677 after fire ravaged most of medieval Southwark. The viewing gallery was used as entertainment for the patrons, and Elizabethan plays were commonly performed within its yard, known as Inn-Yard Theatre. It is certain that The George was familiar (and rumoured to be a favourite place) to Dickens, having been mentioned by name in *Little Dorrit* as the characters visited its coffee rooms early in the book. During his rise to fame Dickens befriended Octavia Hill, the founder of the National Trust. She chose The George Inn to be her first building of sponsorship to be saved. Many believe this to have been at the writer's personal request.

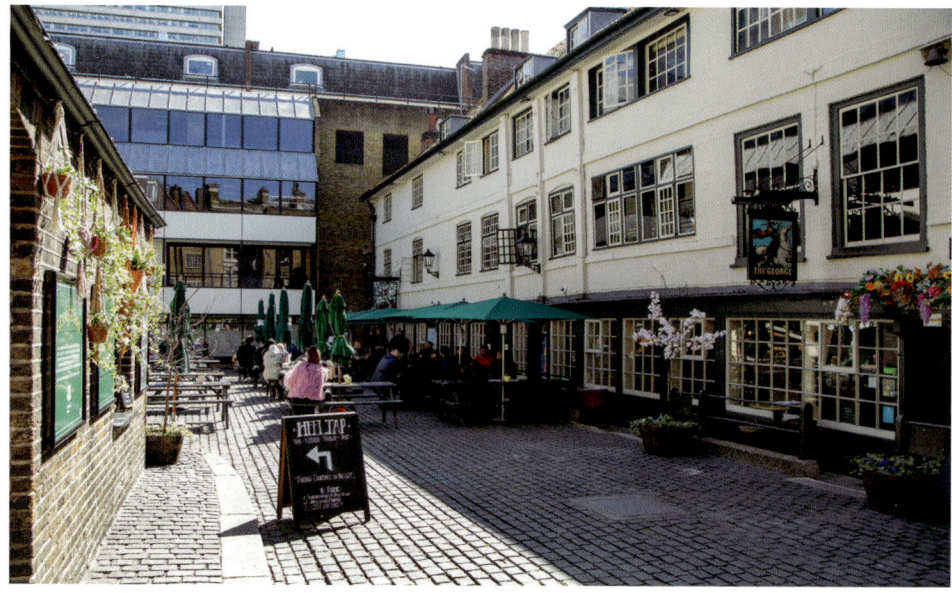

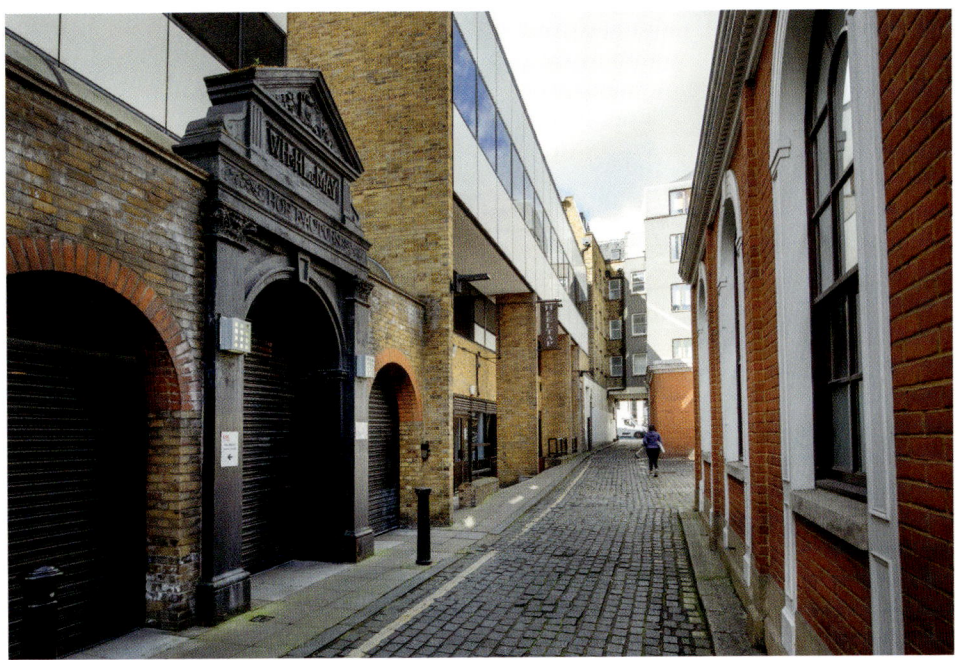

White Hart Yard

Immortalised by Dickens in *The Pickwick Papers*, it is the scene here that allows the author to change the course of the work. The White Hart Inn is where *Alfred Jingle* and *Rachel Wardle* were followed, after their elopement, by *Mr Pickwick*. The writer choses his readers to first meet *Sam Weller* in this location, adding bulk to his intricate descriptive narrative. *Mr Jingle's* demise set here is thought to have been inspired by a tragic incident in 1820 when Elizabeth Wilson neglected to duck after her carriage swept under the coach house entrance, and was killed instantly. Although nothing still survives in terms of the original buildings after its demolition in 1889, 62 White Hart was once the largest coaching inn to have lined Borough High Street. It is steeped in history and held many important meetings. The Mayor and Corporation met here in 1761 to declare war upon Spain.

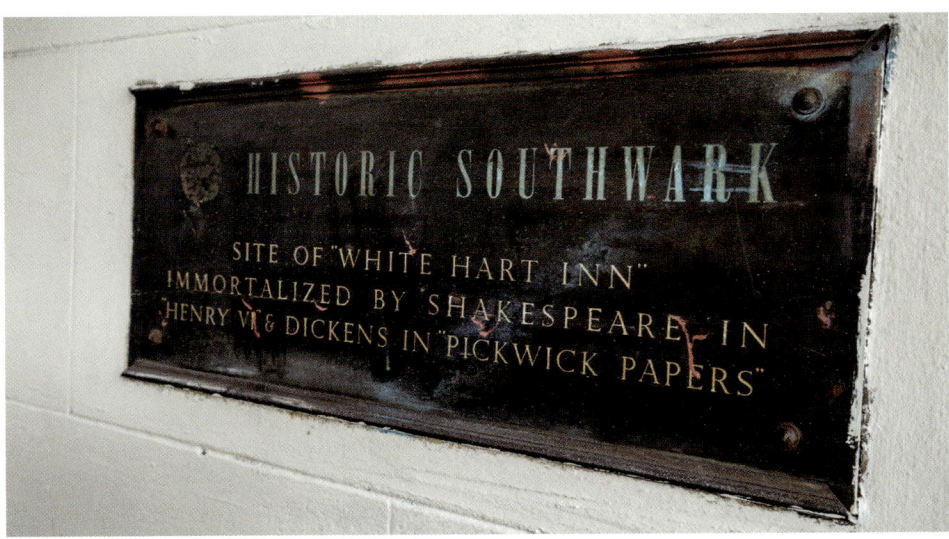

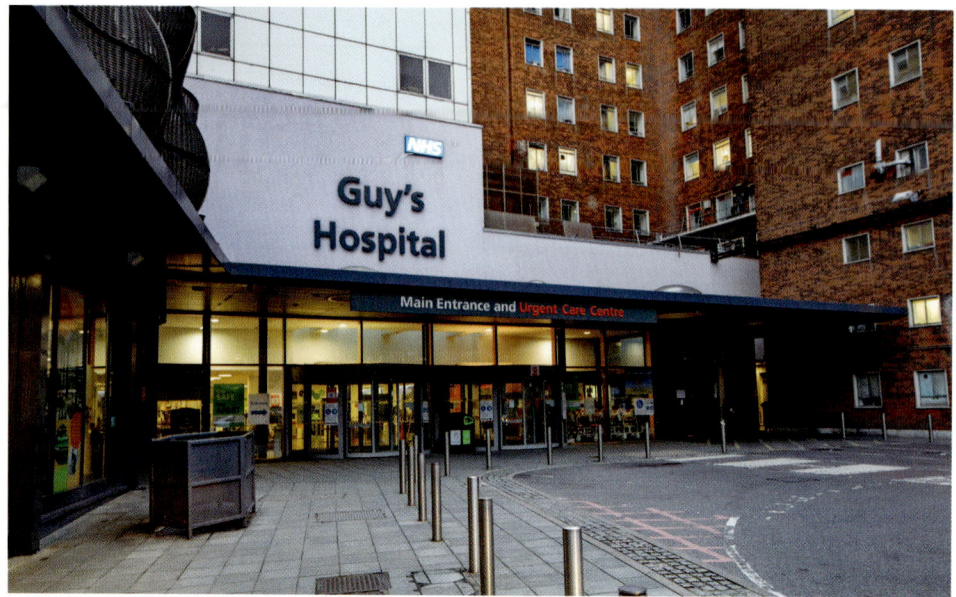

Guy's Hospital

Founded by Thomas Guy in 1721, Guy's Hospital was established to treat incurables discharged from St Thomas' Hospital. Dickens had an affectionate and long connection with many hospitals but mentioned Guy's particularly in his writings. *Bob Sawyer* is depicted as a medical student here along with some other characters in *The Pickwick Papers*, and he also choses it for the setting of the death of *Mrs Gamp's* husband in *Martin Chuzzlewit*. He wrote an article in one of his *Sketches by Boz* entitled 'The Hospital Patient' empathising with the victims of accidents and violence he had witnessed upon his visits. He also doesn't shy away from human illness or disability in his works; notably a major character, *Tiny Tim* (thought to have been suffering from tuberculosis), is memorable for receiving the author's sympathy in *A Christmas Carol*.

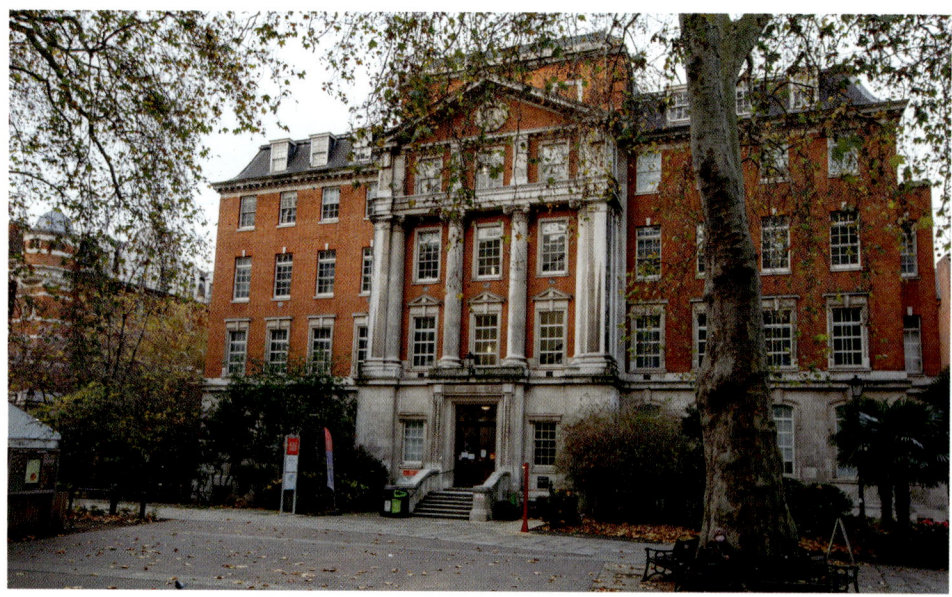

Little Dorrit Court

Previously known as Falcon Court, Little Dorrit Court is a nod to Dickens' beloved character *Amy Dorrit*. After the bombings of the Second World War the council rebuilt much of the area of Southwark, and this is one of several streets and alleys named after a Dickens character. There is also a Copperfield Street, a Clennam Street, a Doyce Street and a Quilp Street close by. Little Dorrit Court is frequently visited and enjoyed by locals and tourists alike due to the aptly named Little Dorrit Park which is around a one-minute walk away. Dickens describes *Little Dorrit's* own childhood as less than jolly – working from a young age and tending to her aging father whilst living inside the Marshalsea. Locals have fondly dubbed it as Little Dorrit's Playground, giving the character some, albeit fictional, reprieve.

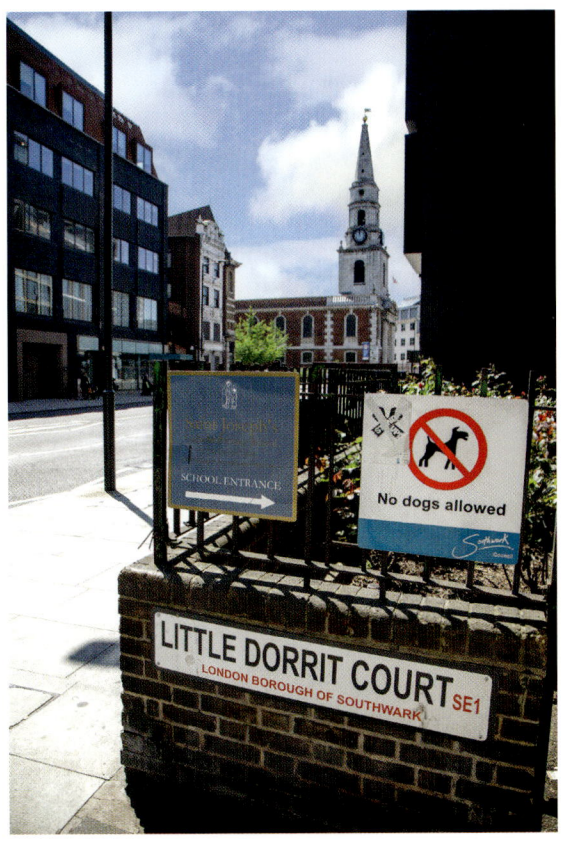

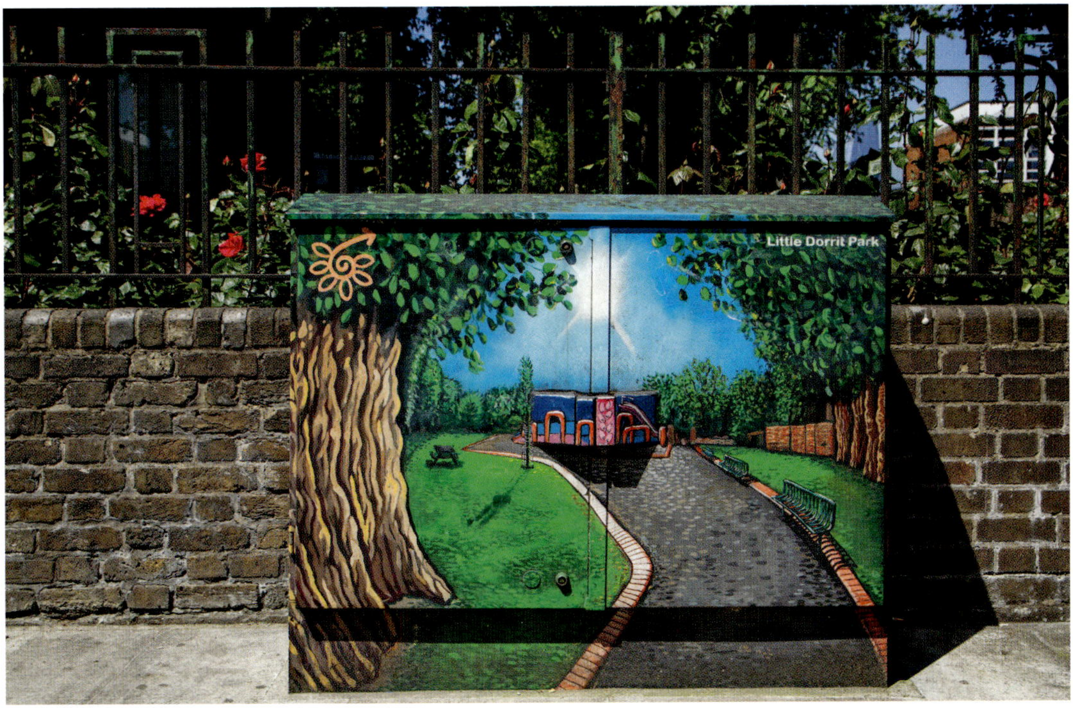

St George the Martyr's Church

Initially constructed in 1122 although it has been rebuilt twice since, St George the Martyr's is often referred to as Little Dorrit's Church. It was the scene for the baptism and marriage of Dickens' heroine within the novel. A figure of *Amy Dorrit* can be seen kneeling in prayer to the left of the altar in a stained-glass window in homage to the character. This church has strong associations with the Dickens family due to the Marshalsea Prison being adjoined to the north side of its churchyard. It was used for many years as a burial ground for the debtors' jail – architectural digs have uncovered the remains of bodies that suffered from malnutrition, some so severely to have quite likely caused their deaths.

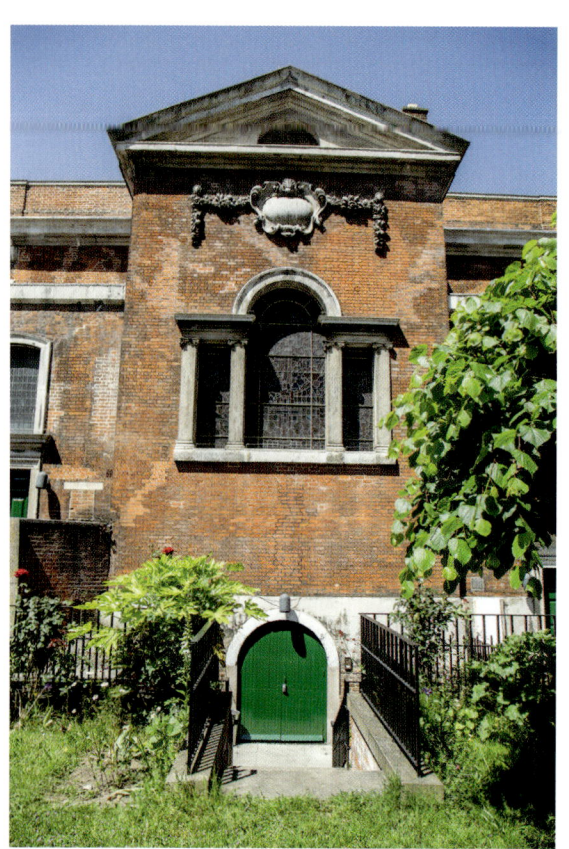

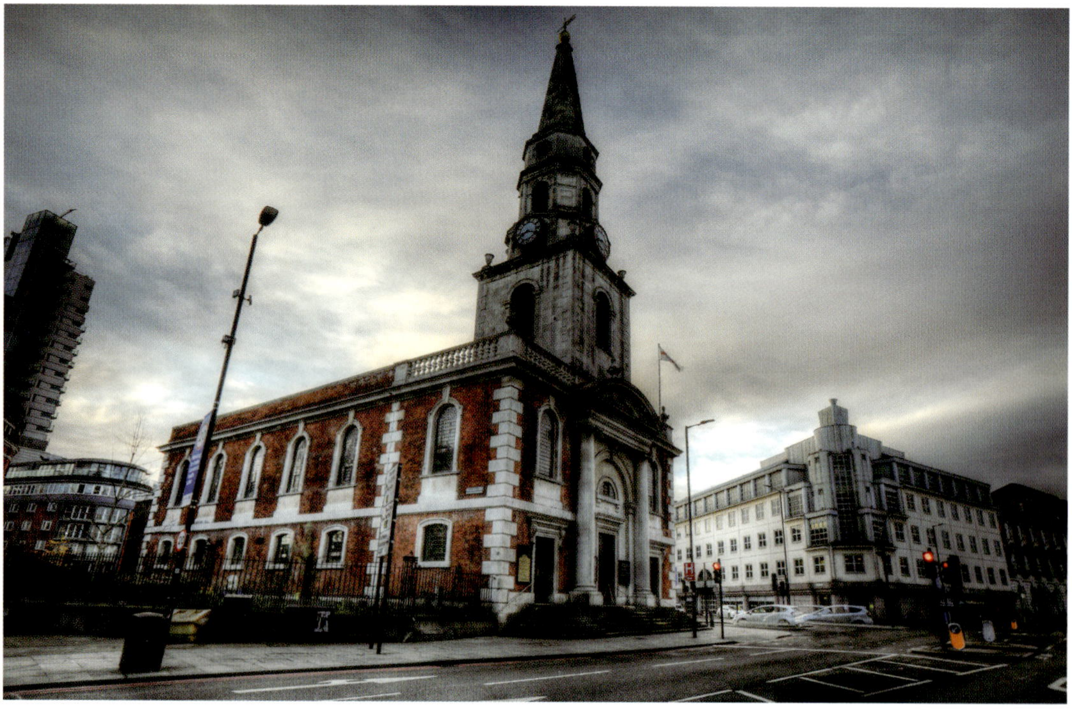

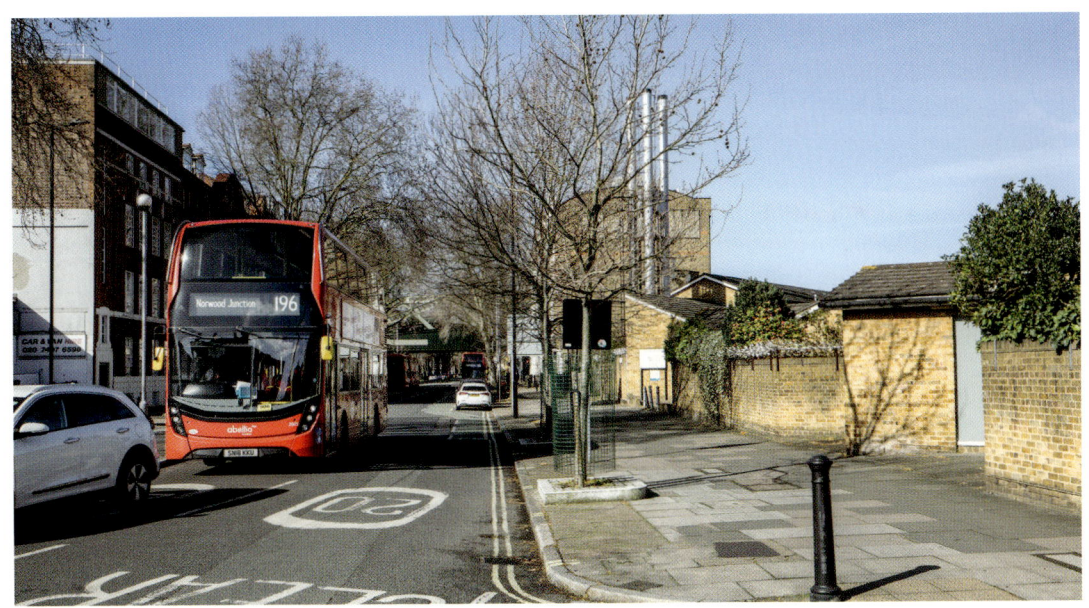

Scovell Estate, Southwark

What is now Scovell Estate was the site of a prison from 1758 until 1880. It is here Dickens chooses as the location to imprison the feckless *Mr Micawber* for debt in his novel *David Copperfield*. This character is thought by most to be unapologetically based on John Dickens, his father, mirroring much of his traits and life choices. Known in Dickens' life as King's Bench Prison it takes its name from the King's Bench Court of Law in which cases of defamation and bankruptcy were held. It had a higher reputation over the Marshalsea for its standards of living. It housed a coffee shop, two public houses, chandlers and butchers. Despite this, most of the occupants were penniless, living in very overcrowded, unhygienic conditions, without bedding or food and many perished due to their situation.

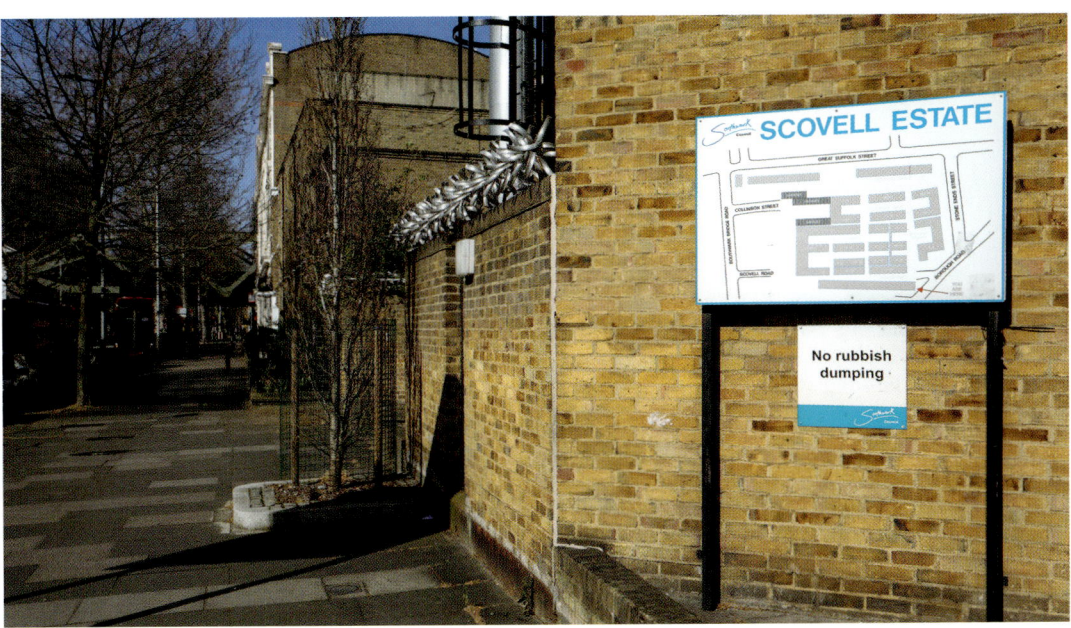

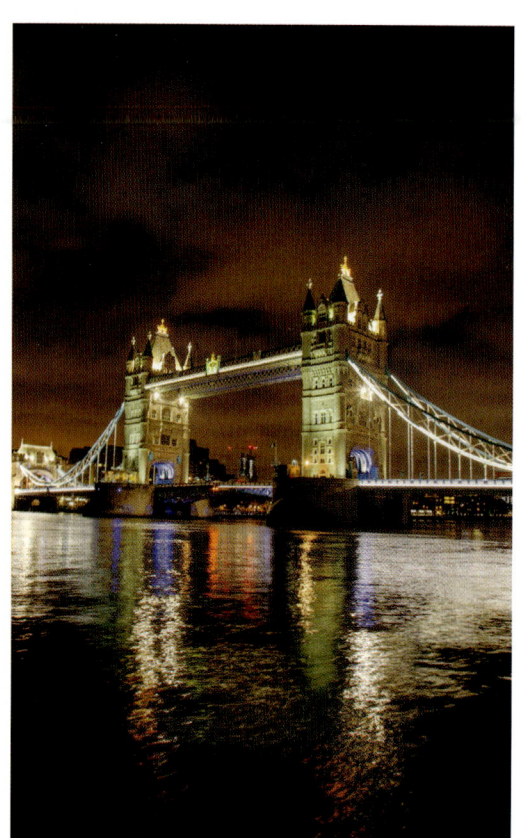

Tower Bridge

Built between 1886 and 1894, this magnificent suspension bridge was constructed to give better access to East London, which was rapidly expanding in commercial potential. Dickens unfortunately never got to see the bridge as it was finished long after his death, but it is heavily linked to a place he did know and used frequently within his writing, the Tower of London. The Tower began its build in 1078 by William the Conquer. This is known as the White Tower and subsequent wings came throughout the years and multiple monarchy reigns. It served as a prison between 1100 and 1952, although this wasn't its primary purpose. It isn't surprising that Dickens called upon the site for inspiration: not only is the Tower an awe-inspiring building of grandeur; it has a dark past full of murder, torture and execution. Most notable references in Dickens' works are when *David Copperfield* takes *Clara Peggotty* here for a day of sightseeing. It is also heavily noted in *Barnaby Rudge* as this is where *Lord George Gordon* is held awaiting trial.

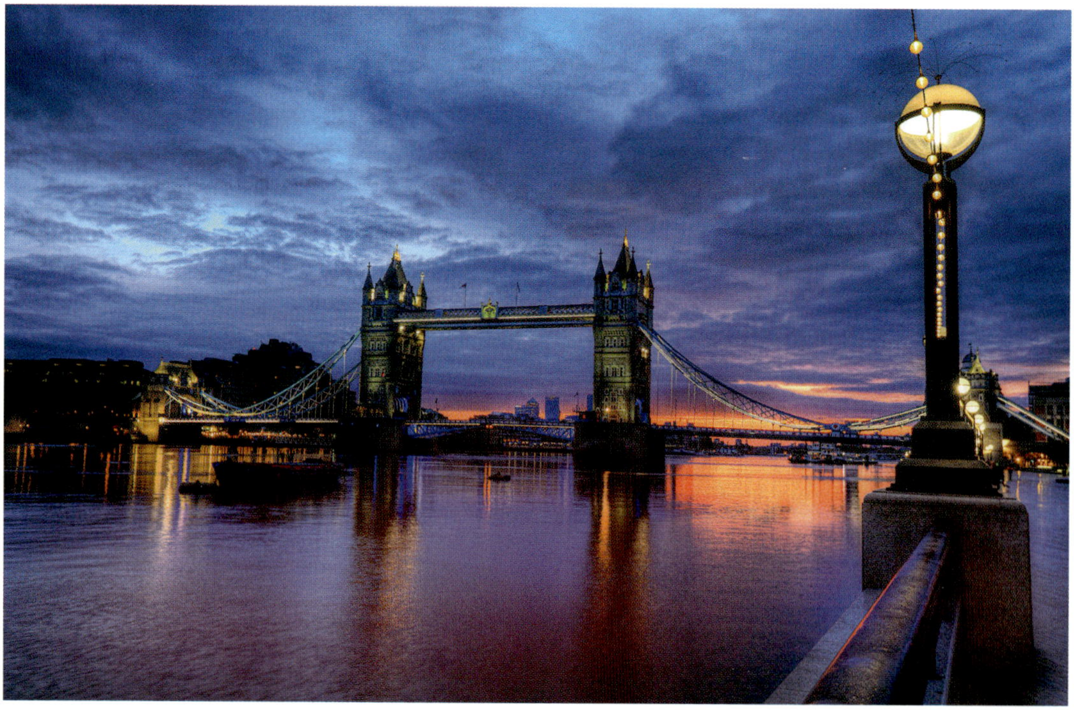

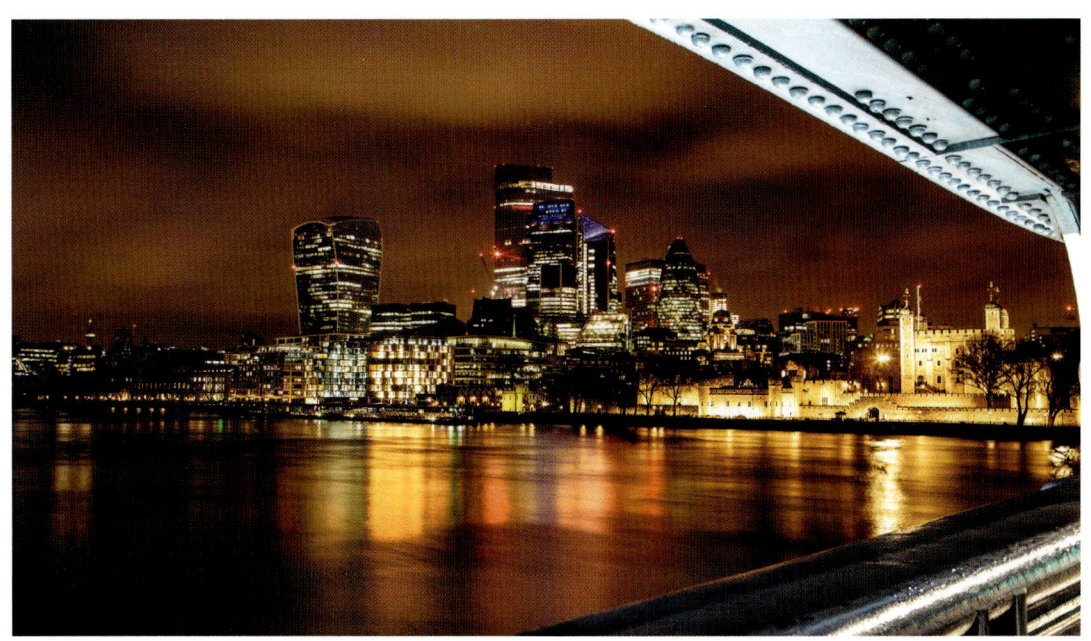

Tower of London

The Tower receives other mentions in Dickens' novels, such as when *Pip, Herbert Pocket* and *Startop* attempt to help *Abel Magwitch* escape England in *Great Expectations*. It also features in *The Old Curiosity Shop*, as *Betsy* and *Daniel Quilp* live on Tower Hill passing the royal fortress. Dickens uses the site to help paint an image of some of his characters' personalities and traits. During a speech to *Mrs Todgers, Seth Pecksniff* unnecessarily recites the gruesome rumour of the smothering of the two young princes within the Tower in *Martin Chuzzlewit*. Dickens is showing the melodramatic and overly confident side of this character.

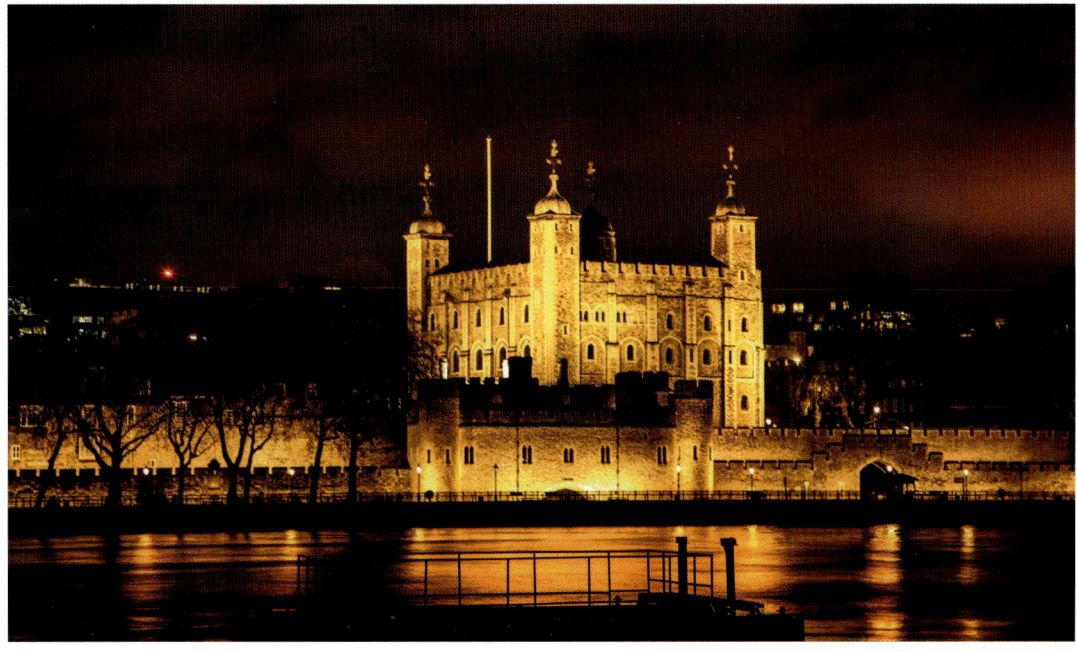

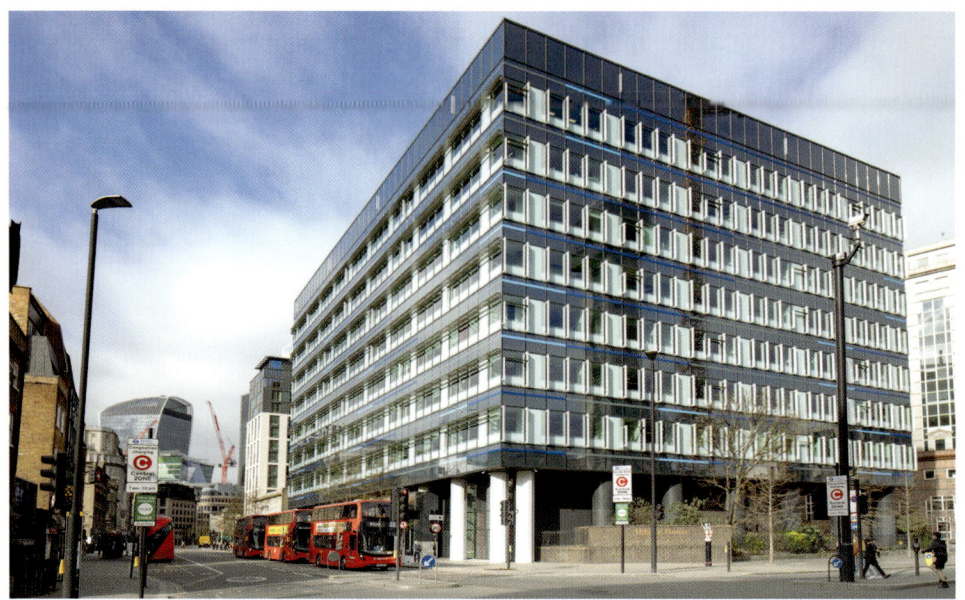

The Bulls Inn, Aldgate

As with most areas of the city, Aldgate was well known to Dickens and as his popularity rose, he became acquainted with some of the city's more exclusive establishments. The Bull Inn's reservable room on Aldgate High Street was frequented by the author as it was known to be a restful place where people of stature could indulge in the house's fine food and drink but remain unapproachable to unwanted attention. In the book *Stage-coach and Mail Days of Yore* by Chares George Harper he describes a conversation with Dickens whilst at a seat within the Bull's parlour: 'Mr Dickens, we know you knows wot's wot, but can you sir, andle a vip?' Remaining modest despite his surroundings, Dickens responded that he could *describ*e one but in the management of a *vip* he was no expert.

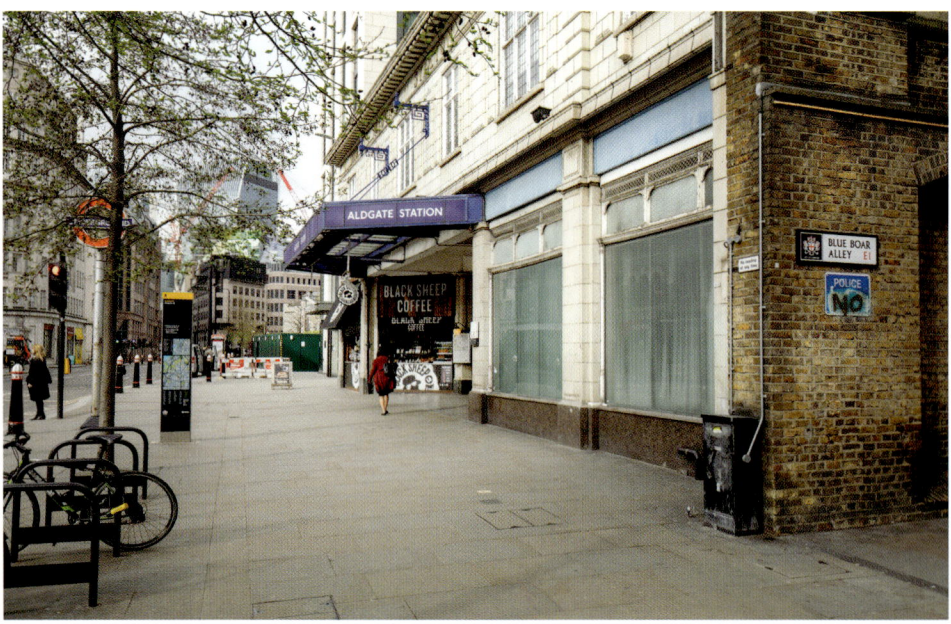

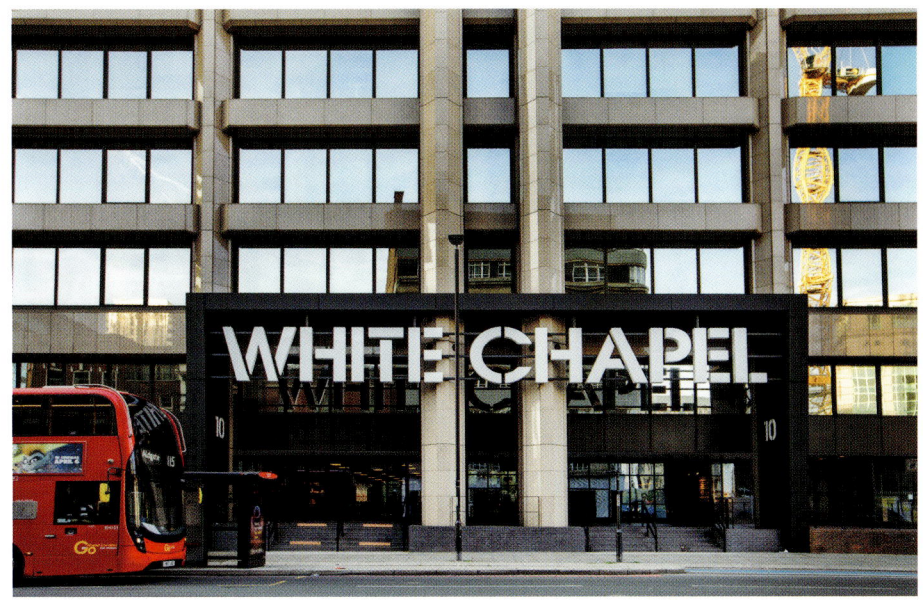

White Chapel Road

The area of Whitechapel in Dickensian times was notorious for filth and poverty. It was where some of the poorest families in London lived and was rife with crime and violence. Nearby Dorset Street was known for a long time as the most dangerous place in London. It is widely believed a local 'fence' going by the name of Ikey Solomon was the basis for *Fagin's* characteristics in *Oliver Twist*. Emphasising the site to outsiders upon arrival, it also features in *The Pickwick Papers* when the *Pickwickian's* arrive via coach from Ipswich. *Sam Weller* reports to others in the carriage 'not a wery nice neighbourhood' and makes way for his famous comment 'It's a wery remarkable circumstance, Sir, that poverty and oysters always seem to go together.' White Chapel Road was of particular interest to Dickens though as it was the site of The Pavilion Theatre (1828–1935) and The Effingham (1834–97). Our author had a great love for the performing arts and attended many productions and stage adaptations here and around the city throughout his life.

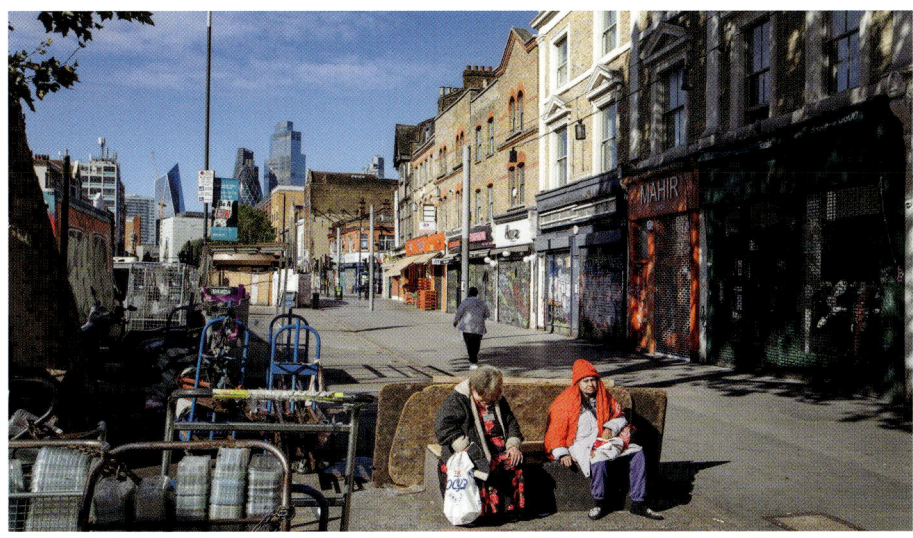

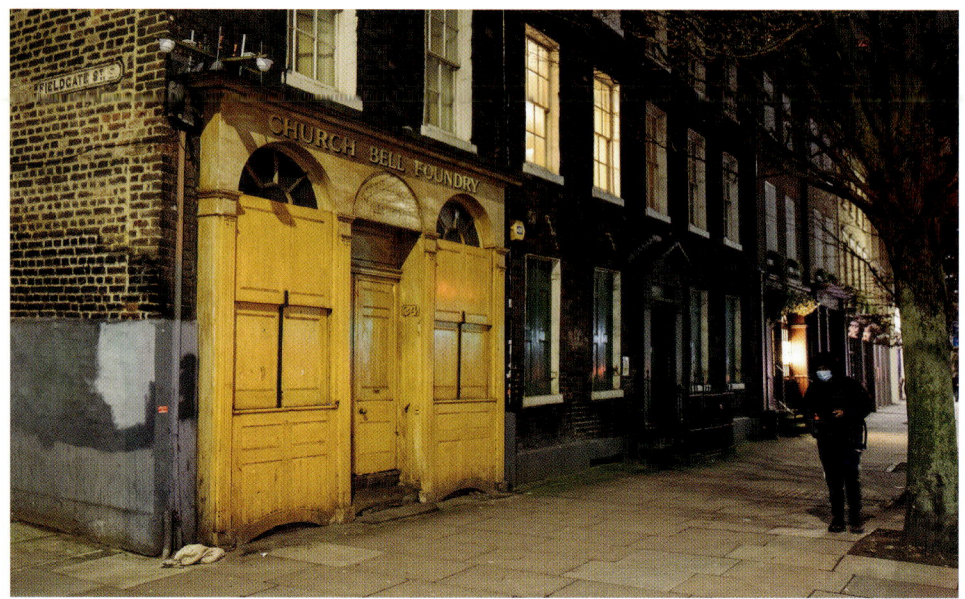

The Bell Foundry

Whitechapel Bell Foundry, having been established in 1570 by Robert Mot, moved to this site due to expansion in 1738. It is the birthplace of some of the world's largest and most well-known bells and their associated fixings. Some of its oldest designs are still in working use at Westminster Abbey from as early as 1583. The foundry is responsible for Big Ben's chimes as well as the original Liberty Bell (1752). It is almost certain the author had a passion for the sound of bells, using them often to set a precedent in his scenes throughout his literary works, even describing one as 'spying on Scrooge' in *A Christmas Carol*. He would have known the business almost exactly as we see it now from the exterior. Sadly, after decades of petitioning, Whitechapel lost the battle with the planning council to save the building. The final bell was cast in 2017 and the business closed its doors.

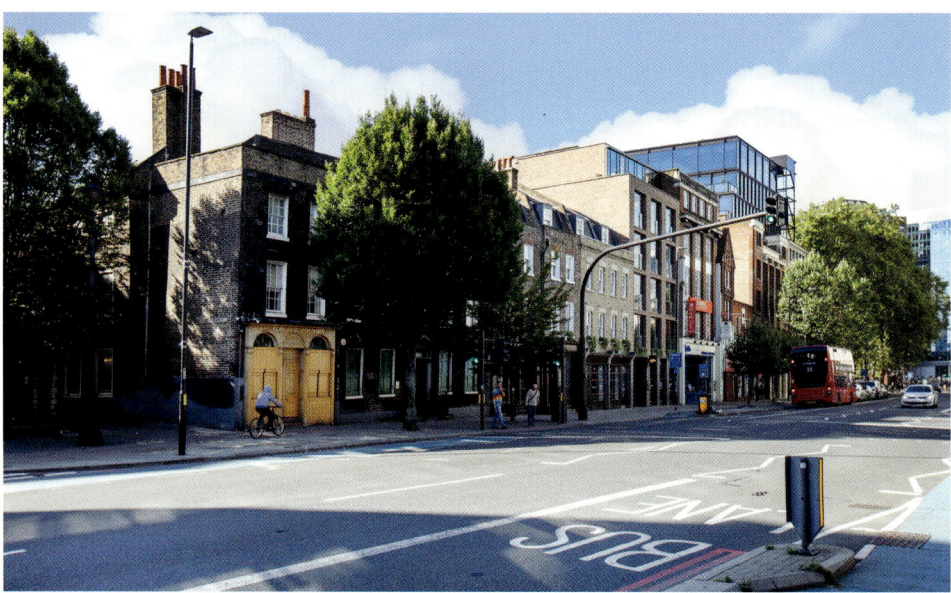

Whitechapel Workhouse

Published in 1850, Dickens wrote an article in *Household Words* under the name 'A Walk in a Workhouse'. It focused upon a visit he had taken at this Whitechapel institute. He was deeply affected by the sight of a young child clearly dead under a sheet being discussed by staff as 'dropped' upon his arrival. He wrote 'The dropped child seemed too small and poor a thing for Death to be in earnest with, but Death had taken it.' Whilst out for a night-time stroll past it's walls in 1855 Dickens came across another startling scene here. In the downpouring rain were several heaps of rags leaned against the entrance stone. Further inspection uncovered that these 'dumb, wet, silent horrors' were in fact young women who due to lack of space were overflow of the workhouse that evening. The author pleaded with the master of the workhouse to find them shelter but to no avail and after gifting them a charitable donation of a few shillings apiece, he had to silently walk away full of reflection on the state of humanity.

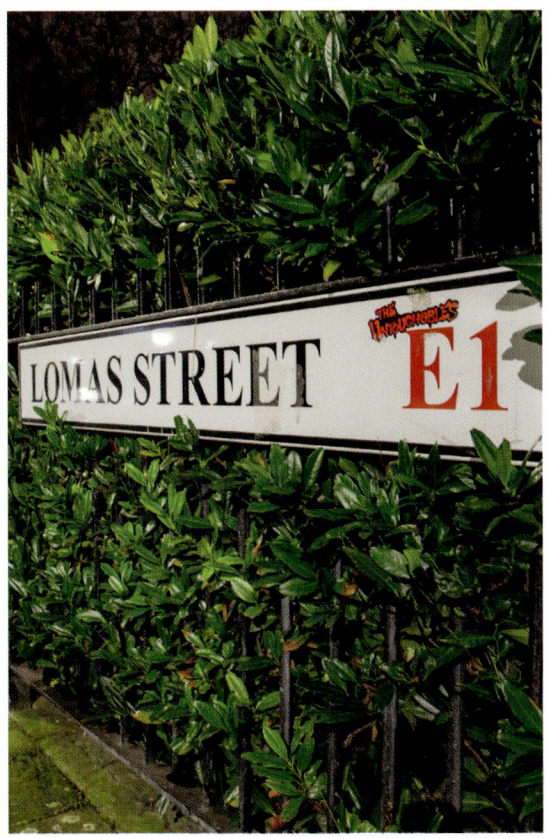

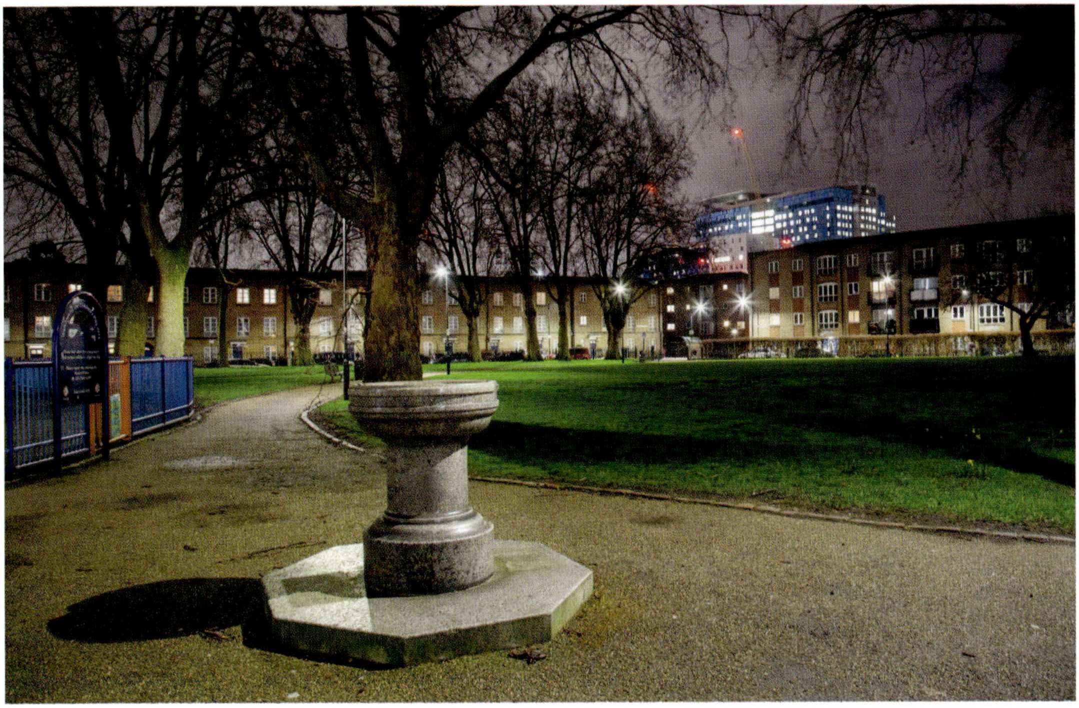

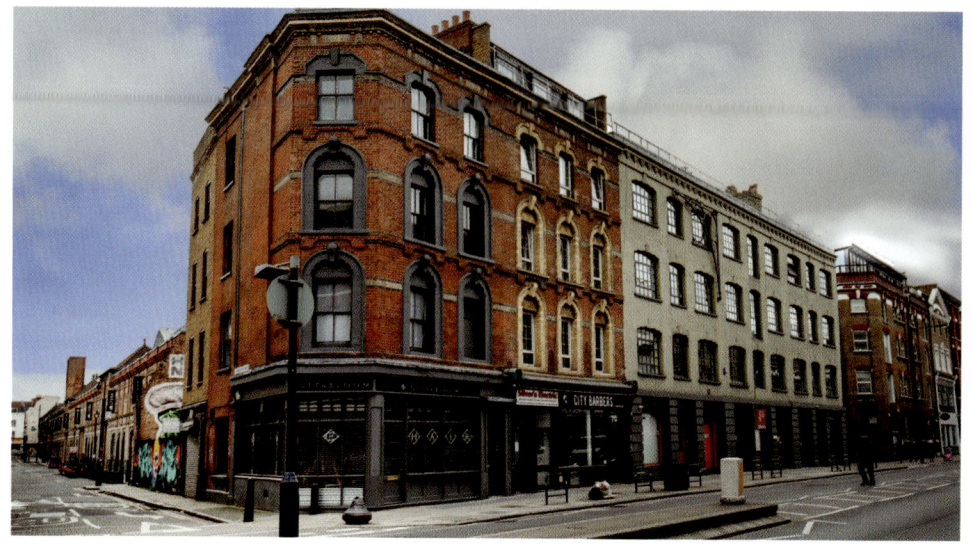

Self-supporting Cooking Depot

The Uncommercial Traveller is a collection of literary sketches Dickens published in his magazine *All Year Round* detailing his jaunts and experiences through the city of London. Originally published in 1863 titled 'The Boiled Beef of New England', the writer is surprisingly delighted to be describing his visit to this self-help project located on the corners of Commercial, Flower and Dean Street. Comfortably seating 300, the working classes could purchase a ticket here for 4.5 pence and be served nutritious meals in clean and dignified surroundings. The author was so struck by the efficiency of the service and quality of the food he states, 'I dined at my club in Pall-Mall aforesaid, a few days afterwards, for exactly twelve times the money, and not half as well.' An advocate for the poor, Dickens was equally pleased that the staff were paid a fair wage and consisted of local girls. His only criticism of the project was that it did not serve beer. He felt this took away from the dignity or choices of the working class.

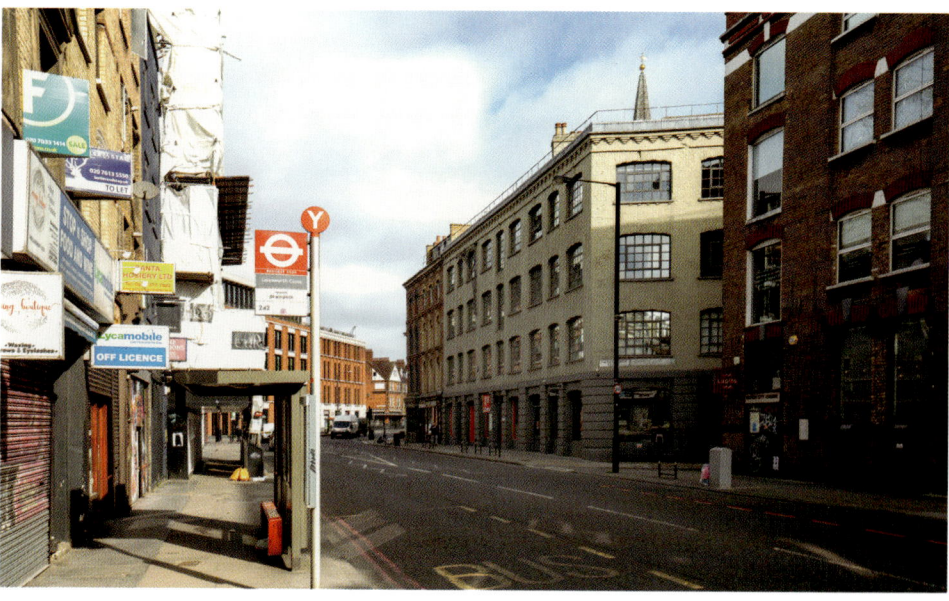

Fournier Street, Whitechapel

The last street to be built on the Wood-Michell estate in Spitalfields, Fournier Street was renowned for being integral to the silk industry. At the height of production in the area there were up to 17,000 looms between 12,000 buildings locally. Eleven and a half Fournier Street was home to seventeenth-century French Huguenots fleeing religious persecution. They mostly galvanised the area's weaving trade at the time. In 1851 early instalments of *Household Words* Dickens wrote a piece dedicated to Spitalfields with his sub-editor, W. H. Wills. It focused on a visit to one of the silk warehouses and its manager, Mr Broadelle, who described how densely populated the area was. He proclaimed the inhabitants to be 'so interlaced and bound together by debt, marriage and prejudice, that, despite many inducements to remove to the country establishments of the masters they already serve they prefer dragging on a miserable existence in their present abodes'.

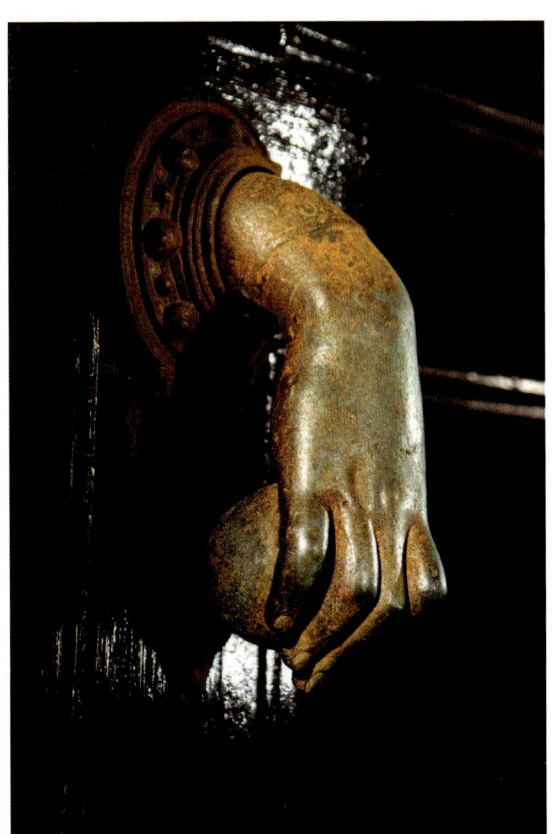

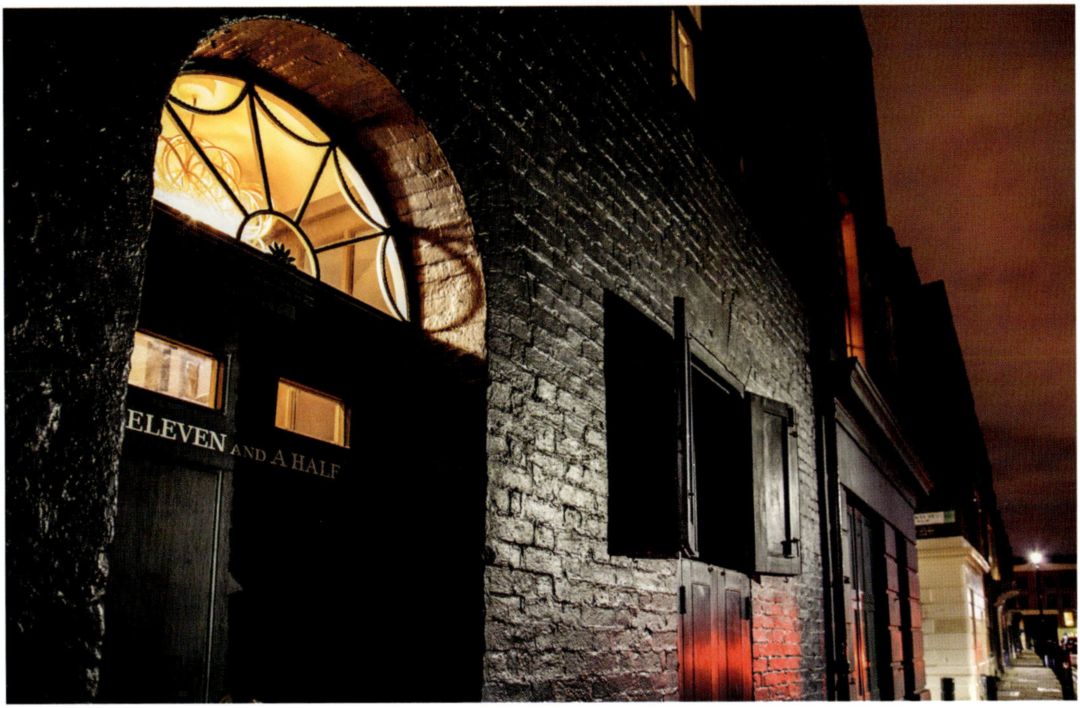

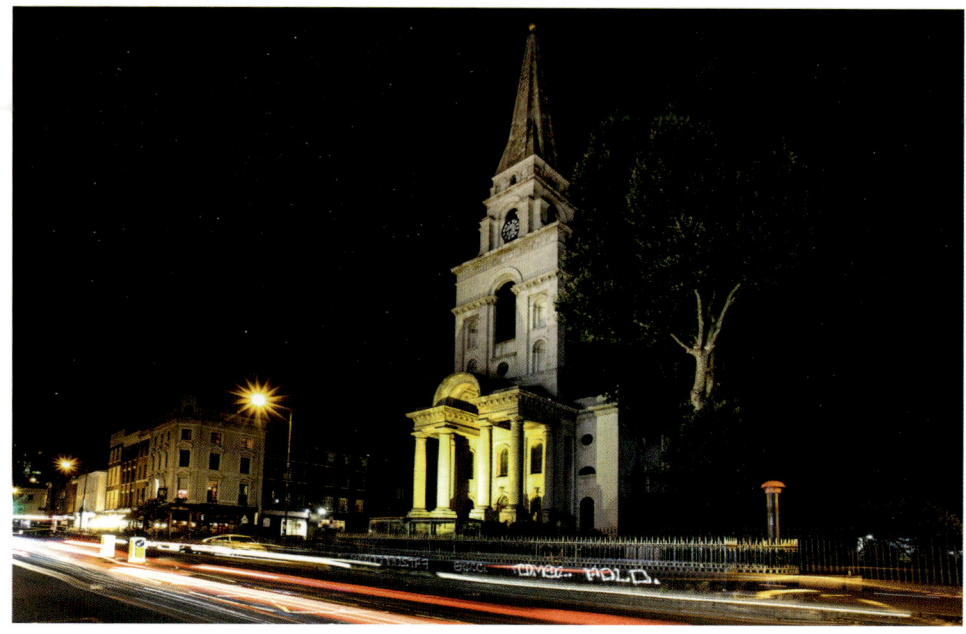

Christ Church, Spitalfields

Designed by Nicholas Hawksmoor and built between 1714 and 1729, Christ Church is the unrivalled and celebrated structure of part of 'The Commission for Building Fifty New Churches' act of 1711's greatest achievement. The reality saw only twelve of the promised built with Hawksmoor designing six of them. Like many architectural masterpieces it lay in ruin from the 1960's until it's restoration in 2004 and has allowed for a booming tourist attraction and heavily booked venue ever since. A regular visitor in to the attached Hugenot chapel Dickens held readings of his works throughout the 1800s. In 1888 it gained further notoriety in holding the strike meetings by the Match Girls preparing for their protest against working conditions at the nearby Bryant and May factory.

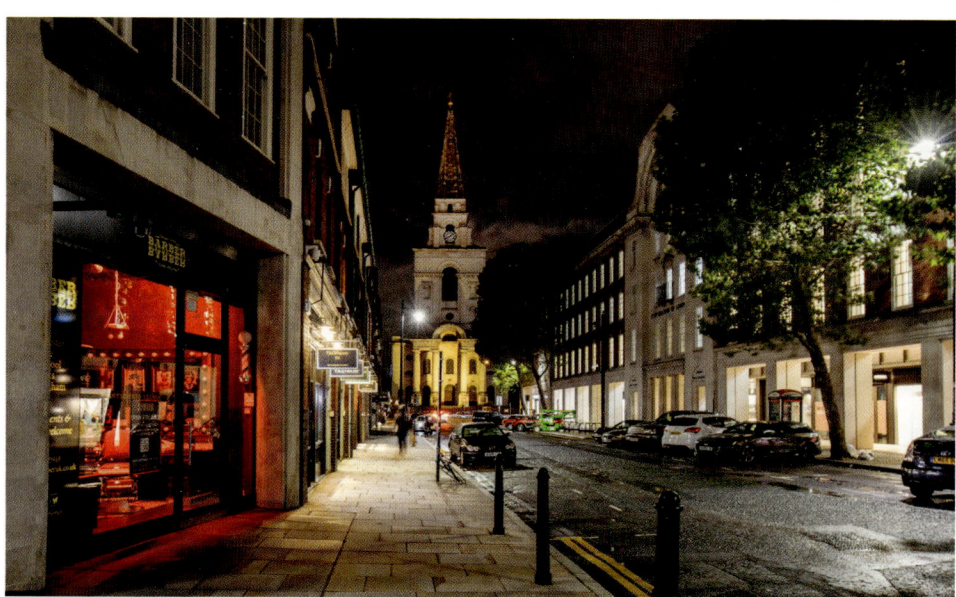

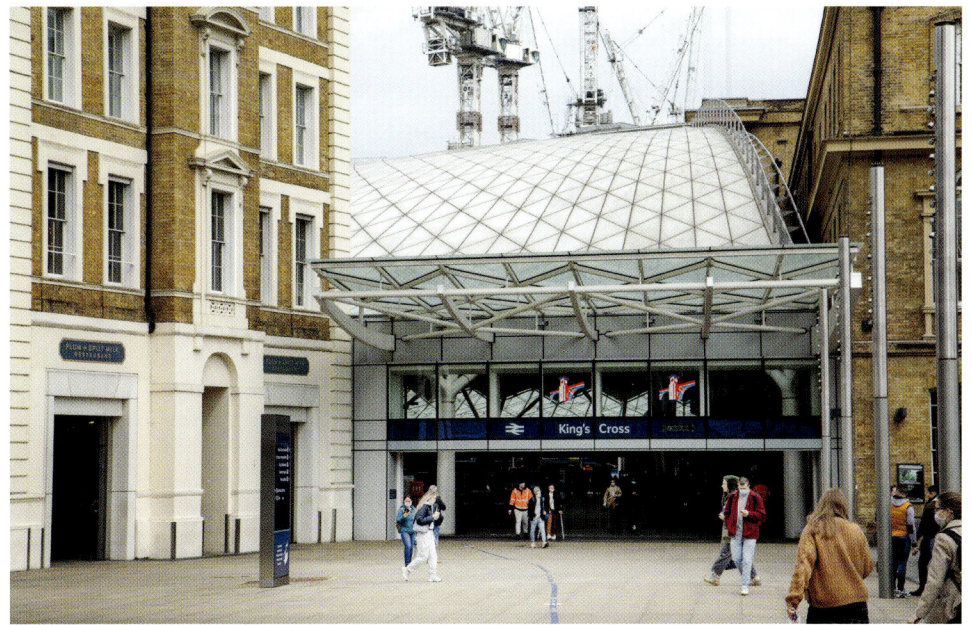

Kings Cross Railway Station
Built in 1851 and a short walk from Doughty Street, Kings Cross station was opened in 1852. It is the largest station in the UK and was well known to our author, who watched its construction with great interest. Its name derives from the Kings Cross building, and its demolition in 1845 appalled Dickens as it was an institute for the care of children with smallpox. Named after his beloved character *Dora Spenlow* from *David Copperfield*, eight-month-old Dora Dickens, his ninth child, died unexpectedly on 14 April 1851 from convulsions. Dickens had spent that day playing with her before travelling to the London Tavern to give a speech. The news was delivered to friend John Forster, who chose to keep the information from Dickens until after the author had made his contribution to the meeting. Many, including Charles, believed Dora was suffering from early signs of smallpox and the fits were brought on by a raise in temperature from the condition. His father, John Dickens, had died a mere nine days prior.

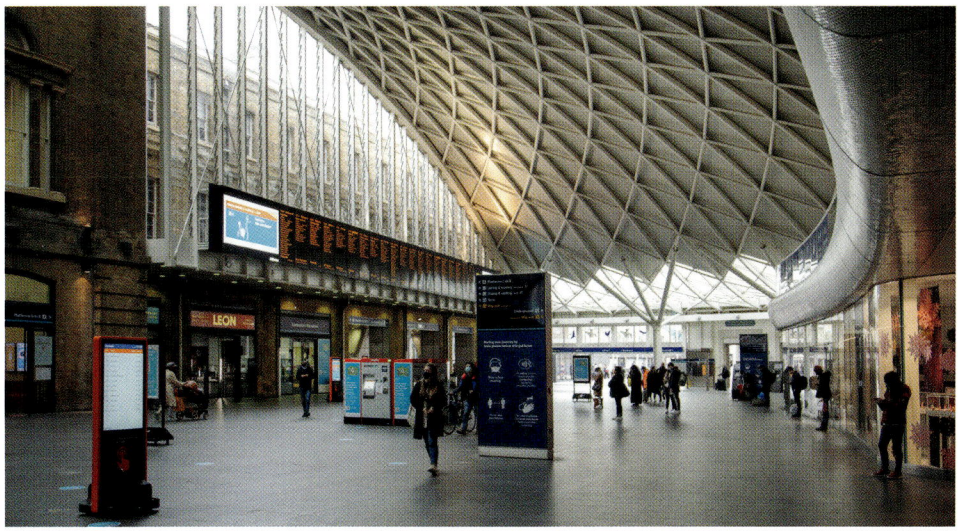

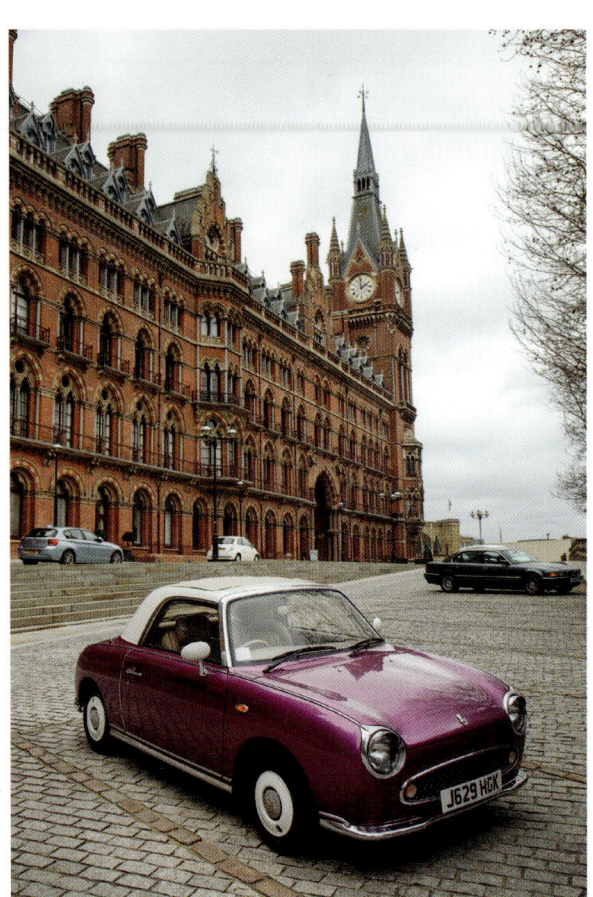

St Pancras Railway Station

Opened in 1868, St Pancras station is a masterpiece of Victorian engineering. The Grade I listed building was beautifully restored in 2007, becoming an international link for Belgium, France and the Netherlands. It maintains its original purpose as the terminus for the Midland main lines connecting Leicester, Derby, Sheffield and Nottingham as well as hosting a high-speed domestic service for commuters from Kent. Despite the opulent new station's reputation as a grand way to travel, it was avoided as an option by Dickens where possible. Whilst travelling with his mistress Ellen Turnan and her mother he had been involved in a tragic railway accident in 1865 which took the lives of ten other people whilst badly injuring forty others. The author escaped unharmed from the Staplehurst rail crash as his first-class carriage was the only one to remain on the tracks after the rest of the locomotive derailed. He tended to the injured and dying before reboarding the train to retrieve the unfinished manuscript for *Our Mutual Friend*.

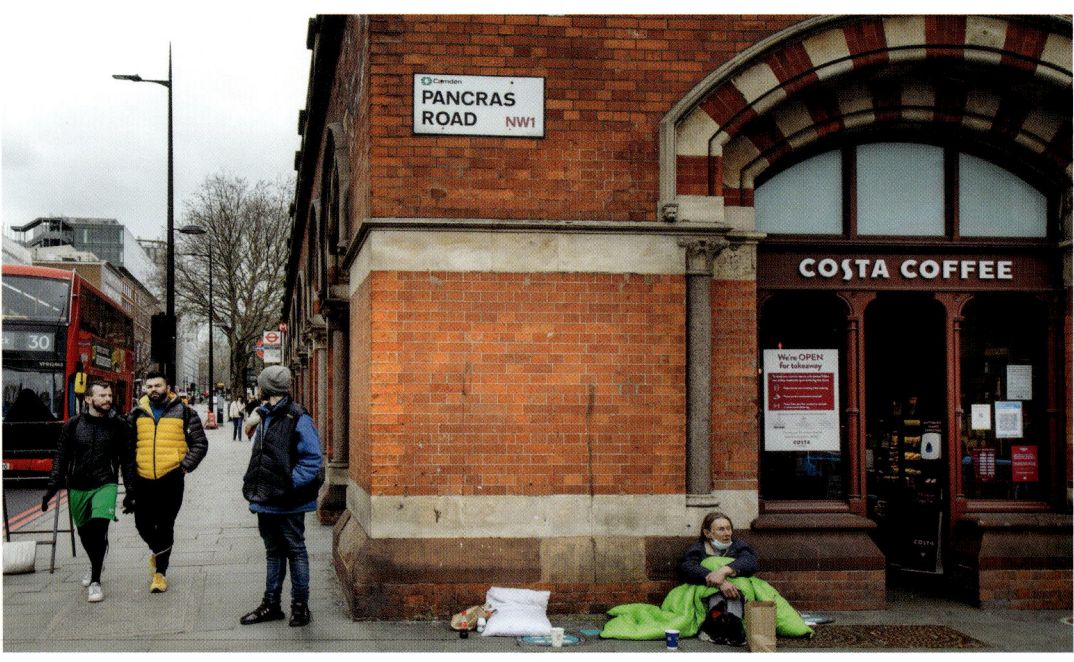

St Pancras Old Church

St Pancras Old Church is believed to be the oldest site of Christian worship in England from as early as the 1500s. Beheaded by Diocletian at only fourteen years of age, Pancras was martyred in Rome in 304. Dickens chose this site for bodysnatching, in his 1859 works *A Tale of Two Cities*, by *Jerry Cruncher* and his son and the burial site of Old Bailey spy *Roger Cly* of the same novel. It is most notably known for the Hardy Tree and it's unusual visual of numerous headstones circling the tree trunk. This came to be in the mid-1860s after young engineer Thomas Hardy was given the task to exhume and relocate many human remains to make way for the nearby railway track plans. In his solution to what to do with the headstones he arranged them around the ash tree as a memorial. Many of the stones have been absorbed by the tree's growth and become part of the tree itself. The grave of Dickens' former schoolmaster William Jones can also be found here.

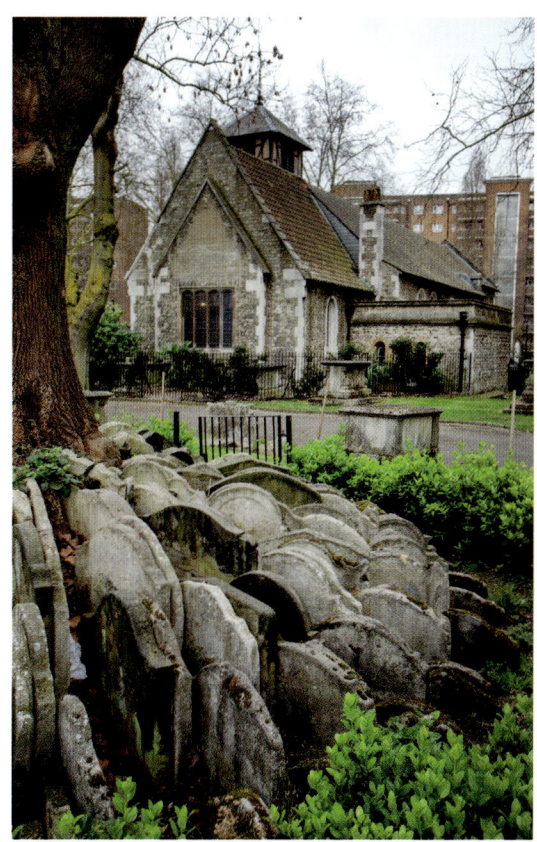

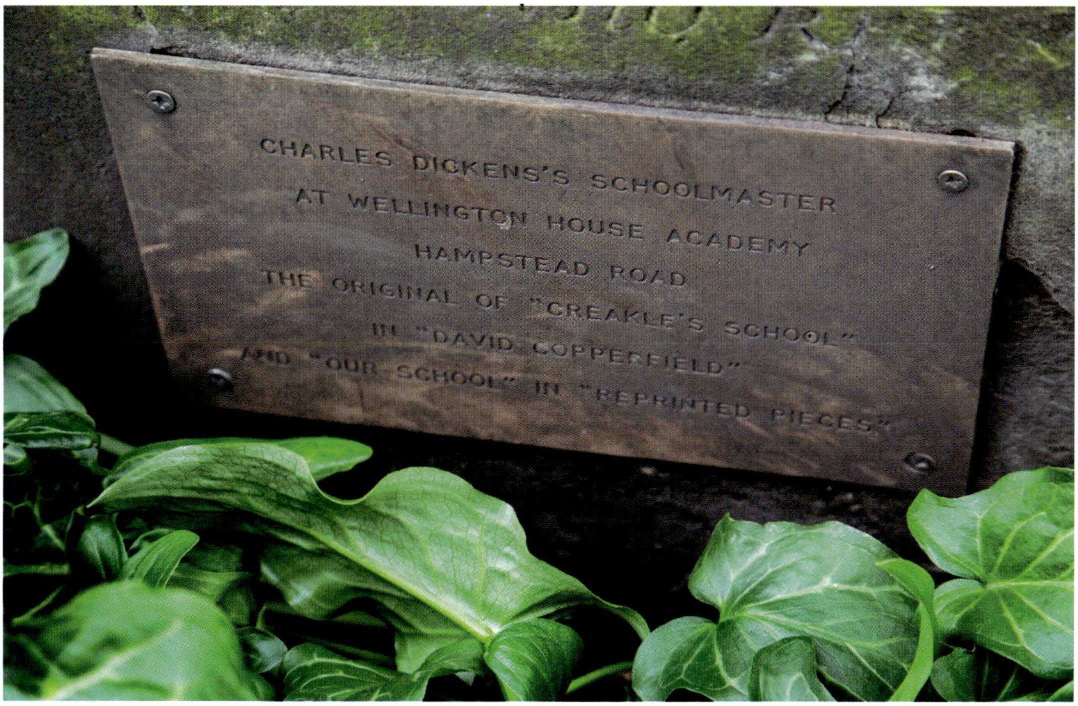

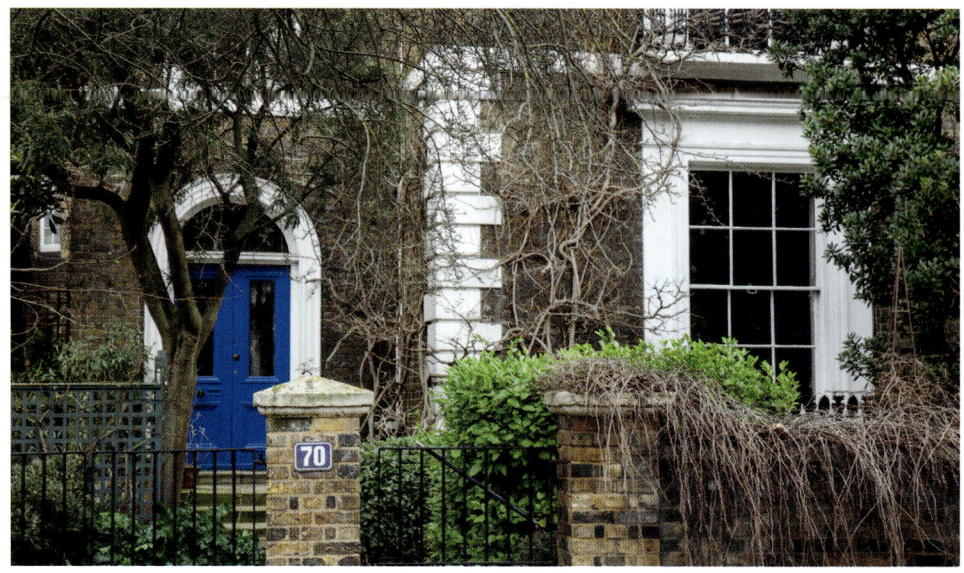

70 Gloucester Crescent

Author, actress and celebrated cook Catherine Dickens (née Hogarth), the wife of Charles Dickens, was often overlooked under the shadow of her husband's acclaim. Married in April 1836, the first of their ten children came along January 1837. Such frequent pregnancies took a toll on Catherine's health, energy and outlook and Dickens was openly resentful of the responsibility of such a large family. Clear disenchantment of the relationship came to light in 1857 when Dickens mistakenly had an engraved bracelet meant for his mistress delivered to Catherine, and a very public legal separation ensued. He moved Catherine into Gloucester Crescent with staff to assist her but never spoke to or visited her again; the children were also discouraged from visiting. She died in 1879 and was laid to rest in Highgate Cemetery. Ellen Turnan, an actress, had starred in a performance of *The Frozen Deep* sponsored by Dickens and he had fallen madly in love with her. She remained his lover until his death, where he made lifelong provisions for her in his last will and testament.

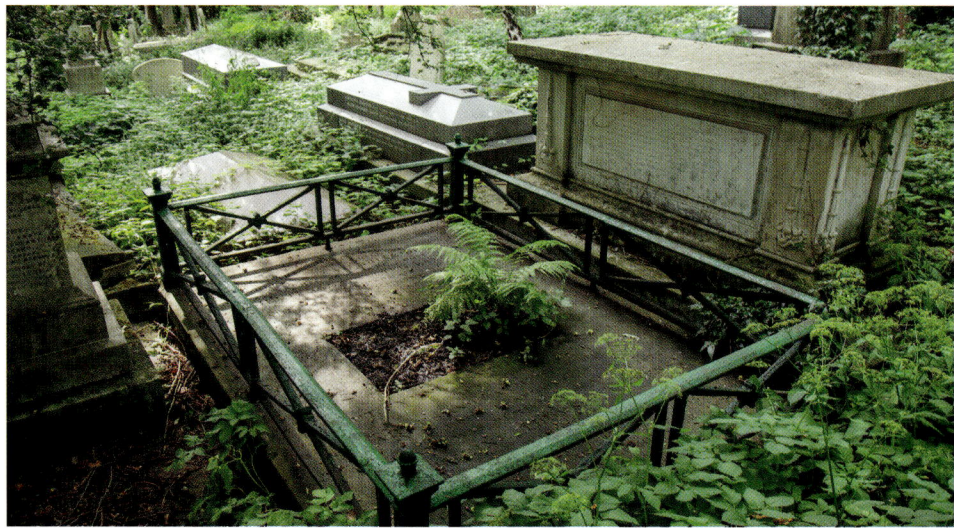

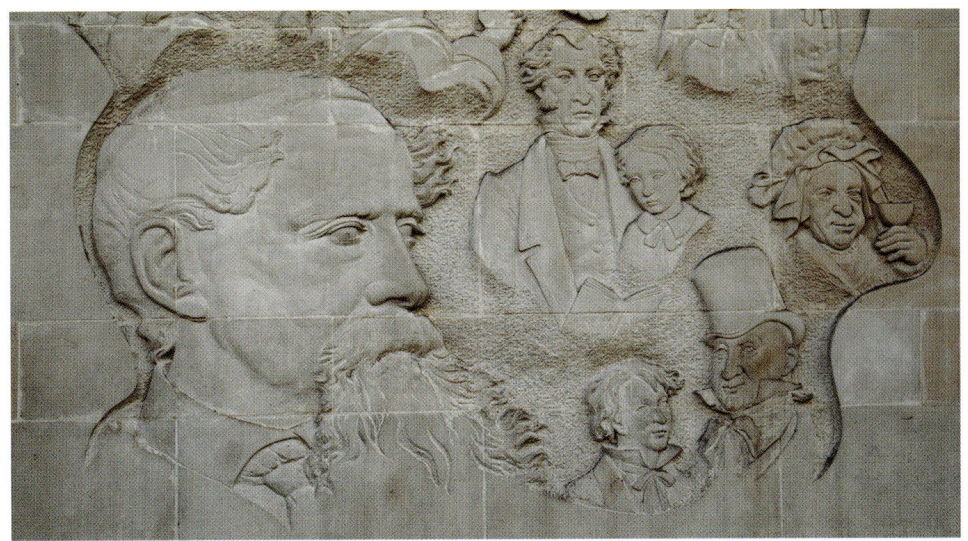

1 Devonshire Terrace

Where once a blue plaque was affixed, it was decided that Dickens should be immortalised in a much grander way in 1960. Estcourt James Clack was commissioned to carve this vast stone mural where once 1 Devonshire Terrace stood. One of Dickens' longest-lived addresses between 1839 and 1851, it was here the author wrote *The Old Curiosity Shop*, *Dombey and Son*, *David Copperfield*, *Martin Chuzzlewit*, *A Christmas Carol* as well as completing *Barnaby Rudge*. The design depicts a character from each of the books he wrote here: *Little Nell* and her grandfather, *The Old Curiosity Shop*; *Jacob Marley*, *A Christmas Carol*; *Mr Micawber*, *David Copperfield*; *Barnaby Rudge* and his raven *Grip* from the sometimes named *A Tale of the Riots of Eighty*; *Sairey Gamp*, *Martin Chuzzlewit*; *Paul* and *Florence Dombey*, *Dombey and Son*; as well as an effigy of Dickens himself. *Barnaby Rudge*'s raven was inspired by Dickens' own pet also named Grip. The author had the animal stuffed upon its death and affectionately kept it close by when writing at his desk.

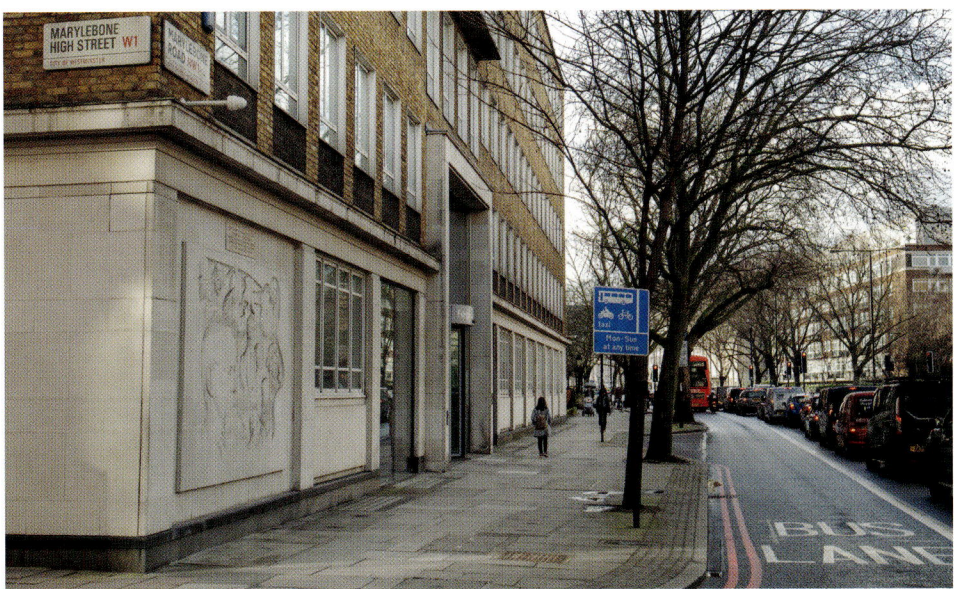

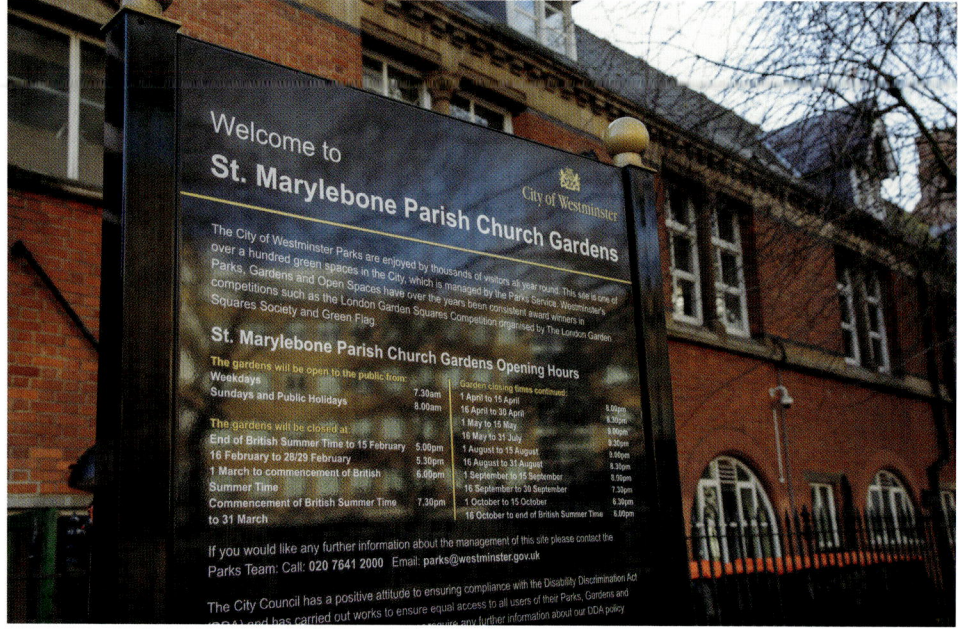

St Marylebone Parish Church

St Marylebone Parish Church is the fourth to serve the area; the original was built in 1200 and stood near Marble Arch. The building as we see it today runs parallel with Dickens' home at Devonshire Terrace and was consecrated by Thomas Hardwicke in 1817. Charles' father John had been baptised at the previous site in 1785. Dickens chose this site for the christening in *Dombey and Son* for baby *Paul*. The author makes particular reference to the organ being the dominant feature, central above the altar, making the setting recognisable to any who knows the building. He also uses this scene to bring some comedic relief to the occasion, describing quite unforgivingly a nuptial ceremony: 'The very wedding looked dismal as they passed in front of the altar. The bride was too old and the bridegroom too young, and a superannuated beau with one eye and an eyeglass stuck in its blank companion, was giving away the lady, while the friends were shivering.'

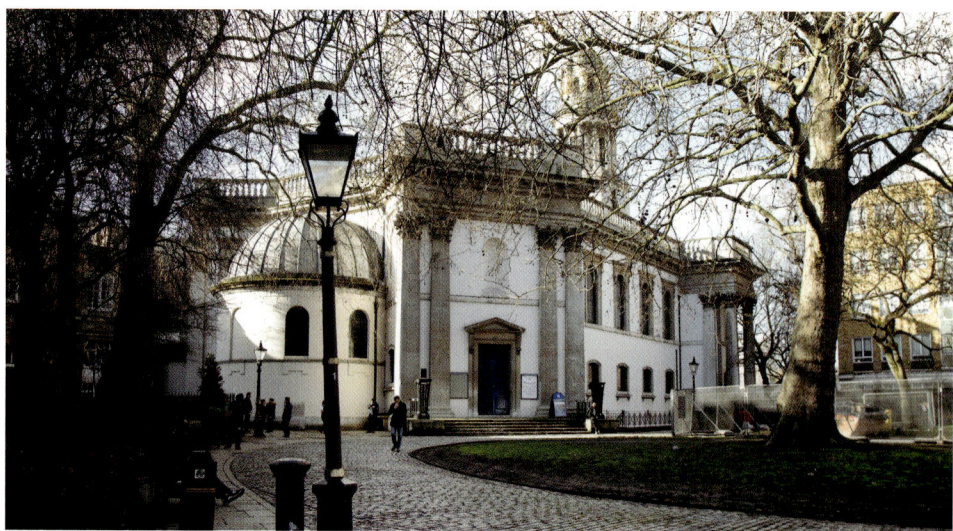

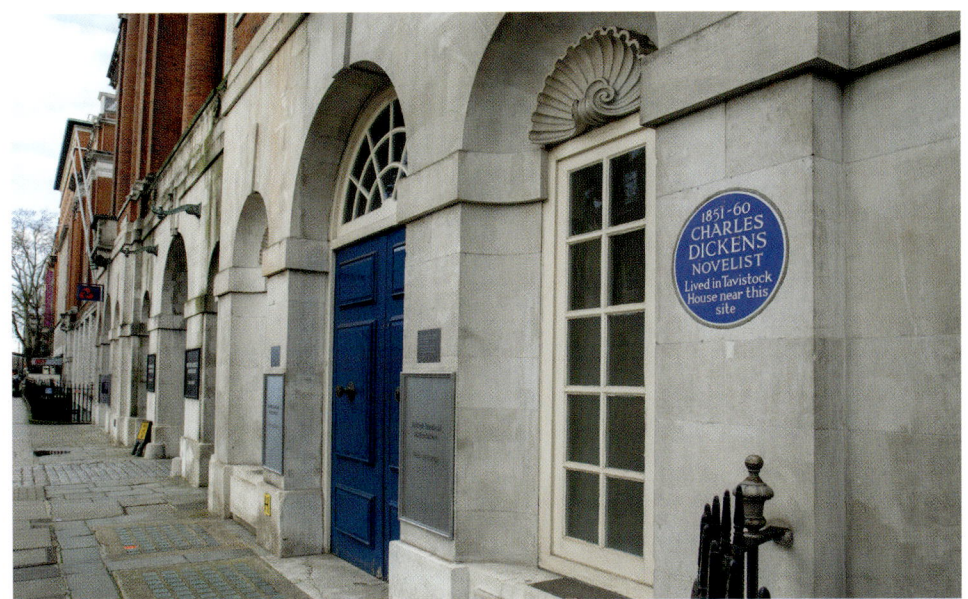

1 Tavistock Square

Becoming the last Dickens family residence in 1851, 1 Tavistock Square was extended and renovated vastly by the writer. He called in the Cubitt building firm who installed a room with outstanding acoustics dedicated to Dickens' love of performance and amateur dramatics. Much of the writer's works produced whilst here in Bloomsbury had a comedic feel about them despite what had become an unhappy marriage in his personal life. In 1857 the couple had stopped sharing a bed and by June 1858 were legally separated, forcing Mrs Dickens to leave the family home. Having failed to persuade a Dr Tuke to have Catherine sectioned under the mental health act in an attempt to save his family-man image, Dickens is said to have left the house in the early hours of the morning and walked over 40 miles to his country home near Rochester. He published a notice in the *London Times* and *Household Words*, explaining the decision to the public shortly after and in 1860 gave up the lease at Tavistock Square to move permanently to Gad's Hill Place in Kent.

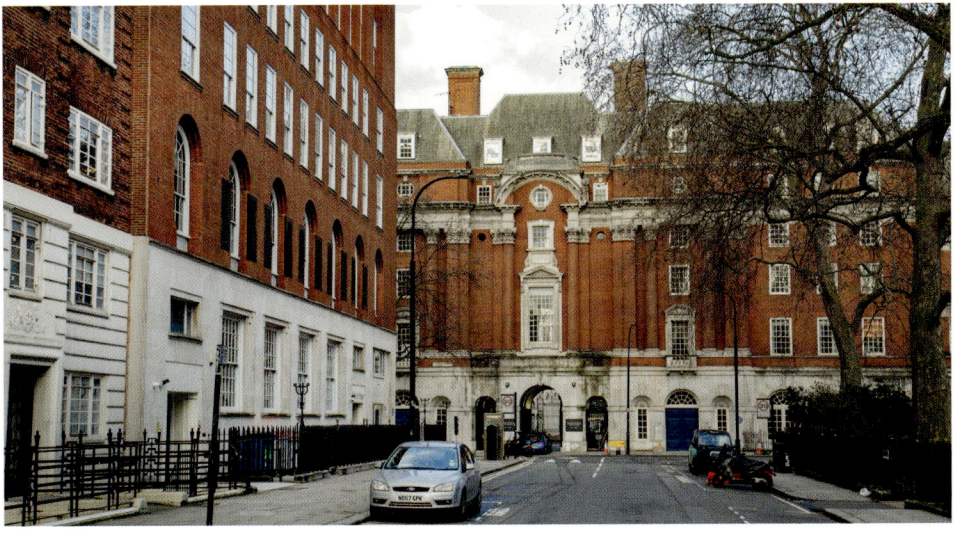

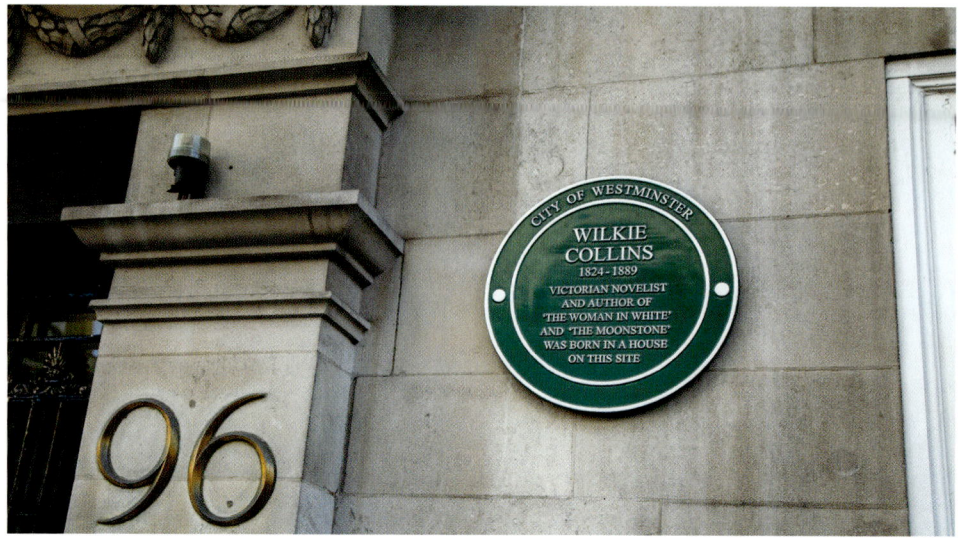

New Cavendish Street

Born on this site in 1824 at what was then known as 11 New Cavendish Street, Wilkie Collins was an author famed for such works as *The Woman in White* and *The Moonstone*. After being introduced via a mutual friend, Augustus Egg, in 1851 Dickens began a close friendship with the novelist which lasted until Charles' death in 1870. They bonded over their love of theatre and Wilkie often published journalistic works with Dickens for *Household Words* and many other pieces. Collins was a firm friend to Catherine Dickens also, a relationship that would predecease the Dickens marriage despite the irony of Collins' script 'Frozen Deep' being the reason for Dickens to meet his mistress Ellen (sometimes referred to as Nelly) Turnan. With an age gap of twelve years, the men shared different opinions of family life. Collins is described as a devoted and loving husband and father whilst Dickens was quite open about the fact that he found the role rather burdensome.

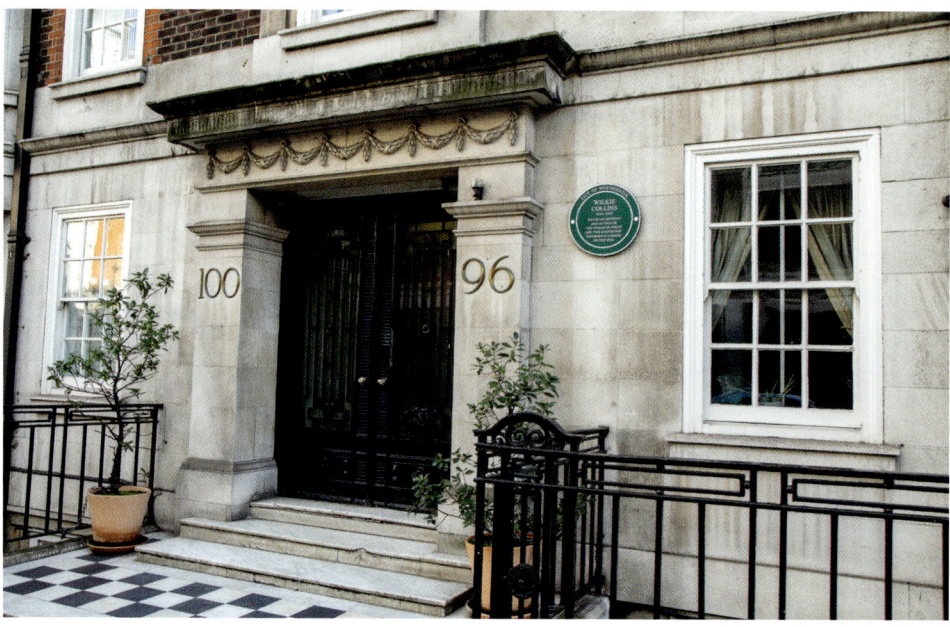

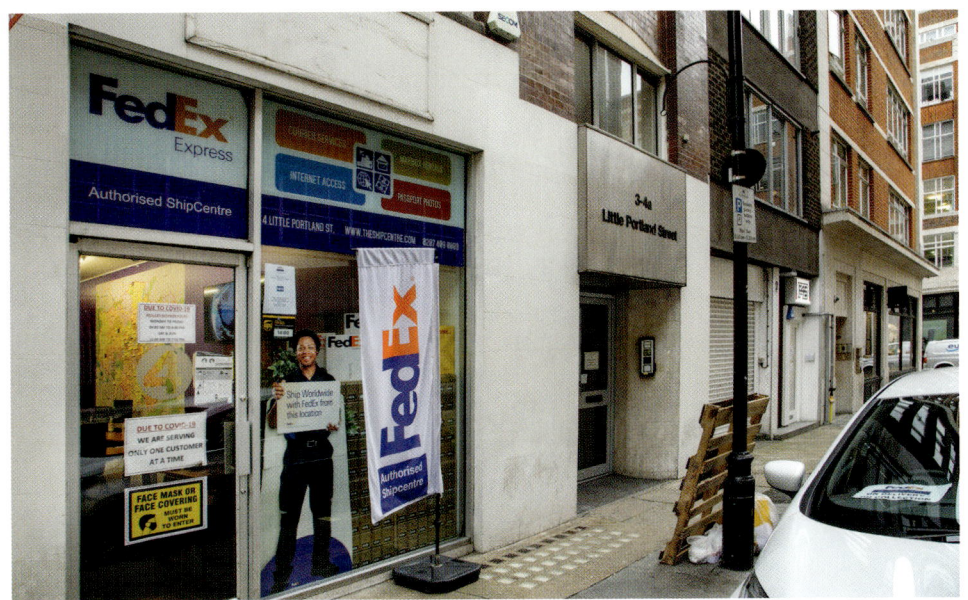

4 Little Portland Street

Like most of London, Dickens knew the area of Fitzrovia very well having lived in many abodes here. His early years had been spent fleeing debt related to his father and the family had moved often. After befriending its minister Edward Taggart, he decided to start attending the Unitarian Church which presided here in 1842. Traditionally bought up in the Anglican Church, Dickens had become dismayed by some of its practices and ethos when it came to humanitarian sensitivity. Upon defending his decision to change denominations, a movement against rationalist and individual trends, he wrote that he was 'disgusted with our Established Church, and its Puseyism's and daily outrages on common sense and humanity'. Concluding that 'I have carried into effect an old idea of mine, and joined the Unitarians, who would do something for human improvement, if they could, and who practise Charity and Toleration.' His interest and attendance, although eager and concentrated at the time, lasted not much longer than a year.

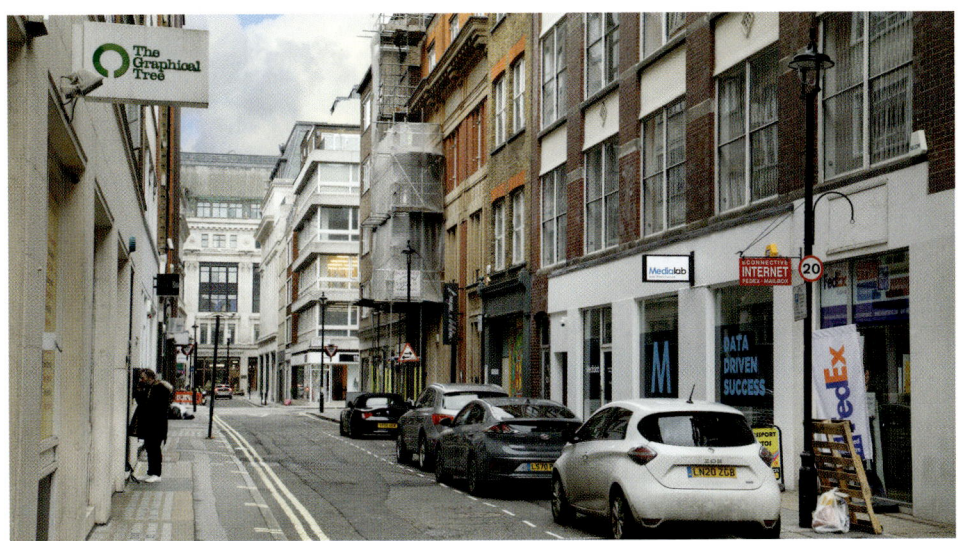

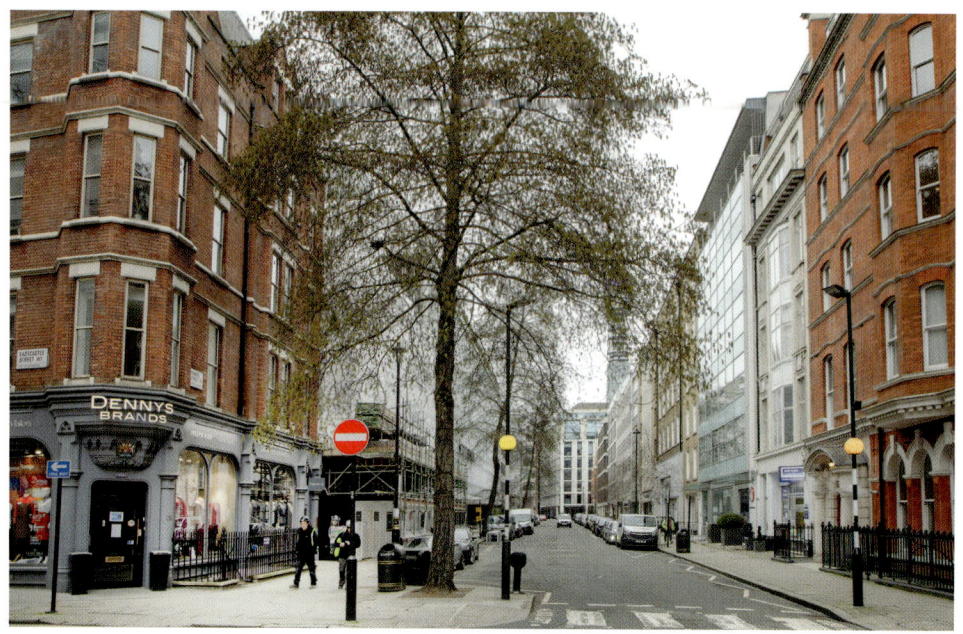

16 Berners Street

Known for being the home of harp and piano makers, Dickens' association with Berners Street came from his maternal great-aunt, Mrs Charlton, who ran a lodging house here. One of the residents, Edward Blackmore, was responsible for employing Dickens in his first clerk's role at Ellis and Blackmore in Gray's Inn, relieving him of his dreadful duties at the Blacking factory. Berners Street was also the inspiration for the complex character *Miss Havisham* from *Great Expectations*. Dickens often saw a middle-aged woman, clearly distressed, roaming the street in a tattered wedding gown. It is suspected a wealthy Quaker had jilted her before marriage, leading her to an eternal mental torment. Dickens used the address at No. 31 to house his secret lover Ellen Turnan, but moved her again quickly within a couple of months when she complained of being sexually harassed by a local policeman. She was the same age as Dickens' eldest daughter when they met.

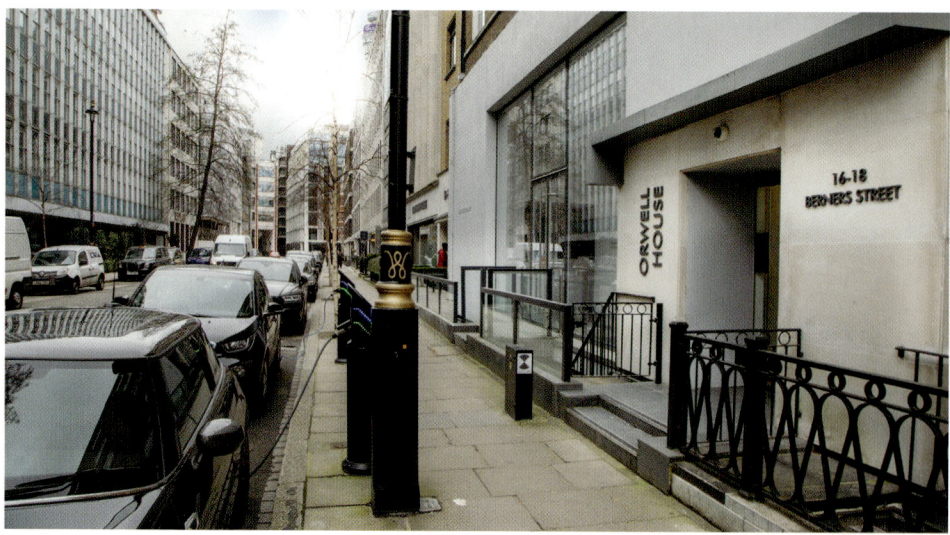

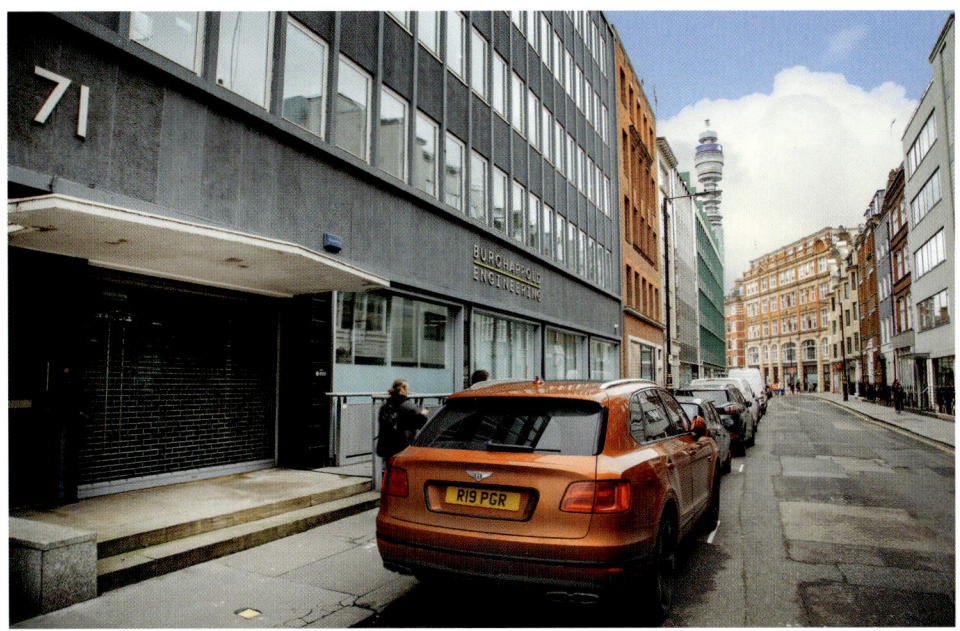

71 Newman Street

This was once the home of noted artist Richard Dadd. Dadd was famed for murdering his own father by taking a blade to his throat in 1843. Vicious drawings portraying the deaths of other friends and family members were found by police inside his rooms here in Newman Street. It is thought the artist suffered from criminal lunacy and in his trial defended his actions as he believed his own father to be 'The Devil'. He was deemed unfit to plead and sent to live out the rest of his days in Bethlehem Hospital but later transferred to Broadmoor Insane Asylum. Dickens took influence from the crime when writing *Martin Chuzzlewit*. The lead's brother, *Anthony Chuzzlewit*, runs a business with his son *Jonas* and despite their considerably comfortable financial position it is implied *Jonas* decides to inherit his father's share in an untimely way when *Anthony* perishes in suspicious circumstances.

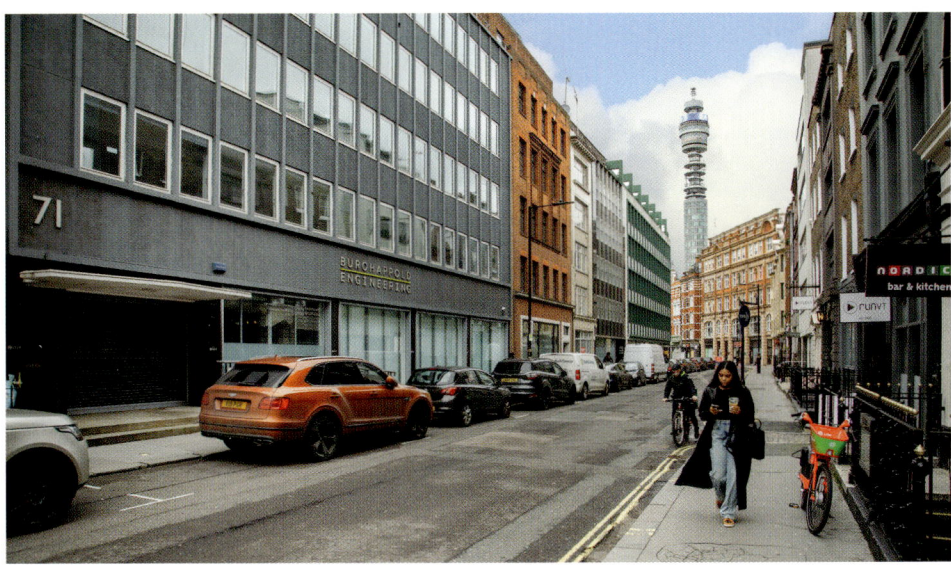

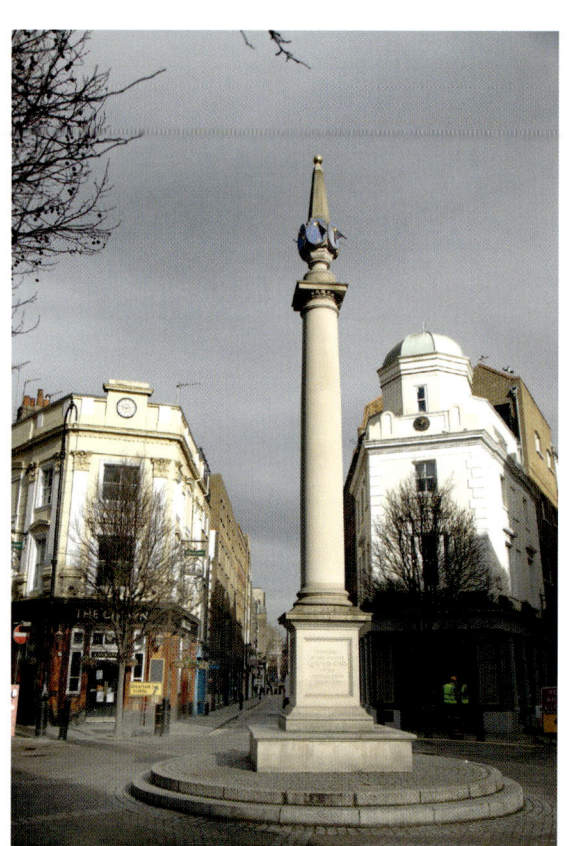

Seven Dials

Marked by a sundial pillar constructed in 1693, Seven Dials had become one of the most notorious slums in Britain by the nineteenth century. An influx of Irish immigrants drowning in poverty paired with numerous gin houses and brothels had made it an avoidable location by most of society. Aptly named, as it is where the joining of seven streets come together in the area of Covent Garden, it was (and still is) a busy thoroughfare with plenty happening. A column marking the intersection makes for an elevated view of the hustle and bustle and was known as a favoured place for Dickens to people-watch. The author describes one such visit in 1835 in his *Sketches by Boz*: 'Streets and courts dart in all directions, until they are lost in the unwholesome vapour which hangs over the house-tops and renders the dirty perspective uncertain and confined.' There were drunken women quarrelling – 'Vy don't you pitch into her, Sarah?' – and men 'in their fustian dresses, spotted with brick-dust'.

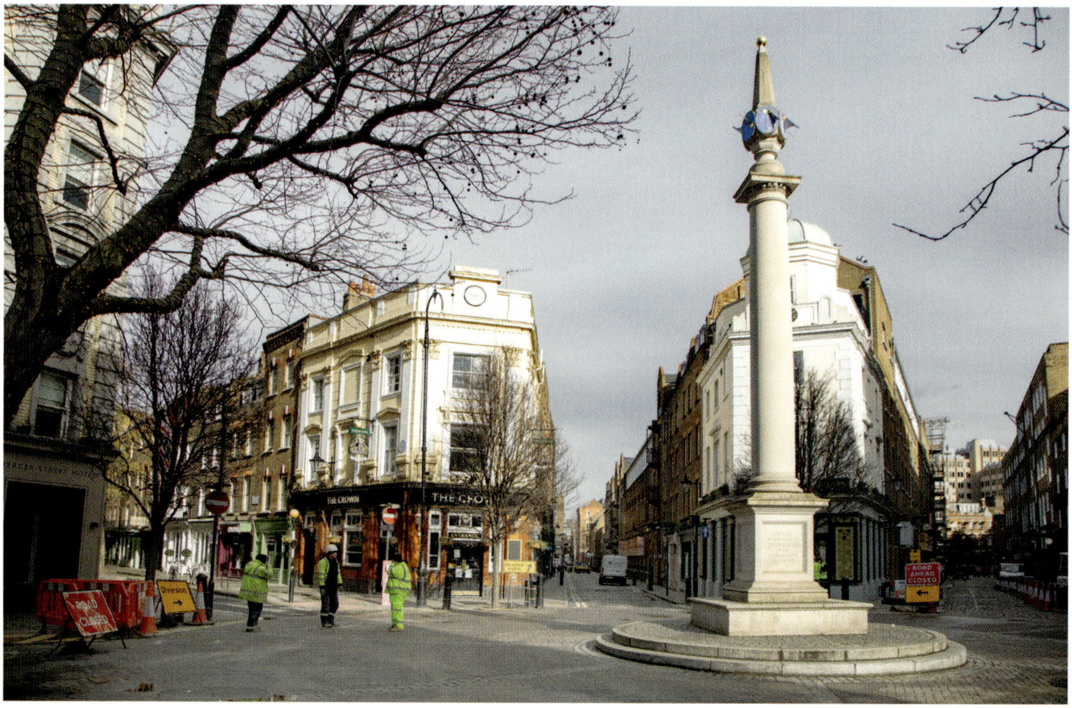

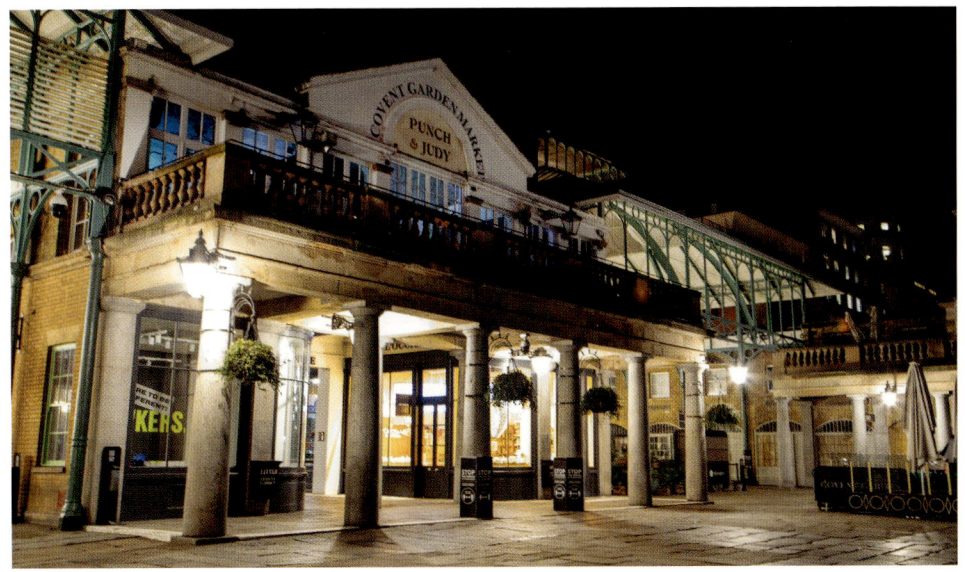

Covent Garden Market

The stallholders who frequented Covent Garden Market were no doubt the inspiration for some of Dickens' more colourful characters. The 'costermongers' purchased to resell anything from fresh produce, silks, to cooked meats and fish. They were rowdy, fearless and in heavy competition with one another. Very few owned a fixed stall and took to using barrow boys to hawk their wares around the site. Dickens produced a loaded, chaotic description of the market's smells and sounds in *Martin Chuzzlewit*. He does choose to end the chapter by quietening the scene and calming his reader though, leading many to believe he found the market quite joyous to visit in reality. Notorious to the market were the Covent Garden flower girls. They attracted sales by singing and calling out to passers-by. It was widely known that many sold not just flowers, and it was a rouse to attract sex work. An industry close to our author, he'd campaigned successfully with philanthropist Angela Georgina Burdett-Coutts to create Urania Cottage in 1847, a refuge for fallen women.

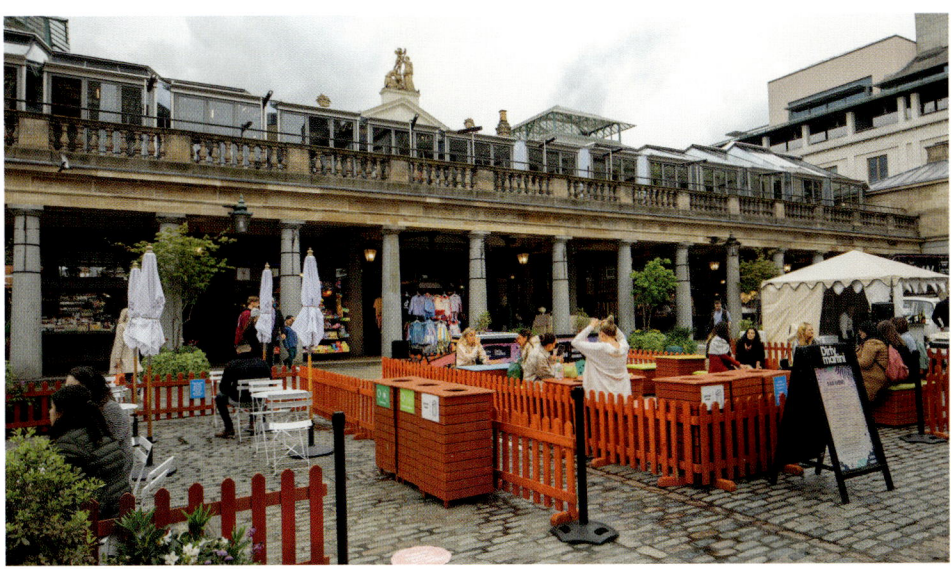

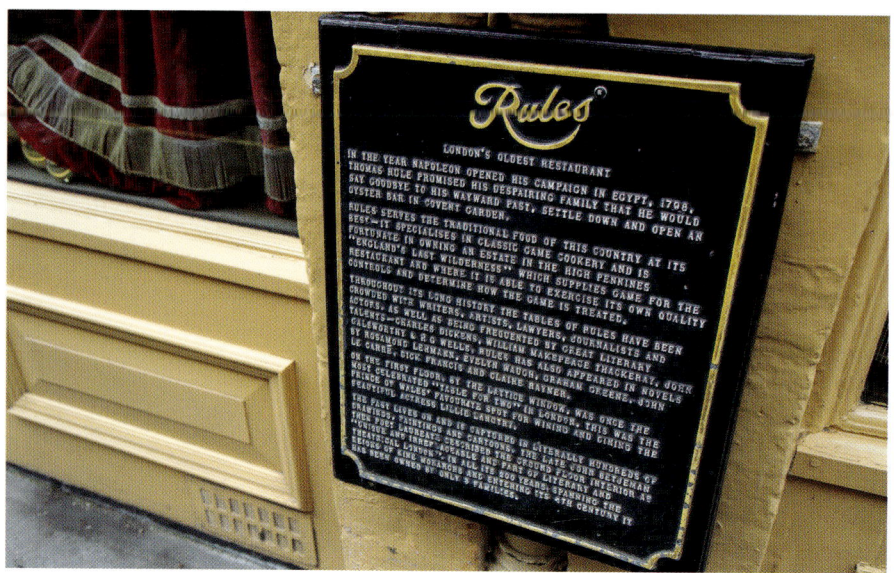

Rules Restaurant

Established by Thomas Rule in 1798, Rules on Maiden Lane boasts the title of the oldest restaurant in London. Dickens was a regular patron, and a private upstairs dining hall was up until recent years named in his honour. He is known to have favoured and reserved a specific table which looked out onto the Blacking factory, most likely a welcome memory of how far he had come in life. Seeing the reign of nine monarchs but only ever owned by three families, the restaurant favours traditional English food, specialising in game, oysters, pies and puddings. Famed diners known to feast here are in vast supply. Charlie Chaplin, William Makepeace Thackeray, Joan Collins, H. G. Wells, Clark Gable, Harrison Ford, Laurence Olivier, Paul Newman, John Prescott and William Hague have all at one time made it their regular haunt. Edward VII chose its discreet location and tactful staff to dine with his mistress, Lillie Langtry. Not such a well-kept secret now though, they named his private dining quarters after him in later years.

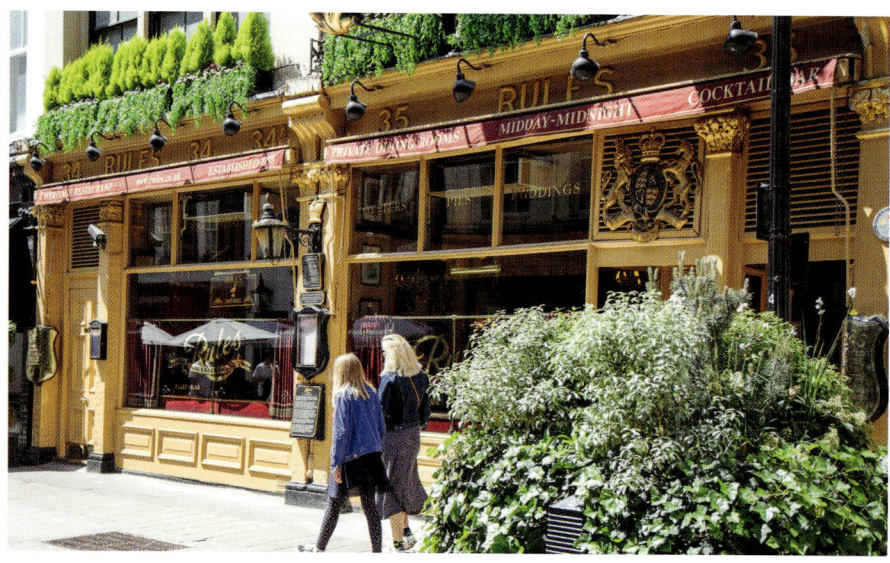

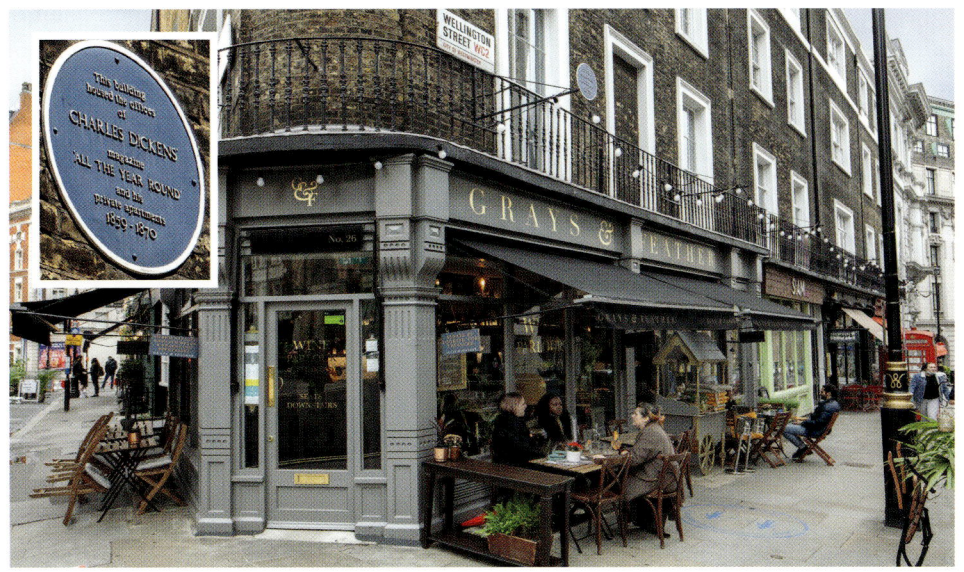

Grays & Feather

Family-run since 2007, this wine parlour stands on the site of Dickens' 1860 two-storey publishing offices. It is rumoured there are caverns running beneath which lead to Covent Garden's theatre district, although quite likely closed now. The Grays & Feather prides itself on bringing affordable yet high-quality sparkling wines from around the globe to London, scouring unexplored producers to bring the champagne-type experience in a Rococo setting to the masses. During his time working here Dickens took a great interest in the reform of women and spent many evenings talking to street walkers and prostitutes of the area. He looked to offer them entrance to Urania Cottage but was surprised by many at their refusal. He took another approach, trying to sell the idea of a clean slate with emigration to Australia at the cost of his own pocket. Many mistook his kindness as a deception to lead them into transportation to the colonies and much to his frustration declined such a concept.

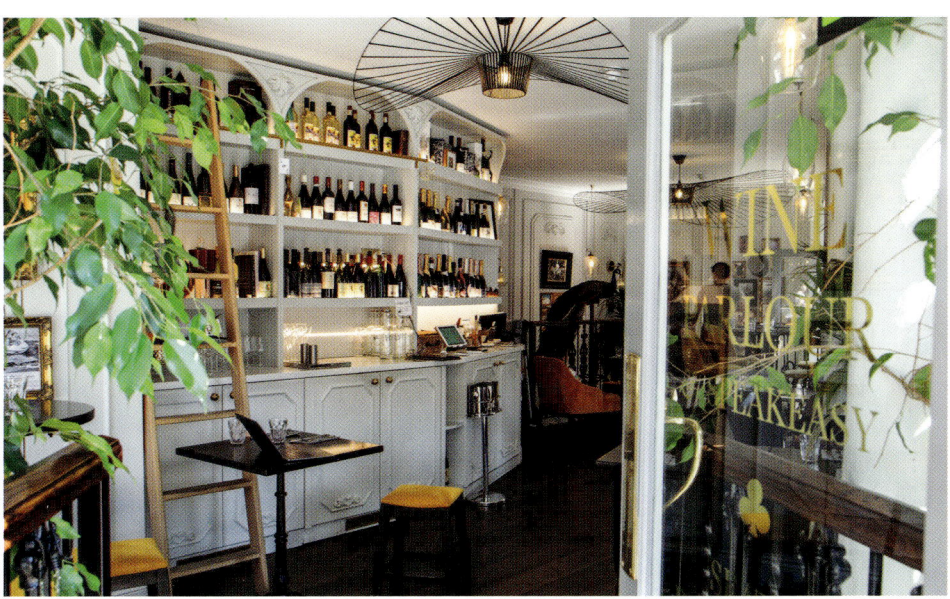

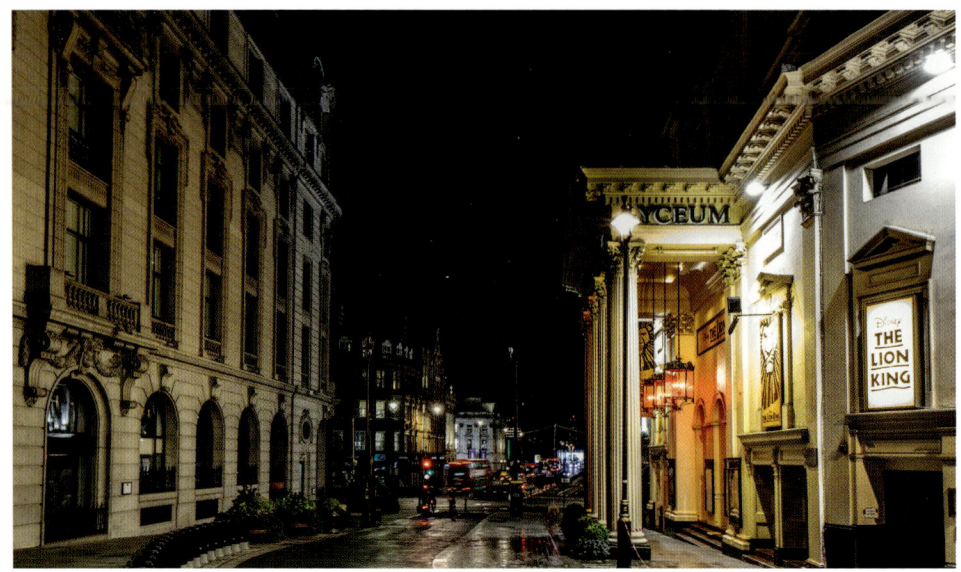

The Lyceum Theatre

Located on Wellington Street just off the Strand, the Lyceum comfortably seats 2,100. Originally built in 1765, it has been re-erected and reconditioned many times after fires and tragedy. The design is unique in its appearance due to the balcony overhanging the dress circle and is how Dickens would have known it before its vast changes in 1904. In 1834 the theatre was known to favour English opera over the Italian productions that had dominated the circuit throughout the centuries. Contractors Peto and Grissell as well as its new owners, Robert and Mary Anne Keeley, allowed adaptions of Dickens' novels to also be performed here, to great acclaim. *A Christmas Carol* and *Martin Chuzzlewit* ran for over one hundred performances, adding to the author's infamy in the city. Closing in 1939, locals fought hard against its demolition. It was eventually converted into a Mecca ballroom in 1951, and after over a decade of abandonment in 1986 it was chosen as the site to host *The Lion King*, which has delighted the masses and kept the performers on the stage since 1996.

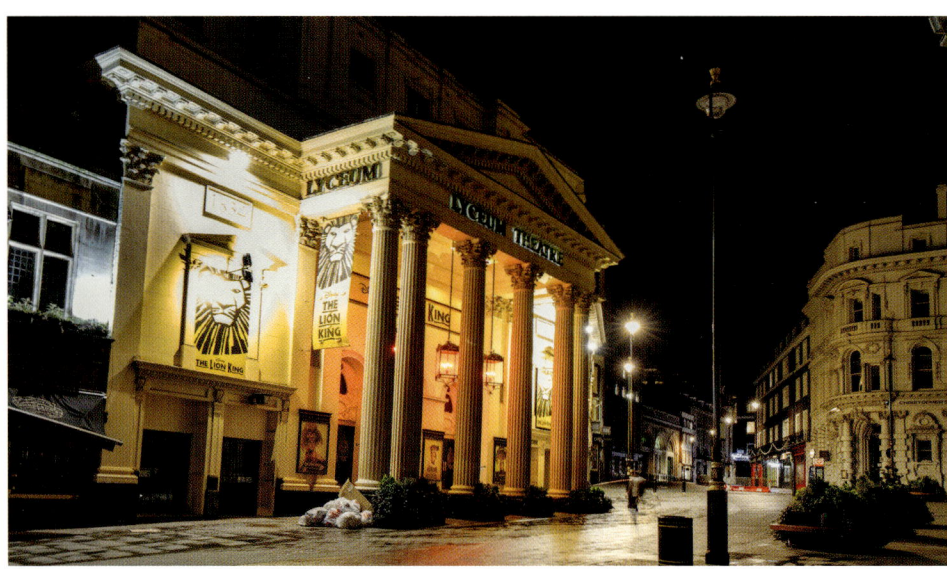

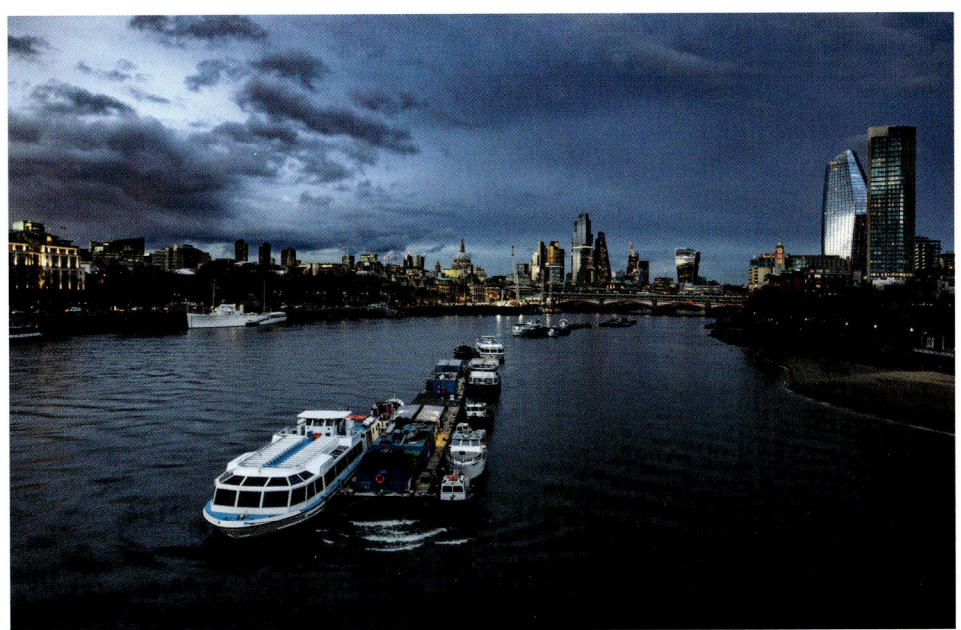

Waterloo Bridge

Opened in 1817, another design by John Rennie, the bridge was originally to be named Strand Bridge. This was overturned in commemoration of Wellington's victory over Napoleon in 1815 and was unveiled as Waterloo Bridge. Demolished in 1939 and replaced in 1945 by Sir Giles Gilbert Scott, the original bridge features many times in Dickens' writing. He produced an article in *Household Words* called 'Down with the Tide' where he follows the 'Pea', who is the Thames police officer keeping an eye on the bridge toll-taker for an evening. In *Bleak House, George Rouncewell* stops here to read a playbill and see a performance at 'Astley's Theatre'. He also chooses its setting for *Sam Weller's* unfurnished lodgings for a fortnight under its dry arches in *The Pickwick Papers*.

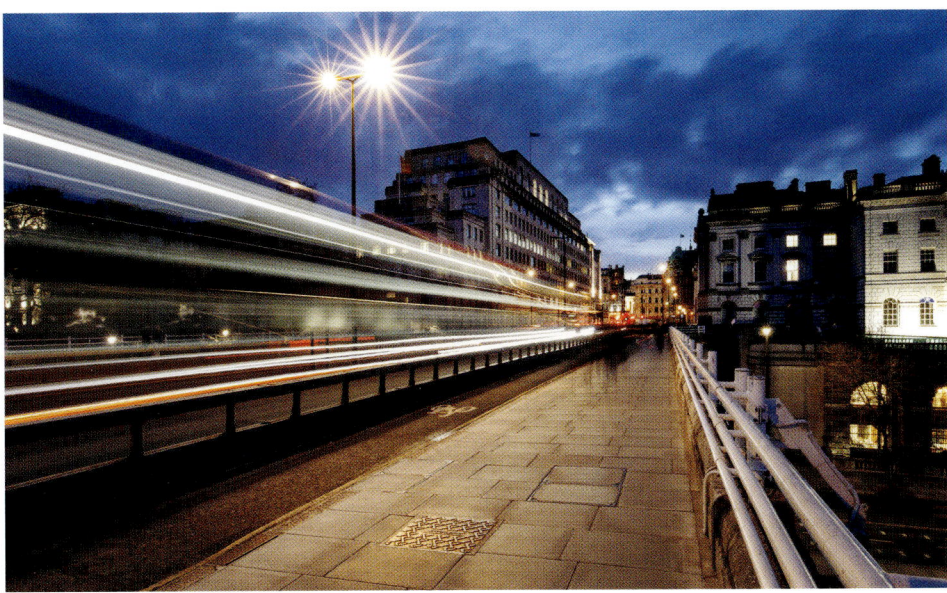

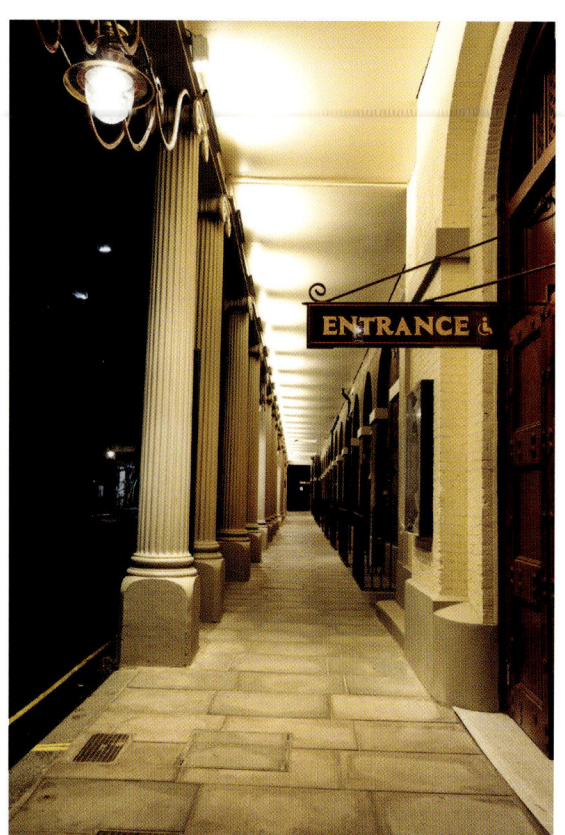

Drury Lane Theatre

Known in Dickensian times for slum-like conditions, a concentration of prostitution and plentiful gin palaces, the origins of the street name and subsequent theatre come from 1500. Sir Robert Drury built what was one of the largest mansions in the city at this time. In 'Gin Shops' of *Sketches by Boz*, Dickens reported of the area, 'There is more filth and squalid misery near those great thorough fares than in any part of this mighty city.' In another article of the same association he chooses to call 'The Pawnbroker's Shop', he makes it known this store of gain on the backs of the impoverished is known to be located here. The author chooses to lighten the mood when using the setting for his fiction, though. *Dick Swiveller* is happily lodged above the tobacconist's in *The Old Curiosity Shop*. *David Copperfield* dines on fine beef at a restaurant here and *Henrietta Petowker* plays a great part for the Crummles Touring Stage Company at the Drury Lane Theatre in *Nicholas Nickleby*.

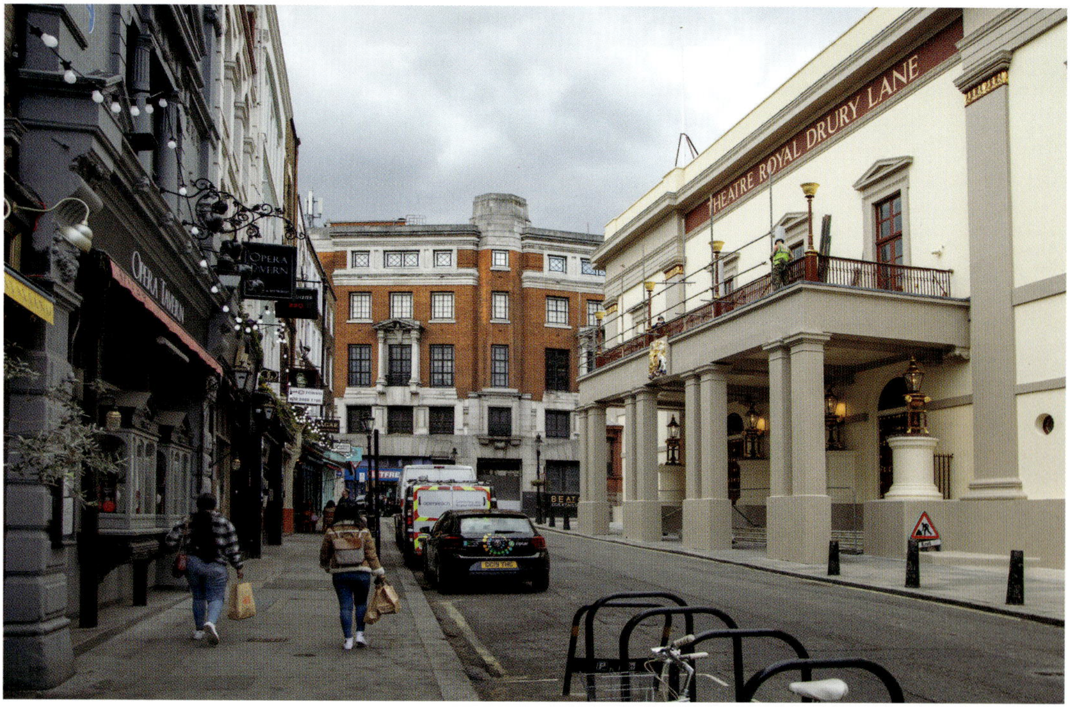

Kingsway

Purpose built and one of the broadest streets in London at 35 metres wide, Kingsway was named after King Edward VII who unveiled it in 1905. Many Dickensian guides choose to start their tours here outside the Holborn station due to it being so central to much of Dickens' work. As with much of London wealth and poverty existed not far from each other and it is believed that somewhere here amongst the Chancery and Inns of Court, the area described as 'Tom All Alone's' in *Bleak House* can be found. It is used as a reminder that we are responsible for the well-being of our fellow humans and the kind-hearted *Mr Jarndyce* as the rightful landlord to some of these homes is in despair that he is forbidden to improve the conditions due to the inheritance dispute to prove he is the rightful owner.

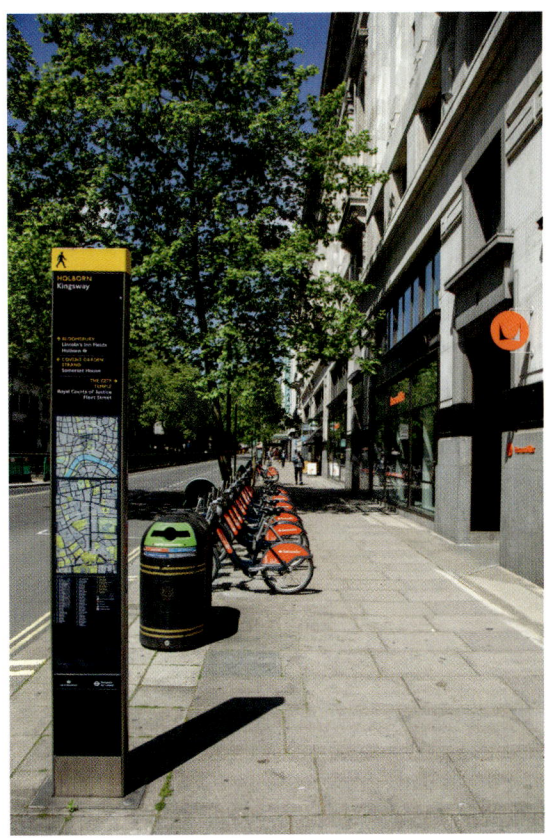

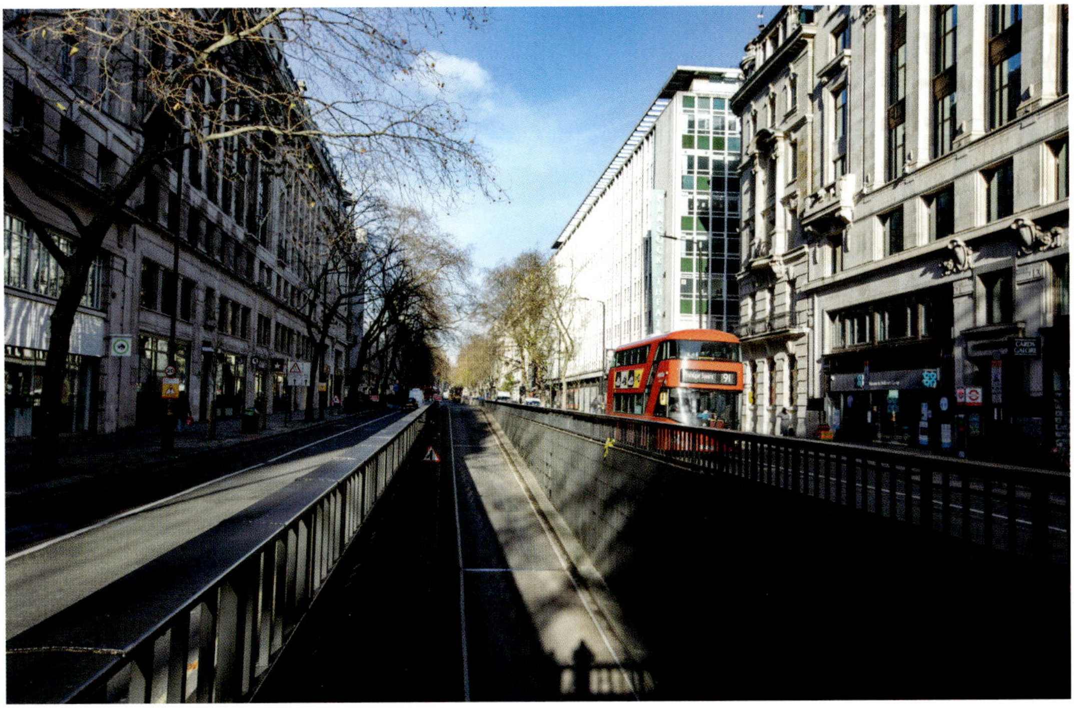

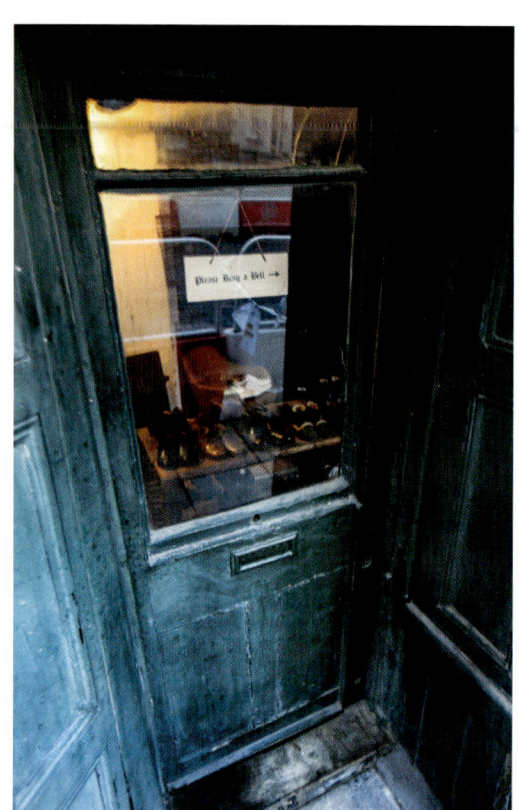

The Old Curiosity Shop

Published alongside short stories with *Barnaby Rudge*, *The Old Curiosity Shop* began its life as a weekly serial in the *Master Humphrey's Clock* between 1840 and 1841. It was so popular that in New York readers stormed the ship bearing it in novel form when it arrived in 1841. The story follows the life of *Nell Trent* and her grandfather (whose name is never revealed in the novel) as she travels throughout England following his antique business, whilst enduring his gambling habits and cold demeanour. It is revealed that his efforts are an attempt of love and stability despite the suspicion of *Fred Trent, Nell's* brother, who schemes to wed her off and indeed dishonour her grandfather's attempts at providing for her. No. 13–14 Portsmouth Street is designed to look like the author's fictional shop. It is owned by the London School of Economics now in an area known as Clare Market. It once functioned as a dairy for the mistress of King Charles II. It is constructed from the timber of old ships and successfully survived the bombings of the Second World War.

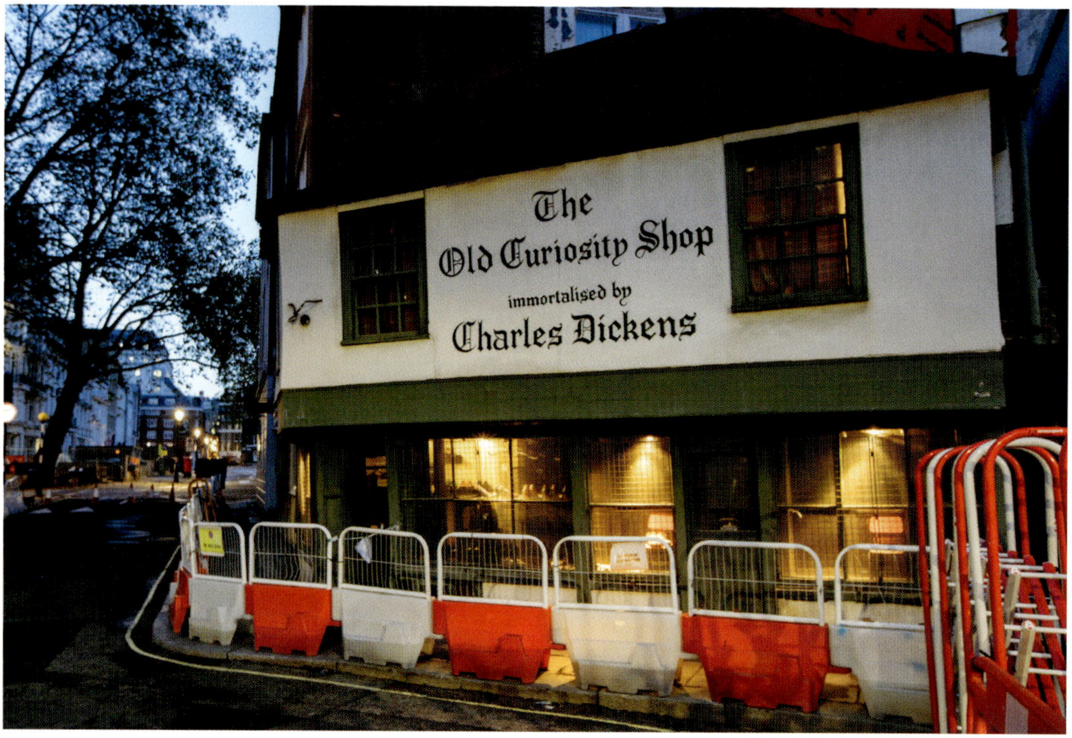

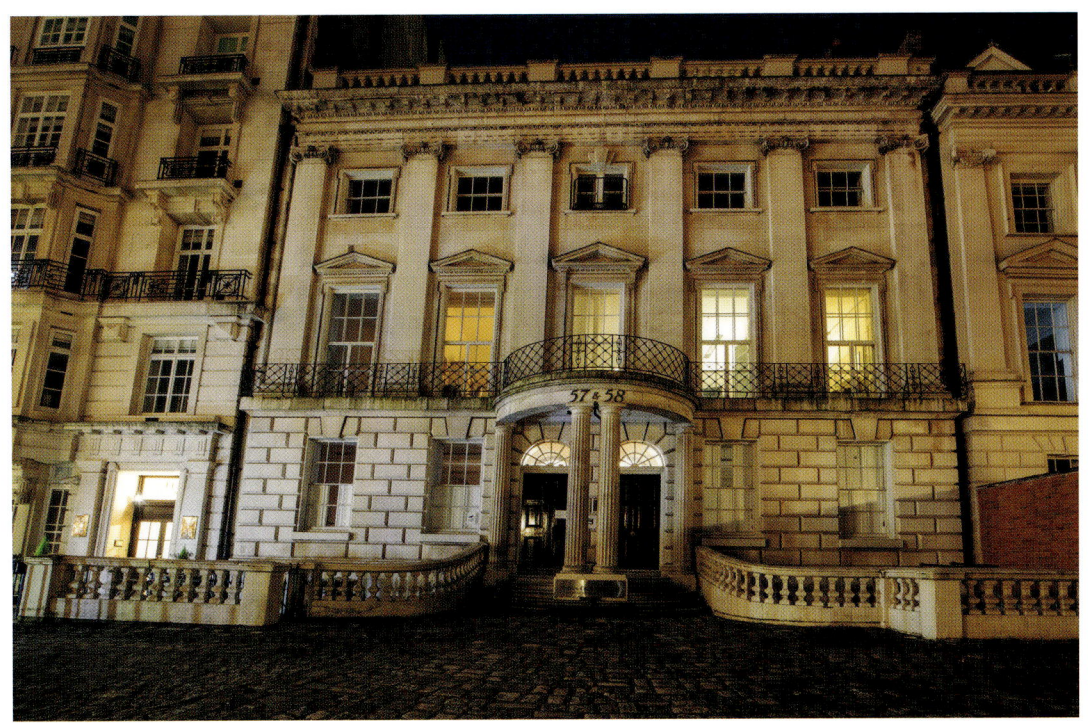

John Forster's House

A fellow critic and reporter, Forster contributed to *The True Sun, Morning Chronicle* and *The Examiner*. He became a prominent figure in the circle of literary men after his publication of *Lives of the Statesmen of the Commonwealth* when he met Dickens in 1836 and they became firm friends. Dickens modelled the bad-tempered *Podsnap* from *Our Mutual Friend* on Forster and is said to have taken inspiration from his basic whilst opulent lodgings at this address for the residence of Tulkinghorn in *Bleak House*. As a trusted muse and advocate for each other's works, Dickens allowed Forster to read most of his manuscripts first and took his critique both seriously and humbly, eventually putting him on the payroll as his literary executor. Despite their undeniable clashes throughout their friendship, John Forster wrote a candid but kind biography of his beloved friend in 1872, two years after his death. He undeniably missed his gifted friend, and *Life of Dickens* is peppered with witty stories and tales of pride for their relationship.

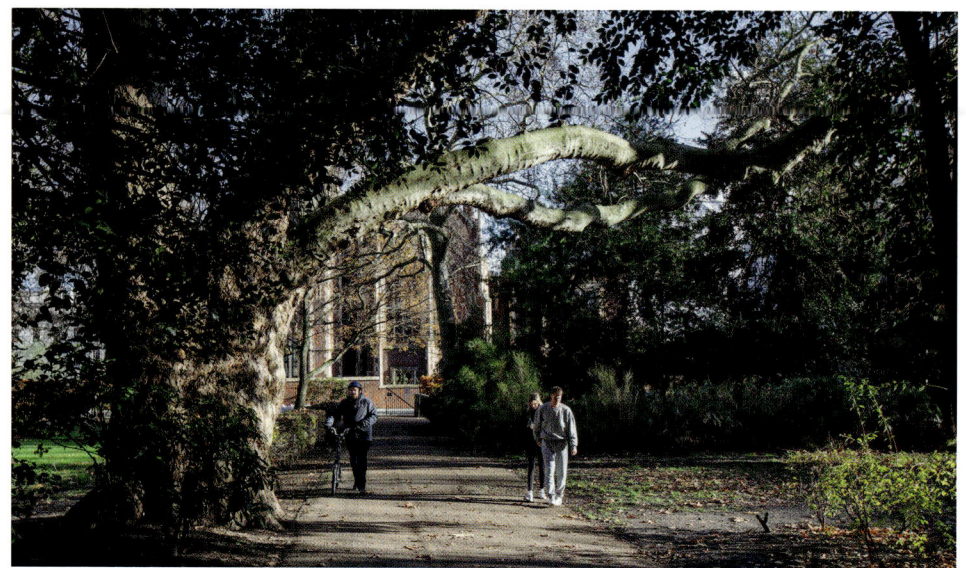

Lincoln's Inn Old Hall

Old Hall, predating 1490. When the New Hall (or Great Hall) was built in 1845, the Old Hall was used as a court of law before being returned to function as a hall for Lincoln's Inn. Dickens used the location for the dispute of inheritance between Jarndyce and Jarndyce in *Bleak House*. The book brims with legal cases and the professionals that worked within the Chancery Lane area of which Dickens had worked until thirteen years prior. The serious structure and site are heavily described using weather and atmosphere in Dickens' usual style. *Bleak House* begins, 'Michaelmas Term lately over, and the Lord Chancellor sitting in Lincoln's Inn Hall. Implacable November weather ... Fog everywhere. Fog up the river, where it flows among green aits and meadows; fog down the river, where it rolls defiled among the tiers of shipping and the waterside pollutions of a great (and dirty) city. Fog on the Essex marshes, fog on the Kentish heights.'

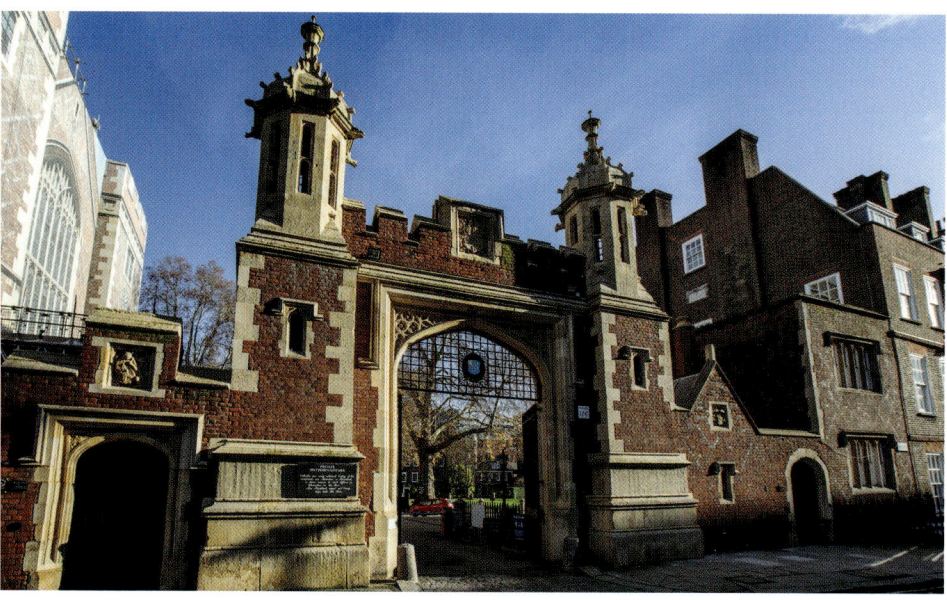

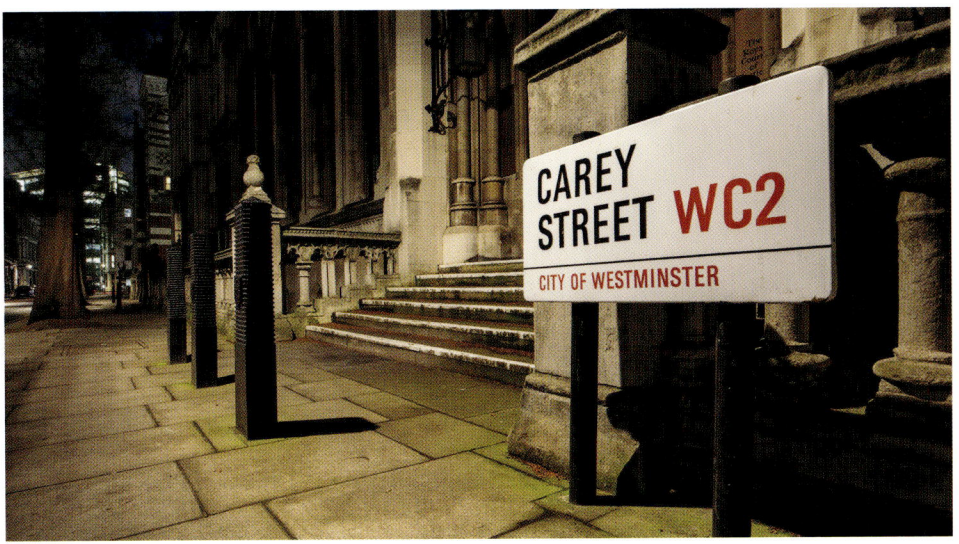

The Seven Stars

Formerly known as the Log and Seven Stars but also The League of Seven Stars and The Seven Provinces of the Netherlands, this Real Heritage, Grade II listed pub is thought to be one of the oldest surviving in London, predating 1602. Still standing at 51–54 Chancery Lane, it began life as a humble drinking hole for the Dutch sailors who had settled in the area. Nearby Shakespearian performances took place in the Middle Temple and the playwright is said to have frequented here. Dickens' propaganda heavily portrays that this site is the model for the Magpie and Stump from the *Pickwick Papers* and the author was also a frequented patron. The bar still carries a Victorian décor and legal theme throughout in homage to Dickens' characters. It is also well known for the ginger house cat (although many times replaced) who roams the grounds greeting the customers wearing a Renaissance ruff collar. Incidentally the word 'Carey' is a euphemism for bankruptcy; the Portugal Street Debtors' Court where John Dickens appealed his insolvency was located close by.

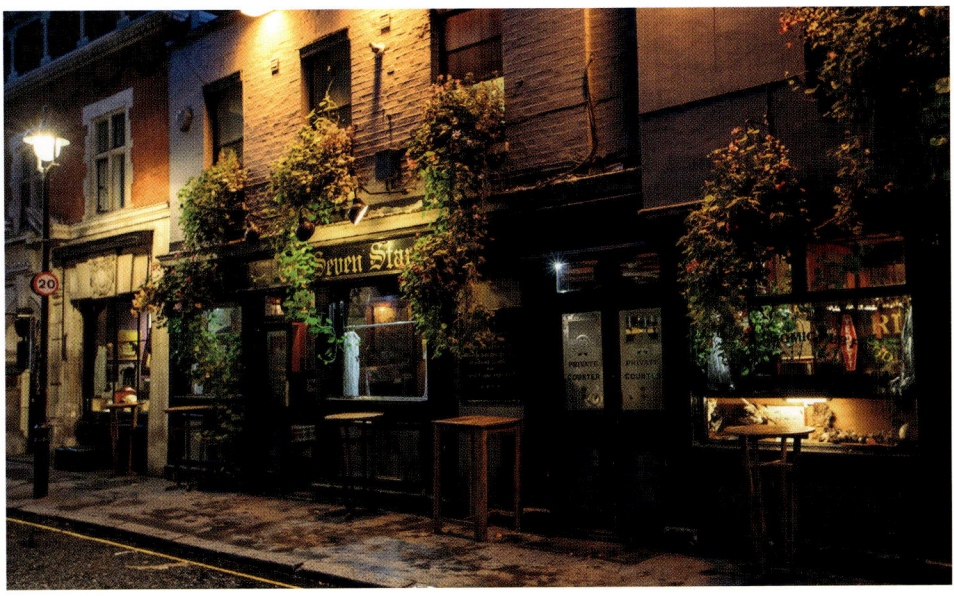

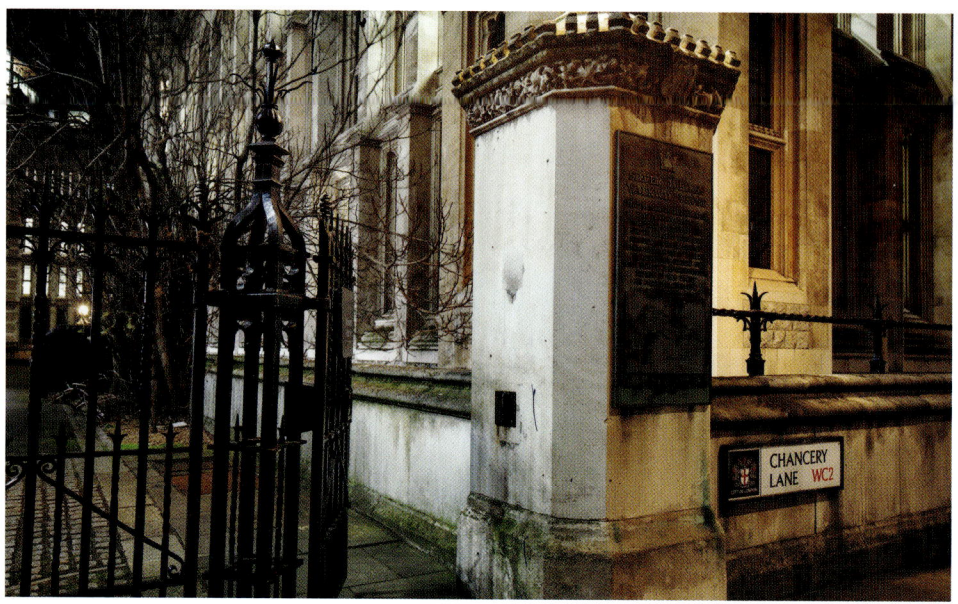

Chancery Lane

Reported on via a sketch he named *London Streets – Morning*, Dickens details the journey many took to their place of work at Chancery Lane, himself included in his early life: 'the early clerk population of Somers and Camden Towns, Islington and Pentonville, are fast pouring into the City, or directing their steps towards Chancery-lane and the Inns of Court. Middle-aged men, whose annual salaries have by no means increased in the same proportion as their families ... no object in view but the counting-house.' He mirrors this in *A Christmas Carol* in the life of *Bob Cratchit* who walks from Camden Town (nearly 4 miles) each day to make a thin living to feed his six children. A familiar area with unpleasant memories was the location of a sponging house here. This is where debtors were kept and urged to borrow from family members before trial sent them to prison. A young Dickens was sent running many times with family belongings up and down Chancery Lane to the local pawnshops in numerous attempts to buy his father's freedom.

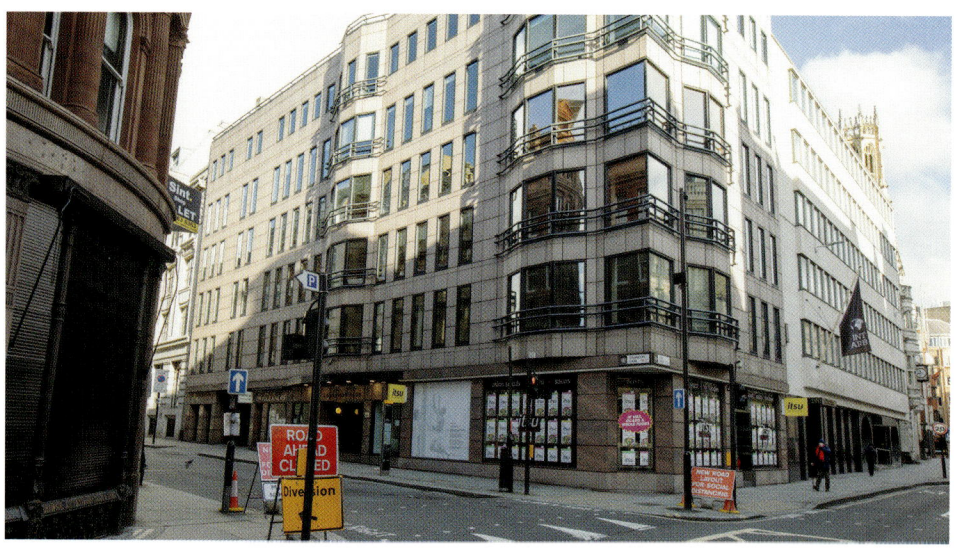

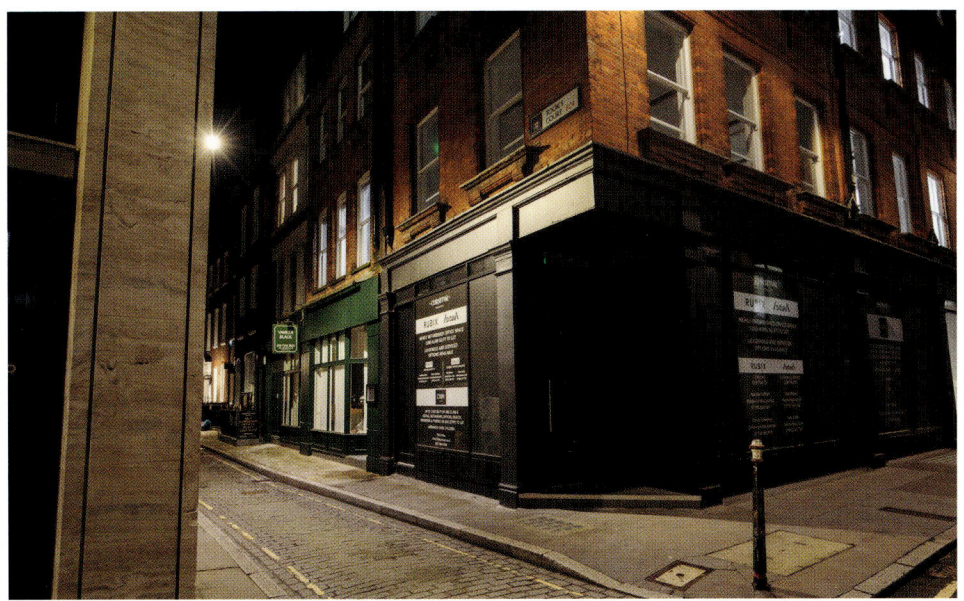

Took's Court

Located off Chancery Lane, 15 Took's Court, built in 1720, was home to young Dickens during his time as a parliamentary reporter. This has been disputed by some who say it is a myth dreamt up by Gryphon Property Partners to back-up their valuation of 2.8 million pounds put on it. The location is named after Thomas Tooke of London Esquyre and what is certain is that Dickens used the location, although renamed Cook's Court for the address of *Mr Snagsby's* legal business in *Bleak House*. The description of the journey leads directly to Took's Court. There is also a story of an unnamed resident who lived in the court, a particular penny-pinching, churlish neighbour who is said Dickens used to add to the traits of the character *Ebenezer Scrooge*. In later years it was a Dr Tukes whom refused Dickens' pleas to commit his wife Catherine into an asylum to hide the reporting on his infidelity. It is maybe why he chose to change the name in his works from Took's to Cook's as the reminder caused a discomfort?

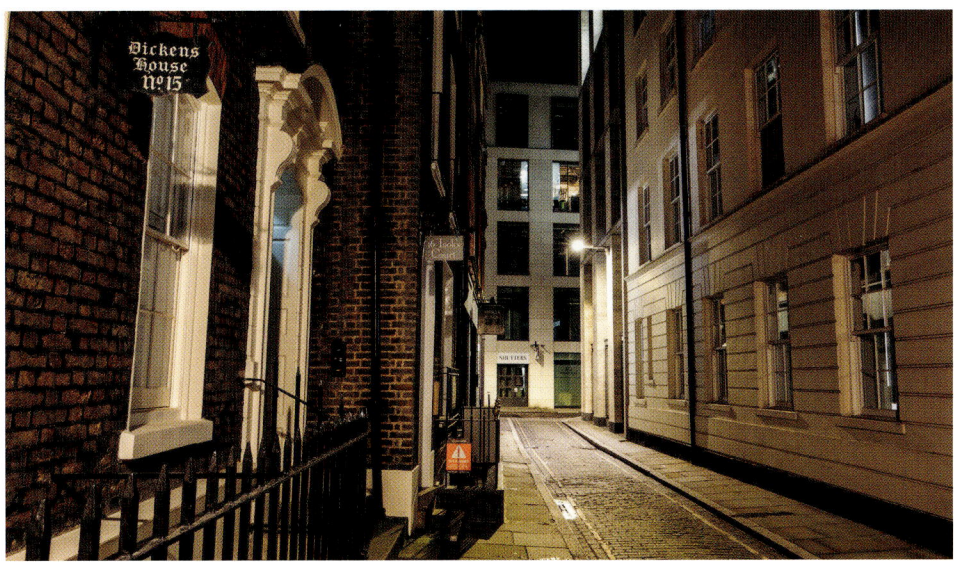

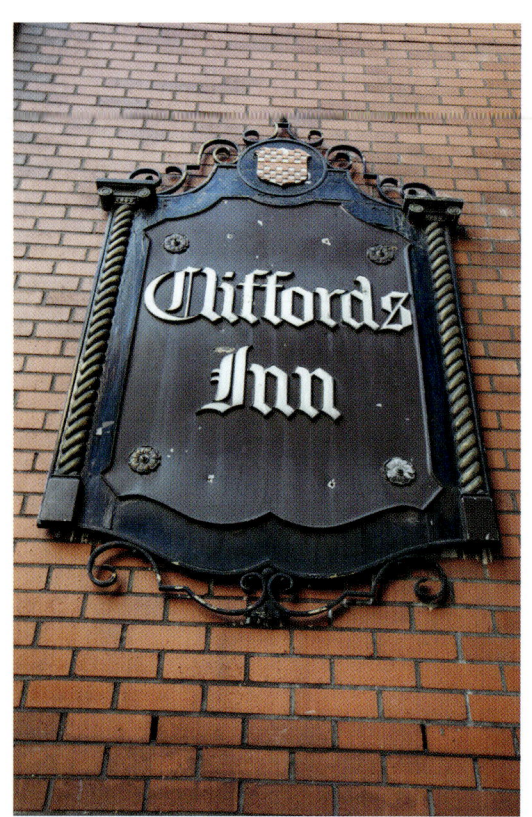

Clifford's Inn

Having the reputation as the longest-surviving Inn of Chancery, Clifford's Inn off Fleet Street dates to 1344. Although rebuilt in 1934, it features the original urine deflectors along its walls. These are the only known surviving Victorian devices designed to keep the stream off the shoes of any gentlemen relieving himself against the walls. It takes its name from the powerful Clifford family who originally rented the land to be used for the education of law students. Tip, the lazy brother of *Amy Dorrit, Fredrick* in *Little Dorrit*, idles as a clerk here before his inevitable termination from the role. John Rokesmith offers *Noddy Boffin* (also known as the Golden Dustman) a quiet place in Clifford's Inn where he can fulfill secretarial duties in *Our Mutual Friend*. It also gets a mention as the practicing place for *Melchisedech* in *Bleak House*.

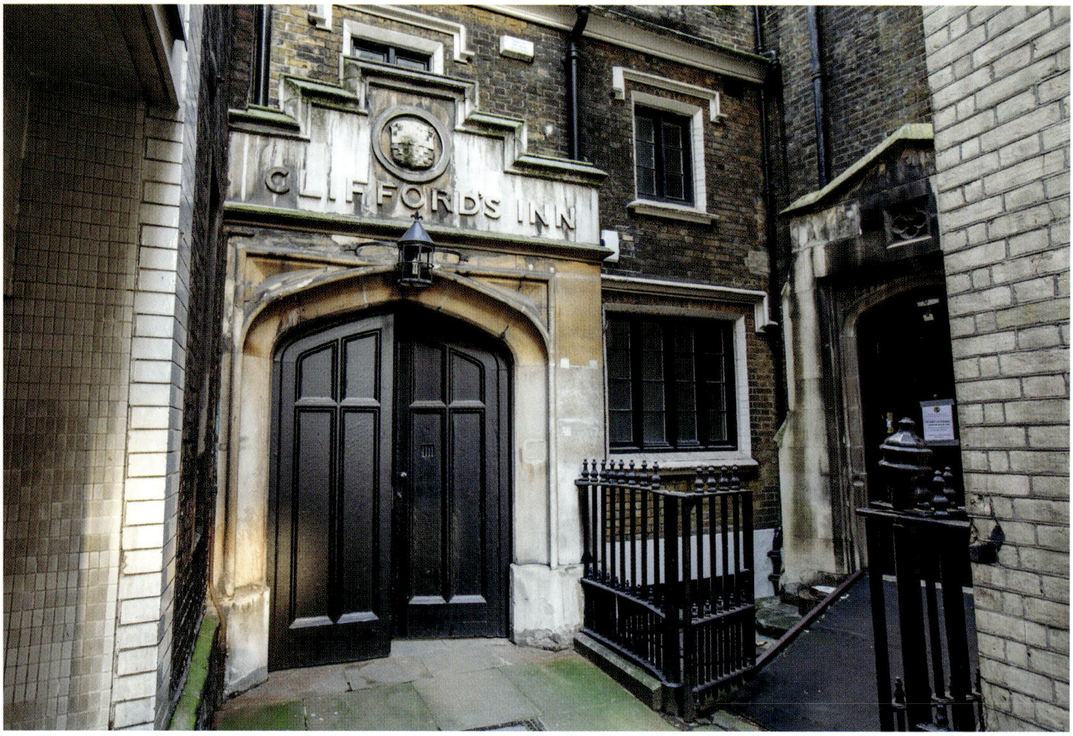

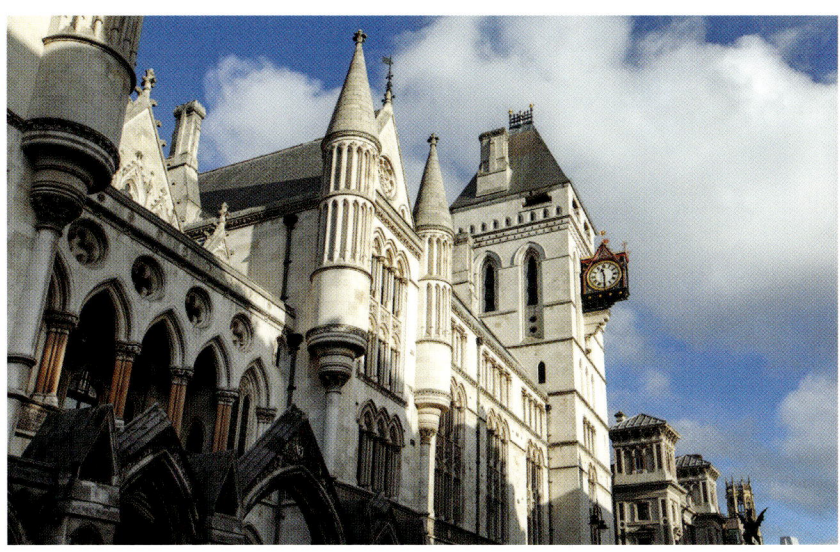

Royal Courts of Justice

In Dickensian London where the Royal Courts now stand was slum housing for more than 4,000 people squeezed into 450 houses. Dickens did not know this building as its construction began three years after his death. The courts featured in his novels were numerously sited around the city and were brought under one roof here in the early 1900s. The Chancery Court appears in *Bleak House* and we are reminded frequently through his writing of the author's relationship with the law. As well as personally experiencing the justiciable system from his own father's imprisonment, Dickens reported veraciously on a variety of news, heavily covering the Doctor's Commons and Parliament. He describes 'The Circumlocution Office' in *Little Dorrit* which, although a satirical fantasy, explains how Dickens viewed the path to innocence as being set up to be purposeful and confusing for those seeking a fair trial. Even Queen Victoria expressed the hope that 'the uniting together in one place of the various branches of Judicature in this Supreme Court will conduce to the more efficient and speedy administration of justice to my subjects'.

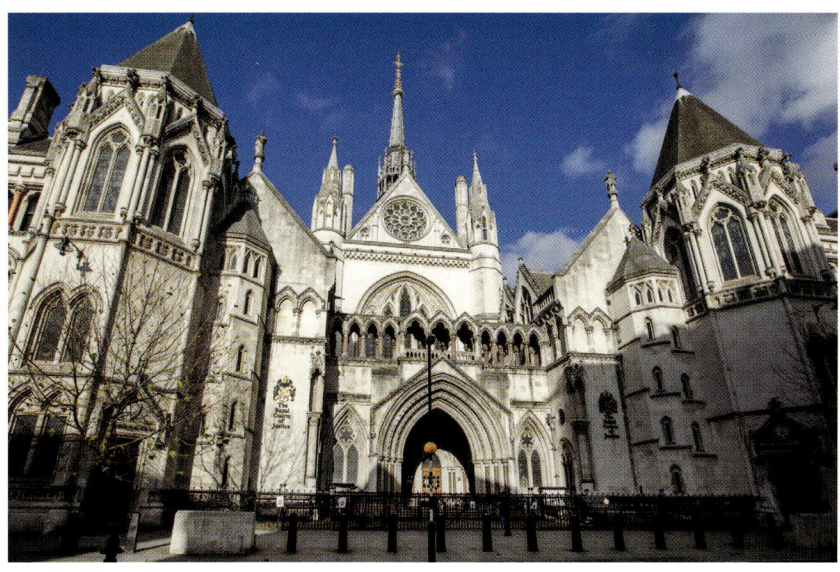

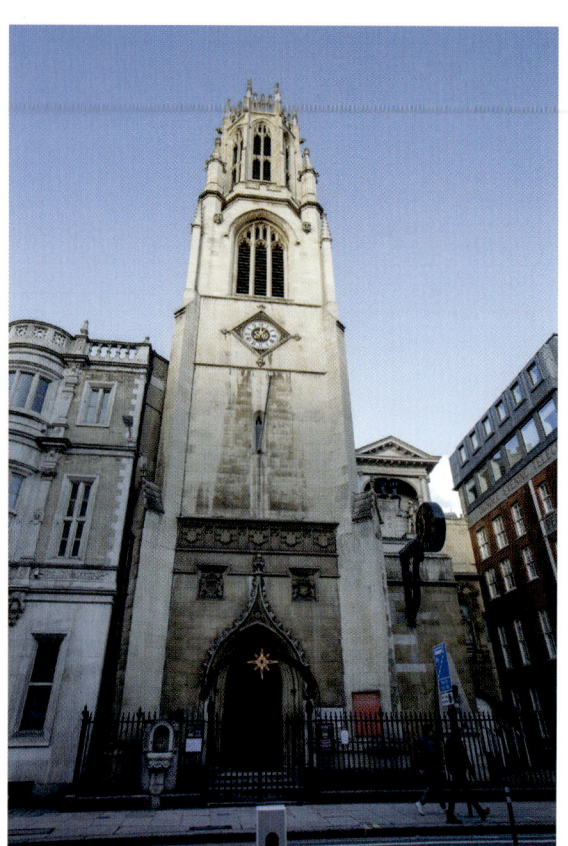

St Dunstan's in the West and Hanging Sword Alley

Noted in *Barnaby Rudge* and *David Copperfield*, St Dunstan's of Fleet Street housed a concert venue with performances on most Wednesday and Friday afternoons. The church itself, demolished and rebuilt in 1830, features a clock held by two stone giants who strike its bells every fifteen minutes. It was the first public timepiece in the city to have a minute hand. Although nowadays the sound is drowned out by passing traffic, *Betsy Trotwood* takes a young *David* in *David Copperfield* to see and hear the strike of the bells – the stone giants have movement in their workings. They hope to 'catch them at it at twelve o'clock' in the book. Nearly directly opposite sits Hanging Sword Alley. A quite unremarkable site today, in Dickensian times this alley was infamous for being a slum area of residence – presumably why it is chosen for the home of the ghastly character *Jerry Cruncher* in *A Tale of Two Cities*.

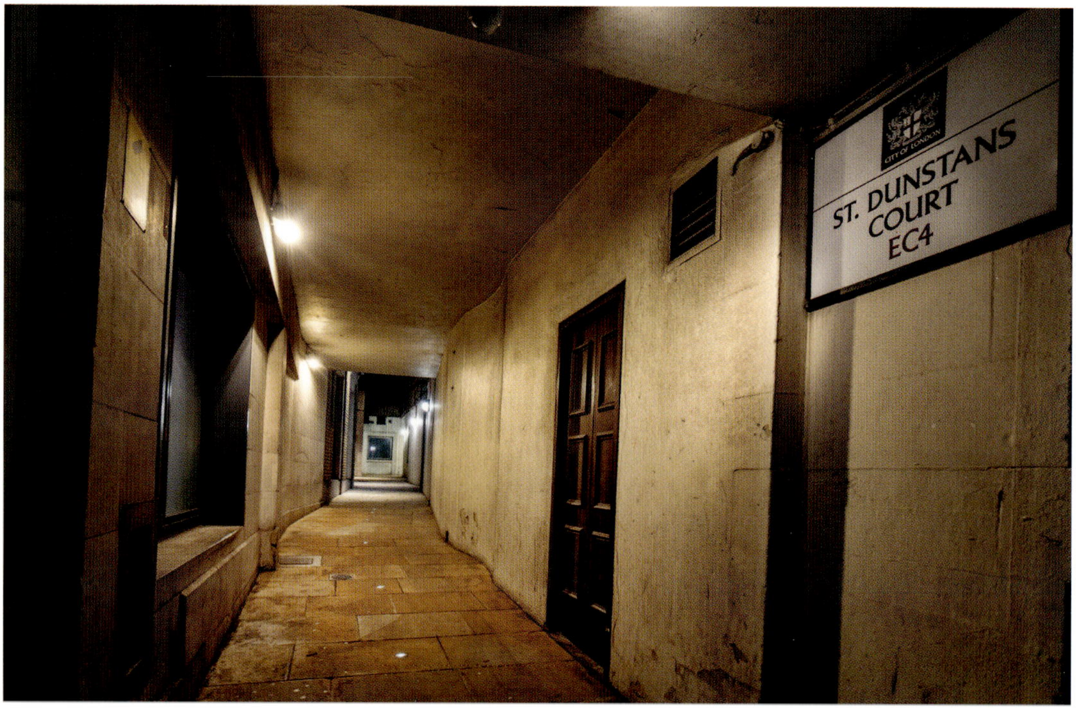

Fleet Street

Home to London's newspaper district, Dickens worked here for a few weeks as the editor for the *Daily News* – his role was short-lived due to his opinion on the paper's ethics, and he quickly resigned. Known to many is the historical legend of 'Sweeney Todd'. Operating in 1785 from 186 Fleet Street, the barber was rumoured to have murdered over a hundred clients before selling their flesh to Margery Lovett to add to her pies in nearby Bell Yard. There is no real evidence of this crime happening and few believe the story to be entirely factual. Dickens also used the area for the setting of his tales. *David Copperfield* takes *Clara Peggotty* on a trip to the Fleet Street Waxworks whilst Tellson's Bank is located here in *A Tale of Two Cities*. A directional change in narrative is also made here in *Martin Chuzzlewit* when *Tom Pinch* meets *Mr Fips* to be escorted from the Temple Gate to his new place of business.

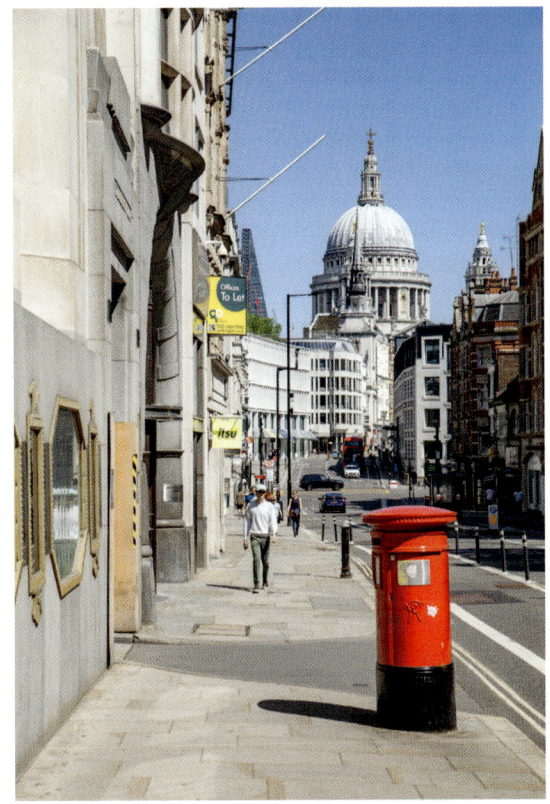

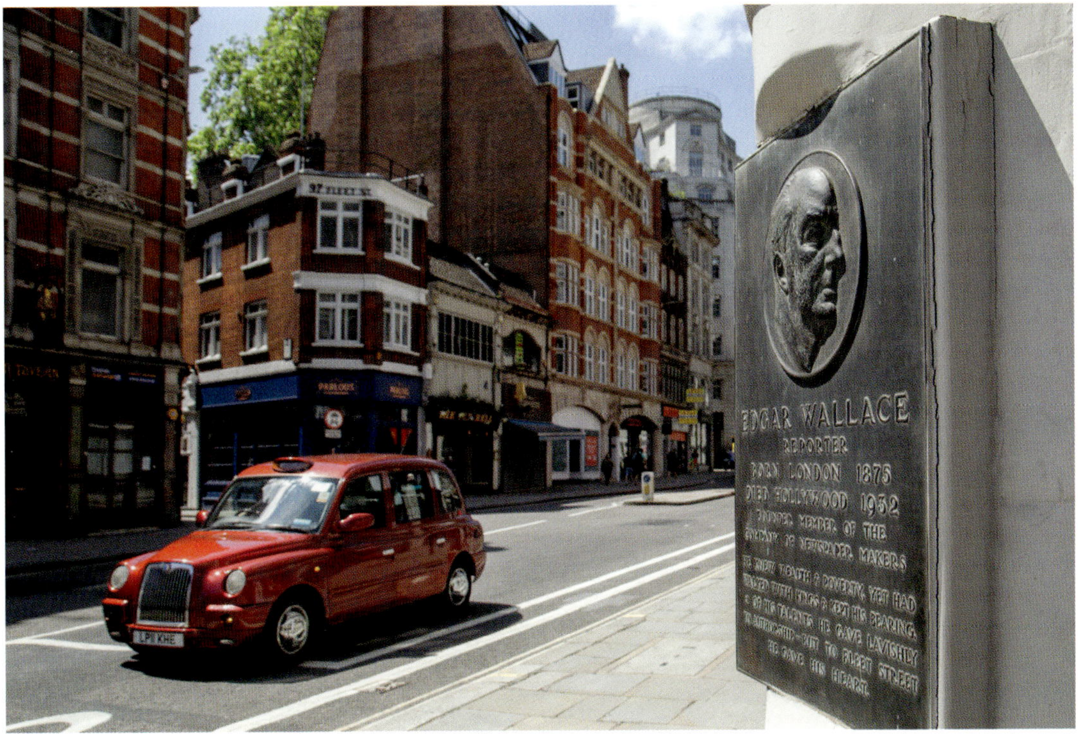

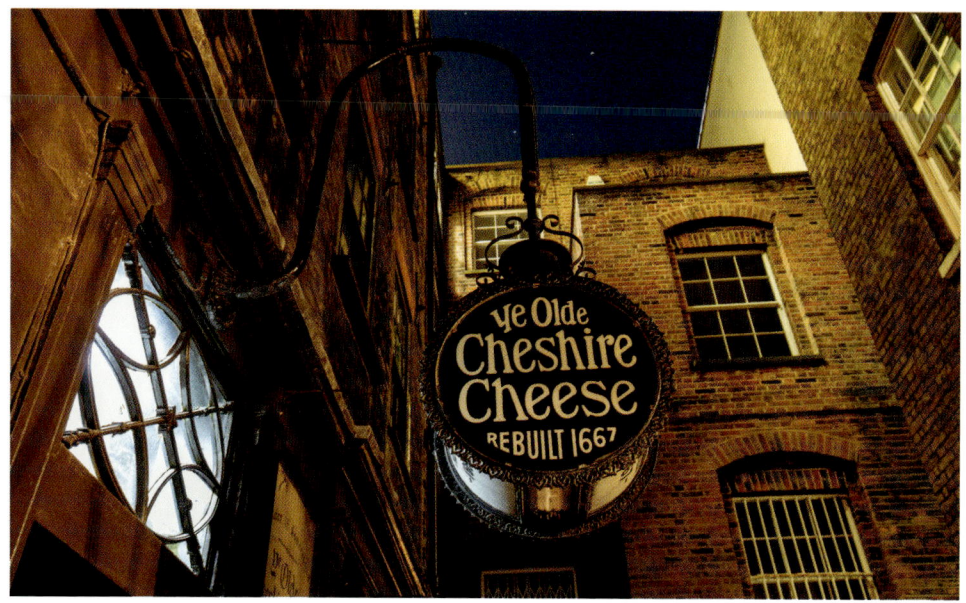

Ye Old Cheshire Cheese

Renowned for its literary associations, this Grade II listed watering hole was rebuilt shortly after the Great Fire of London, 1666. A regular haunt of both Dickens and Mark Twain, the Fleet Street tavern was one of many on the road. Scenes from *A Tale of Two Cities* are set here, where *Charles Darnay* recuperates and gains his strength back. Run now by the Sam Smith Brewery, the strict rules Humphrey Smith enforces on his patrons ensure this venue remains a true time capsule. The lack of fruit machines, music, phones or devices allow people to enjoy timeless hospitality in a traditional setting. One inhabitant who would not have passed the Smith Brewery's rules is the stuffed African parrot above the bar. Polly lived in the tavern for over forty years, dying in 1926. She was infamous for foul-mouthed tirades and the odd attack on patrons.

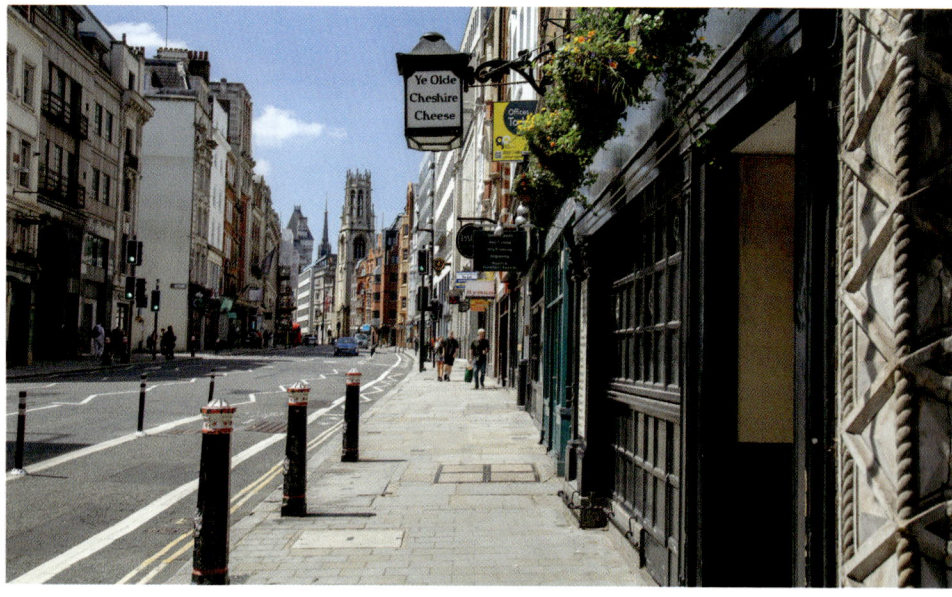

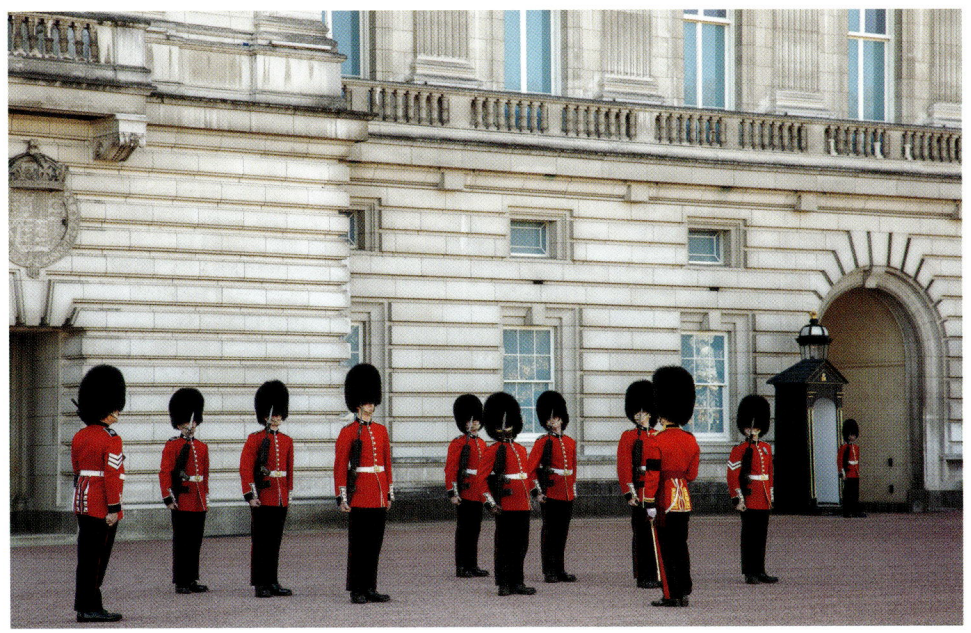

Buckingham Palace

Serving as the official residence of the sovereigns since 1837, Buckingham Palace remains as the administrative headquarters of today's monarch. After starring as *Fagin* in the West End adaptation of *Oliver Twist,* Mr Bean actor Rowan Atkinson was among the guests as Queen Elizabeth hosted an event at Buckingham Palace to celebrate Charles Dickens in 2012. *X-Files'* Gillian Anderson, who had played the character of the jilted bride *Miss Havisham* from the BBC's *Great Expectations* and *Lady Dedlock* from *Bleak House*, showed her gratitude at the invite, which is rumoured to become a centennial event in the author's honour. Queen Victoria is said to have been a fan of the writer's works and fond of reading them to her children – she had met Dickens not long before his death. Upon hearing of his passing, she sent a handwritten condolence to Catherine Dickens despite the couple's legal separation in June 1858.

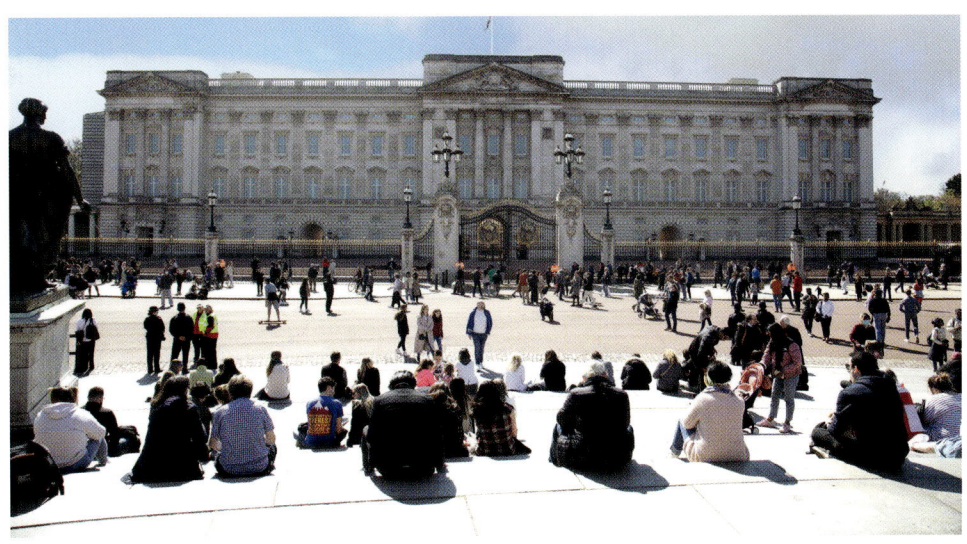

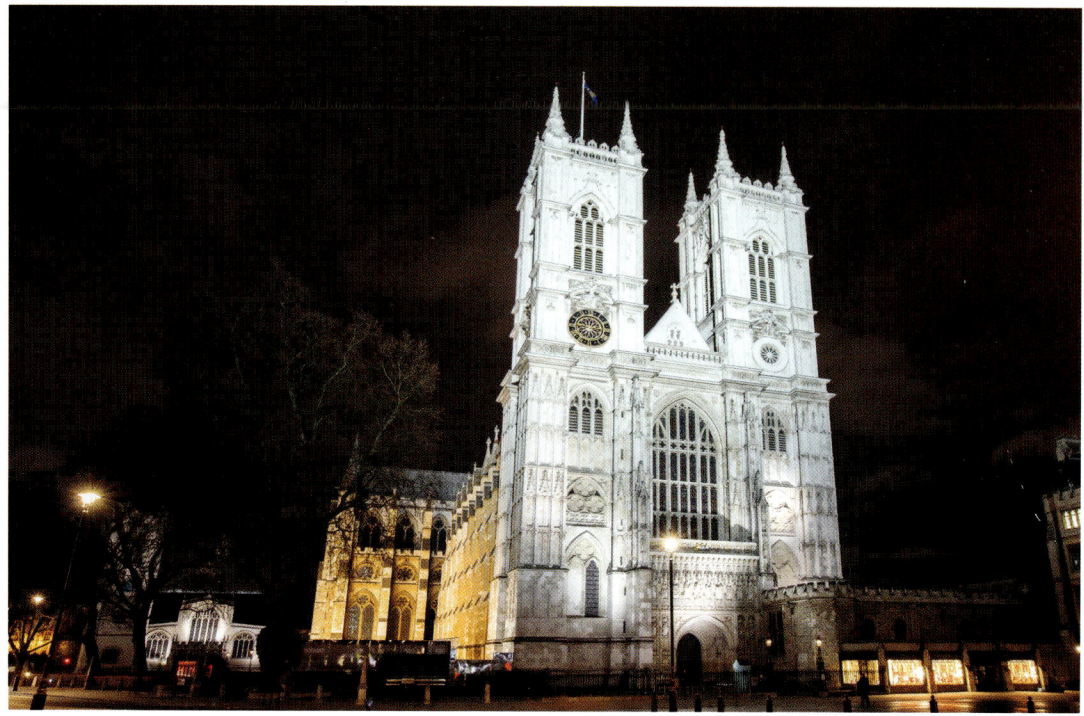

Westminster Abbey

Poets' Corner at Westminster Abbey is the final resting place of our writer after his death at the age of fifty-eight from a sudden stroke on 9 June 1870.

Marked by a small stone with a basic inscription, the author was buried in a low-key service that included only twelve family members and friends. Dickens' wishes in his will to be buried in Kent at Rochester Cathedral under a wall and tree with no publicity were ignored and his grave remained left open to be visited by the public and reporters until it was filled on 16 June. The *Times* newspaper led by public opinion demanded that the Westminster site was the only place worthy of a burial of someone with such distinction. His friend John Forster persuaded the Dean of Westminster of the same. The grave was dug at night and the quiet funeral service was read from the 1662 Book of Common Prayer. The plain coffin was adorned with ferns and roses. Thousands of flowers were added in the following days by mourners and a memorial sermon was preached on Sunday 16th for the public. Dickens lies between George Frederick Handel, Richard Brinsley Sheridan, Richard Cumberland and the ashes of Thomas Hardy and Rudyard Kipling.